THE ST PAUL
SAINTS

THE ST. PAUL
SAINTS

BASEBALL IN
THE CAPITAL CITY

STEW THORNLEY

MINNESOTA
HISTORICAL
SOCIETY PRESS

www.mnhspress.org

The Minnesota Historical Society Press
is a member of the Association of
American University Presses.

Manufactured in the United States
of America

10 9 8 7 6 5 4 3 2 1

∞ The paper used in this publication
meets the minimum requirements of
the American National Standard for
Information Sciences—Permanence
for Printed Library Materials,
ANSI Z39.48–1984.

International Standard Book Number
ISBN: 978-0-87351-958-8 (paper)
ISBN: 978-0-87351-959-5 (e-book)

Library of Congress
Cataloging-in-Publication Data
available upon request.

This and other Minnesota Historical
Society Press books are available from
popular e-book vendors.

Design and layout: Diana Boger

Acknowledgments

Jim Hinman produced a manuscript, *Brief History of the St. Paul Saints,* in 1998. Although this manuscript was not published, the information in it was helpful, along with Jim's willingness to share information from his notes as well as photos.

Joe O'Connell was generous in sharing his research and memories, which include his many trips to Saints games at Lexington Park and Midway Stadium.

Society for American Baseball Research members Dan Levitt, Kristin Anderson, Rich Arpi, Steve Steinberg, Armand Peterson, Dave Kemp, Tom Flynn, Dave Trombley, Brian Madigan, and Anthony Bush provided insights and information that was valuable.

Nick Chanaka and Jim Rantz played in the Northern League that existed until 1971 and shared their memories.

Many members of the current St. Paul Saints helped enormously: Marvin Goldklang, Mike Veeck, Annie Huidekoper, Sean Aronson, Tom Whaley, Derek Sharrer, Bob Klepperich, and Sam Hovan; as well as former Saints employees Dave Wright, Rusty Kath, Kris Atteberry, Anthony LaPanta, and Amanda Rodriguez.

Miles Wolff, a pioneer in independent baseball, was gracious and helpful during a telephone interview about his background and involvement in the minor leagues. Jim Gilligan, who managed the independent Salt Lake City Trappers during a 29-game winning streak in 1987 and later coached Kevin Millar at Lamar University, answered questions and shared his memories.

Bert Blyleven talked about the help he received with his curve ball from former Saints pitcher Ed Roebuck after Blyleven's junior year of high school.

Kevin Luckow has a blog, *10th Inning Stretch,* that documents his experiences with the Saints starting in 1993. I referred to his writing to get a sense of the community spirit prompted by the Saints.

Other people in the St. Paul baseball community allowed me to interview them, including Steve Winfield, Bill Peterson, Dennis Denning, and Jack Morris.

I've always enjoyed dealing with the professionals at Minnesota Historical Society Press; I worked with Pam McClanahan, Josh Leventhal, Ryan North, Shannon Pennefeather, and Dan Leary on this project.

Through the years I've had the chance to interview and/or exchange letters with a number of people in some way connected with the Saints and Minnesota baseball, and I appreciate their courtesy and help: Mike Augustin, Buzzie Bavasi, Al Brancato, Lou Cardinal, Ray Christensen, Don Dix, Dave Frishberg, Angelo Giuliani, Halsey Hall, Jerry Kindall, Norm Larker, Gene Mauch, Tom Mee, Andy Nelson, Oscar Roettger, Larry Rosenthal, Howie Schultz, Tom Sunkel, Eric Tipton, John Van Cuyk, Charley Walters, Mark Wegner, Leo Wells, Frank White, Stan Williams, Gregg Wong, and Don Zimmer. Many of these people with connections to the historic Saints also donated to a fund to purchase a plaque marking the site of Lexington Park. This plaque is now part of a plaza display erected by TCF Bank on Lexington Parkway.

Introduction

In 1993, the formation of the St. Paul Saints baseball team in the newly formed Northern League marked a pivotal moment in the history of baseball in Minnesota's capital city. Ever since the Minnesota Twins arrived in 1961, first settling in Bloomington and then moving to downtown Minneapolis in 1982, the major-league club had been the primary baseball focus in the state. The Saints turned some of that focus back onto St. Paul, a city that traces its baseball roots back to 1859—one year after Minnesota was admitted as the thirty-second state in the nation, with St. Paul as its capital.

Interest and participation in amateur baseball grew quickly in the 1860s, and professional baseball soon took over the scene. No longer the domain of local lads, baseball in St. Paul was being played by professionals who arrived from all over. Still, the fate of the team and its players, wearing shirts that said St. Paul, became a matter of civic pride and ignited the passions of area fans.

The original team known as the St. Paul Saints played in the American Association minor league from 1902 until 1961. While the Saints played at Lexington Park, one of their top rivals in the league, the Minneapolis Millers, played a short streetcar ride away at Nicollet Park. The long-standing rivalry between the cities played out on the diamonds and in the grandstands of those two ballparks, as well as in the teams' subsequent homes of Midway Stadium and Metropolitan Stadium.

Many great players passed through St. Paul to play for the Saints on their way to the major leagues. Most came from elsewhere, but the city also produced some stars for the local team. Hank Gehring, Angelo Giuliani, Larry Rosenthal, and Howie Schultz are just a few who grew up in St. Paul and had memorable baseball careers with the Saints. Relationships with major-league ball clubs—first informal arrangements, later official affiliations—brought to

St. Paul such future Hall of Famers as Miller Huggins, Leo Durocher, Lefty Gomez, Duke Snider, and Roy Campanella.

Even after the demise of the original Saints team, St. Paul continued to produce tremendous baseball talent. Both Dave Winfield and Paul Molitor launched their baseball-playing days on the diamonds and sandlots of St. Paul before leading the University of Minnesota Gophers baseball team to the College World Series. Both went on to Hall of Fame careers in the majors, each returning home late in his career to play for the Twins, for whom they picked up their 3,000th career hits. Jack Morris likewise had his most notable seasons with other teams but had an unforgettable year with the Minnesota Twins in 1991. Five years later, at the age of forty-one, Morris would return to his St. Paul home in an attempt to revive his career as a member of the Saints. Joe Mauer, possibly the greatest all-around athlete ever in Minnesota, was one St. Paul native who stayed with the hometown team, coming up to the Twins in 2004 and winning the American League Most Valuable Player award five years later.

Starting in 1961, area baseball fans united behind the Twins, a team that represents not just the Twin Cities metropolitan area or the state but an entire region of the Upper Midwest. But St. Paul has always maintained its own baseball identity, which was made especially clear when the new St. Paul Saints team began play in 1993. The Saints were part of the independent Northern League, an organization that had no affiliation with Major League Baseball. Such a setup seemed destined to become a short-lived footnote in local baseball history, as minor leagues had survived only as affiliated organizations throughout the preceding decades. But the Saints and the rest of the Northern League defied the odds, thanks to a fresh approach to the game and by building a loyal fan base.

Right away, this new organization was attracting attention that went beyond mere curiosity or novelty. Fans were purchasing season tickets, and the Saints were selling group ticket packages for family and workplace outings. Before anyone knew it, the opening home weekend was nearly sold out.

To be sure, a team whose co-owners included storied, second-generation baseball owner Mike Veeck and famous comedian/actor Bill Murray would not be a staid affair, and fans knew surprises were always in store at Saints games. A real live pig delivering baseballs to the umpires and a nun giving massages in the stands were only part of the fun at Midway Stadium.

The Saints also gave fans the chance to watch baseball outdoors and to tailgate before and after games, things that were not options with the big-league club in Minneapolis. The atmosphere fostered a community connection among the fans and with the players. The small-town feel of minor-league baseball in the second-largest city in the state was producing a phenomenon that soon attracted national attention.

The Northern League, led by the Saints, thrived in most of its home cities. Its success led to the formation of more independent leagues, and a new force in baseball had been created. Major-league teams ultimately recognized the independents as another source of players for their organizations.

As the demand for tickets increased in St. Paul, the team expanded its existing facility at Midway Stadium. A push for a new riverfront ballpark downtown didn't gain much traction at first, in part because of the affinity fans had for the simple pleasures of Midway Stadium. But as other Northern League teams upgraded their stadiums, and as the Twins unveiled their own new ballpark gem in downtown Minneapolis, the drive for a new Saints ballpark in the Lowertown area of St. Paul gained momentum and, eventually, became a reality. In addition to Lowertown's connections to the city's early history—a landing below the bluffs of the Mississippi River when the river was the main road into the burgeoning metropolis of the late 1800s—the new ballpark is located near where the first baseball in St. Paul was played prior to the Civil War.

The St. Paul Saints: Baseball in the Capital City tells the story of this beloved and unique baseball team as part of the broader history of the game in the city. Longtime fans will remember the Saints of Lexington Park, a team that established a proud history through nearly sixty years in the American Association, long before the torch of St. Paul baseball was passed to the current incarnation. The histories of both teams—the players who donned Saints jerseys and the championships won in both the American Association and the Northern League—are chronicled within these pages to trace the rich, long-standing traditions and the vibrant, groundbreaking innovations on the baseball fields of Minnesota's capital city.

THE HISTORIC SAINTS

CHAPTER 1

Early Baseball in St. Paul

MINNESOTA'S FIRST ORGANIZED LEAGUES

In 2014, construction began on a new ballpark in the Lowertown area of St. Paul. The ballpark is home to the city's most prominent baseball team, the St. Paul Saints. On the fringe of downtown, this area was also home to the city's first baseball team. In 1859 the Olympic club put a diamond on a common area at Ninth and Olive, within mere blocks of the site of the new ballpark of the St. Paul Saints more than 150 years later.

The game of base ball (two words then) grew in St. Paul during the 1860s, as it did through Minnesota and across the United States. The first contest between teams from Minneapolis and St. Paul took place in May 1867, launching a nearly century-long baseball rivalry between the cities, which reflected a larger struggle between two emerging metropolises vying to become the dominant city in Minnesota.

Later that year, the North Star Club of St. Paul took the lead in the creation of the Minnesota State Association of Base Ball Players, which also included teams from Dundas, Faribault, Hastings, Lake City, Northfield, Owatonna, Red Wing, St. Cloud, and two from Minneapolis. The first state tournament was held in the city in late September, and the North Stars came away with the first-place prize in its class.

As baseball became increasingly popular, clubs began to realize there was money to be made in the sport by charging fans to attend games. This, in turn, led to the inevitable shift from amateur to paid professional players.

One significant occurrence during this transition was the establishment of the League Alliance in 1877. This collection of clubs from the Midwest and East included representatives from both St. Paul and Minneapolis, the Red Caps and Brown Stockings, respectively. The League Alliance is considered one of the first true minor leagues in organized baseball since it acknowledged the position of the National League, formed a year earlier, as the sole major league.

The League Alliance also marks the first encroachment of professionalism on the Minnesota baseball scene. Baseball historian Rich Arpi states that St. Paul was a fully professional club when the league got underway and that Minneapolis achieved such status by the end of the 1877 season. Arpi also notes that the clubs started with amateurs, gradually adding professional players beginning in late 1875 and 1876.

Professional baseball continued to grow in the 1880s. In 1882, the American Association (not to be confused with the minor leagues of that same name in the twentieth and twenty-first centuries) joined the National League as a major league. Two years later an organization called the Union Association formed as a third, competing major league. Minor leagues also ballooned in 1884, with the number of leagues more than doubling from the year before.

The Northwestern League had started as a minor league in 1883 with teams in Ohio, Michigan, Indiana, and Illinois. The league added new teams in 1884, including three in Minnesota: St. Paul, Minneapolis, and Stillwater. (The Stillwater roster included Bud Fowler, who, ten years earlier, had become the first black player in organized baseball.)

St. Paul was the beneficiary of the shortsightedness of Ben Tuthill and Joe

MAJOR PLAYERS *in* MINNESOTA

The Twin Cities were decades away from being on the big-league circuit in the nineteenth century, but the locals still got to watch some of the best players in baseball during that time.

The Chicago White Stockings won the National League's first pennant in 1876 and then came to Minnesota on a barnstorming tour following the season. Boasting some of the top players in the game, Chicago's roster included Albert Spalding, Deacon White, and Adrian "Cap" Anson—who are now in the Hall of Fame in Cooperstown, New York. Cal McVey, Ross Barnes, and Paul Hines were also on the team. The White Stockings played both Minneapolis and St. Paul, as well as Minnesota's St. Croix Club of Stillwater. The National League champs won all five games they played in the state.

The White Stockings swung through Minnesota again in July 1877. Chicago first won a game in Winona and then came to the Twin Cities. They swept the three games they played in Minneapolis and St. Paul before returning to Chicago to resume their National League schedule.

Another grand team came to town about a dozen years later. Spalding organized a round-the-world tour featuring the White Stockings and a group of stars called the All-Americas during the winter of 1888–89. After a game in Chicago, the teams arrived in St. Paul the morning of Sunday, October 21. That afternoon, in front of approximately 2,500 fans, the White Stockings beat the All-Americas 9–2. The game was called after six innings so that the winners could play

Murch, the manager and owner, respectively, of the Minneapolis club. The pair passed over local talent, opting instead for "real ball players," which led a number of local Minneapolis stars to go elsewhere—Joe Visner to Stillwater and Billy O'Brien, Charley Ganzel, and Elmer Foster to St. Paul.

The Northwestern League regular season opened on Thursday, May 1, 1884. St. Paul lost 13–1 to Milwaukee in a game called on account of rain after six innings.

None of the Minnesota teams got off to a good start, and two quickly fell to the bottom of the pile. The standings after May 24 that year had St. Paul in 11th place with a record of 2 wins and 14 losses, ahead of only 0–16 Stillwater, which finally got a win in its next game.

The local teams had started their seasons with a month-long road trip and didn't get to Minnesota until the second week in June. St. Paul opened on its home grounds with a 6–1 loss to Quincy (Illinois) on June 10. The team played at the Fort Street Grounds, also known as the Seventh Street Grounds, on a small patch of land to the west of Fort/Seventh Street where a modest structure had been hastily erected.

St. Paul was at home for its first game against Minneapolis, on Monday, June 23, before a large crowd mixed with fans from both cities. "The friends of the visiting club were present in full force at the game, and were anxious and

St. Paul. In that game, St. Paul beat the White Stockings 8–5.

The All-Americas and Chicago were scheduled to play a game the next day in Minneapolis, and then a second game was added. Bothered by the loss to St. Paul, Anson arranged for a rematch. On October 22, before a crowd of about 1,800 to 2,000, the All-Americas beat Chicago, and Chicago then faced St. Paul. "Despite the fact that it was mostly a Minneapolis crowd, it was very apparent that it was all united against the common enemy, Anson and his men," reported the *St. Paul Dispatch*. However, this time Chicago won 1–0. The touring teams left Minnesota and headed west, playing games along the way before departing for foreign lands.

WHAT'S *in* A NAME?

The 1884 St. Paul club is often cited as the "Apostles" in modern references. However, contemporary newspapers at the time did not mention nicknames, and it is unclear if teams and fans of the time referred to the team as the Apostles, Saints, or any other name beyond the geographic designation. Eventually, the club in St. Paul did become identified as the Saints.

willing to place their shekels upon the result, with the Minneapolis club as their choice," reported the *St. Paul Dispatch*. "So eager were they to obtain bets that they gave odds of ten to eight, with only few takers."

Fortunately for the Minneapolis bettors, St. Paul fans were reluctant to take those odds. Foster pitched a shutout, leading St. Paul to a 4–0 win. The *Minneapolis Tribune* was anything but magnanimous in its reporting of the game, blaming the Minneapolis loss on the condition of the field and on the umpire:

> The St. Paul grounds are beyond all question supremely the worst in the Northwestern League, and after Sunday evening's shower were in a condition wholly unfit for any kind of showing by a team not used to scrambling through the mud and over such uneven country as that of St. Paul. To the umpire, in addition to this, St. Paul has reason to tender her warmest thanks for valuable assistance received. The gentleman who acted as that important functionary, and who is known as Mr. Keenan, left no room for doubt as to his magnificent capabilities for one-sided judgment. His decisions were placarded at the outset with his manifest determination to give the victory to St. Paul, and give it he did as far as lay in his power.

The *Tribune* did note that three of St. Paul's best players—Foster, Ganzel, and O'Brien—were "Minneapolis men, and last year played in the 'scrub' nine organized in the city."

Foster was on the mound five days later for the first meeting between the teams in Minneapolis. He struck out 15 batters, but his team lost 6–4. The *Pioneer Press* had earlier written that Foster "pitches a very hard ball to hit, and were it not that he is a little wild, would rank among the best in the league." Walks, along with poor work in the field behind him, were Foster's undoing in Minneapolis.

St. Paul played well through the summer but lost its star hurler when Foster sprained a tendon in his arm. For the next three weeks he remained in the St. Paul lineup at other positions before resuming his spot in the pitcher's box. The St. Paul crowd greeted his return to pitching enthusiastically on August 26, but Foster's season came to an end on the very first pitch of the game. The *Pioneer Press* reported on the injury: "The first ball he delivered went away over between the first baseman and catcher, and the attention of everybody was arrested by a loud snap, which was audible all over the grounds. Foster was immediately surrounded by the other players, who announced to the crowd his arm was broken between the elbow and shoulder, whence the ominous snap so distinctly heard." As Foster was taken to a doctor for treatment, an appeal was made of the St. Paul fans for financial help, noting that Foster "was the sole support of an aged mother; also that he had always labored

John "Scrappy" Carroll played for St. Paul in the Union Association in 1884 and rejoined the St. Paul club in 1888 and 1889. He also spent time with teams in Minneapolis and Duluth.

conscientiously for the success of the St. Paul club. . . . The hat was circulated and the handsome sum of $172.50 was collected."

The Northwestern League, similar to many other professional leagues in 1884, struggled to stay afloat, as most of its teams were financially unstable. Bay City (Michigan), riding a record of 40–13, was the first team to disband, on July 25. The carnage continued as other teams folded until only three were left. Winona (Minnesota) was added to the extant Milwaukee, Minneapolis, and St. Paul franchises as the league struggled to continue operations. On September 3, however, the Minneapolis club folded. Four days later, the league's final game was played, with St. Paul losing in Milwaukee.

Following the collapse of the Northwestern League, St. Paul immediately left on a barnstorming tour to the west. Meanwhile, Milwaukee looked to join the Union Association to finish out its season.

Founded by St. Louis millionaire Henry V. Lucas, who also served as league president and manager of the St. Louis team, the Union Association joined the National League and American Association as a major league in 1884. The new association—an outlaw league—eschewed baseball's reserve clause, which locked players into their current teams, and, as a result, was able to lure players from other leagues. In the end, though, this practice caused the Union Association's own demise, as its players were, in turn, raided by the other leagues.

Altoona (Pennsylvania), Baltimore, Boston, Chicago, Cincinnati, Philadelphia, St. Louis, and Washington, DC, were charter members of the Union Association, but only five of the original eight survived the entire season. Other teams were brought in to replace those that disbanded, and in late September

CARROLL, R. F., St. Paul
COPYRIGHT BY GOODWIN & CO., 1889.

ST. PAUL *in the* UNION ASSOCIATION

September 27	at Cincinnati	Cincinnati 6	St. Paul 1
September 30	at Cincinnati	Cincinnati 6	St. Paul 1
October 1	at Cincinnati	Cincinnati 7	St. Paul 0
October 3	at St. Louis	St. Louis 8	St. Paul 5
October 5	at St. Louis	St. Paul 1	St. Louis 0
October 8	at Kansas City	St. Paul 9	Kansas City 5
October 9	at Kansas City	Kansas City 7	St. Paul 2
October 12	at Kansas City	Kansas City 4	St. Paul 4
October 14	at St. Louis	St. Louis 14	St. Paul 1

the Union Association added Milwaukee and St. Paul, the two survivors from the Northwestern League.

Starting in Cincinnati on September 27 and then moving on to St. Louis, St. Paul lost its first four games. The team finally won on October 5, despite being held hitless. St. Paul scored a run against St. Louis on two errors and a stolen base in the fourth inning. The game was called by rain after five innings, giving St. Paul a 1–0 victory.

St. Paul then went to Kansas City and won its second game in a row, despite committing 13 errors (Kansas City made 15). Over the next week, in Kansas City and back in St. Louis, St. Paul lost two games and played to a 4–4 tie, finishing their brief stint in a major league with 2 wins, 6 losses, and 1 tie, ranking them ninth among the 12 teams that played in the Union Association that season.

The Union Association lasted only that one season. The St. Paul Base Ball Club also disbanded at the end of the 1884 season. It would be nearly seventy-seven years before Minnesota had a major-league baseball team again.

RISE AND FALL OF THE WESTERN LEAGUE

Over the next ten years, St. Paul was represented in a variety of minor leagues. Teams commonly played at fields across the Mississippi River from downtown, an area known as the West Side, since it was on the west bank of the river. Special motor trains transported fans from the foot of Jackson Street to games across a drawbridge spanning the Mississippi River.

The West Side was on low ground that, to this day, is prone to flooding. The spring baseball schedule was occasionally disrupted by a submerged ballpark. One of the West Side parks, Athletic Park on State Street, was designed by the prominent architecture firm of Gilbert and Taylor, the former being Cass Gilbert, who later designed the Woolworth Building in St. Paul, the Supreme Court Building in Washington, and the state capitol in St. Paul.

In 1894, a new minor league, the Western League, was formed with the idea of eventually transforming it into another major league to challenge the National League. Cincinnati sportswriter Ban Johnson and Charles Comiskey, who had been a star first baseman in the 1880s, were the main forces behind the new league. However, Johnson had to act alone initially because Comiskey was still under contract to manage, and occasionally play for, Cincinnati in the National League.

In its first season, the Western League had a team in Minneapolis but not in St. Paul. When Comiskey was freed from his National League obligations at the end of the 1894 season, he was awarded the Western League's Sioux City (Iowa) franchise with the agreement that he would transfer it to St. Paul. Comiskey acted as the owner, manager, and part-time first baseman. In April of 1895 he secured a permit to build a ballpark in the block between Dale and St. Albans streets and Aurora and Fuller avenues.

With Comiskey's dad on hand to supervise construction, the ballpark was completed with a 1,500-seat grandstand and two sets of bleachers with 750 seats each. According to Harold Seymour in *Baseball: The Early Years,* "Comiskey rearranged the position of the diamond so that the right field fence would be located a short distance beyond first base, to give the seven left-handed hitters in his St. Paul line-up an inviting target."

While the park was being built, Comiskey assembled his squad in Cincinnati, where they played a practice game, and then headed to St. Paul, playing exhibition games along the way. The Apostles, as the team was then called, also got in some preseason games on their home grounds. Two Sunday games were played, but objections from neighborhood residents put an end to that.

A Minnesota statute on "Sabbath breaking" prohibited many recreational activities on Sunday for religious reasons. Local clergy and neighborhood groups pushed for extending enforcement of this statute to baseball. The May 1, 1895, *Pioneer Press* quoted a protester at a meeting the previous night as saying, "We will get fifty men, arm them with rifles and send them down to clean out the entire base ball park, if the mayor does not enforce the law and stop this nuisance."

The mayor, Robert A. Smith, responded by saying, "We have many laws on the statute books, and I should not wish to see them repealed, but if we were to enforce all the laws we might as well put a fence around the town and be done with it."

Protests over Sunday baseball weren't new, nor were they confined to St. Paul. In 1890 a St. Paul team was playing in Des Moines, Iowa, when local authorities stopped the game after one inning and arrested all the players for violating an ordinance against playing on Sunday. Scenes such as this were common in the 1890s. Sometimes clubs played on Sunday as a means of challenging local blue laws.

The Apostles weren't trying to test the laws when they played in St. Paul; Comiskey merely wanted to be free to play games at home any day of the week. Two weeks after the neighborhood protest, however, a judge granted an injunction against Sunday games. Over the next two seasons, Comiskey had his team play either at Minnehaha Driving Park in Minneapolis or back at the previously used ballpark on the city's West Side, areas where local opposition to baseball on the Sabbath was either nonexistent or more muted.

Another problem emerged during the exhibition games prior to the 1895 season. Comiskey noticed people watching the game from outside the ballpark, on a hill along St. Albans Street. He put an end to their freeloading by erecting additional stands on that side of the field, and as the *Pioneer Press* reported on

May 7, 1895, the morning of the first regular-season game, the "congregation of person who would otherwise probably not pay their half-dollar to see the game will be disappointed." That same season, Comiskey learned that more than 200 peepholes had been bored into the outfield fence to allow free views of the field. He plugged those freeloaders' viewpoints by building a second fence six inches inside the outer one.

Prior to the first official game, the Apostles and their opponents, the Milwaukee team, toured the city in trolley cars, led by a car containing a band. The parade ended at the ballpark, where the teams worked out for a couple hours before the game's 3:30 start time. Despite the rainy weather, which delayed the game for about a half hour in the third inning, 3,000 people showed up to the ballpark. St. Paul's starting pitcher was Tony Mullane, who in the previous decade was a five-time 30-game winner in the major leagues. Mullane also homered against Milwaukee, and the Apostles won the game 18–4.

As the season progressed, Comiskey's frustration with the resistance to Sunday baseball in the neighborhood around the ballpark continued. He began

Owner Charles Comiskey (center) poses with his St. Paul baseball team in 1897.

seeking a new home for his team. The St. Paul team had another new ballpark in 1897. Lexington Park opened one year after its counterpart in Minneapolis, Nicollet Park. Both parks lasted sixty seasons and became closely associated with each city's rich baseball history.

Edward B. Smith, who operated a St. Paul real estate company and had been a part owner of a National League team in Buffalo in the 1880s, built the new ballpark for Comiskey. Located on the southwest corner of Lexington Avenue and University Avenue, approximately one mile west of the park the team had been using, Lexington Park occupied a lot 600 feet square, large enough to provide for generous field dimensions. In addition to University and Lexington avenues, the park was bounded by Dunlap Street on the west and Fuller Avenue on the south. Smith leased the ballpark to the Saints until 1910, when he sold it for $75,000 to George E. Lennon, a clothing merchant who owned the team at that time.

The *Pioneer Press* praised the new grounds in a story on Friday, April 30, 1897, the day Lexington Park opened: "St. Paul fans will see a ball ground that is not excelled in the West, and those who are familiar with the National league parks say that few, if any, of them surpass the St. Paul park." The laudatory comments continued in the next day's paper—following the Saints' 10–3 win over Connie Mack's Milwaukee team in the ballpark opener—citing gasps of "amazement and delight" from fans as they "gazed out over the wide open plain of rich green and brown earth, as smooth as a billard [*sic*] table. . . . The more the arrangements and conveniences of Lexington Park are studied the stronger becomes the impression that it is not excelled anywhere in the United States."

The St. Paul team played at Lexington Park—on every day of the week, including Sundays—for three years. After the 1899 season, Comiskey moved the team to Chicago, part of Ban Johnson's grand plan to upgrade his league to major-league status. A year later Johnson changed the circuit's name to the American League, reflecting a national rather than regional perspective.

Despite the name change, the American League was still a minor league in 1900 because it remained loyal to the National Agreement, a pact that governed all of professional baseball and recognized the National League as the sole major league. The agreement expired at the end of 1900, and the American League did not renew its participation in it.

By this time, Johnson was getting the financial backing he needed to make his final move, and in 1901 the American League declared itself a major league. Minneapolis and several other midwestern cities were cast aside, left to continue in the depleted Western League. In 1902 Minneapolis and St. Paul joined up with other current and former Western League cities to form a new minor league, the American Association.

St. Paul Saints in the American Association

WITH BOTH HOME CITIES left behind as the Western League transformed itself into a major league, the St. Paul Saints and Minneapolis Millers became charter members of a new minor league, the American Association, in 1902. They were joined by the Toledo (Ohio) Mud Hens, Columbus (Ohio) Senators, Louisville (Kentucky) Colonels, Indianapolis Hoosiers (later Indians), Kansas City Blues, and Milwaukee Brewers.

During its first two years, the American Association was considered an outlaw league since it was not part of the National Association of Professional Baseball Leagues, which was formed in 1902 as the umbrella organization for organized baseball. In 1904 the American Association became affiliated with the National Association and was subject to the operating rules and procedures of the other minor and major leagues.

Although the league was no longer independent, its teams were still free from affiliations with major-league teams, as were all minor-league clubs at the time. Later in the century, nearly all minor-league teams became part of a farm system, owned or controlled by a major-league parent. In the early 1900s, however, minor-league teams had control of their own operations. Many players came back to the same team year after year, rather than getting plucked away and promoted the moment they started to play well. The Saints and Millers had informal working relationships with different major-league teams at various periods, but it wasn't until the 1940s that they lost their independence entirely and officially became part of major-league farm systems.

EARLY SUCCESS FOR THE SAINTS

The Saints and Millers emerged as the best of the bunch over the life of the American Association. Both of the Twin Cities teams won nine pennants

between 1902 and 1960, more than any other team, and the Millers and Saints had the best overall winning percentages among all members of the American Association during this period.

During their decades in the American Association, the Saints and Millers also maintained the great rivalry that began with the cities' earlier amateur teams. The intercity battle brought increased attendance to games and, during tough economic periods, were a boon to the owners—"pay days" is how former Saints player Oscar Roettger characterized games between the teams. Highlights of every season were holiday doubleheaders—on Decoration Day, the Fourth of July, and Labor Day—with the teams playing a morning game in one city and an afternoon game in the other. The rivalry was hot no matter where the teams were in the standings.

St. Paul got the early jump in the American Association, finishing third in 1902, well above the seventh-place Millers. The Saints then won the Association pennant in 1903 and 1904.

The 1903 American Association champion St. Paul Saints.

MINNESOTA HISTORICAL SOCIETY COLLECTIONS

The 1903 pennant-winners relied on speed. Six players had at least 30 stolen bases. Second baseman Miller Huggins—who would become a Hall of Fame manager with the New York Yankees—led the team with 48 and was one of five regulars on the team with a batting average over .300. Third baseman and outfielder Phil Geier led the entire league with a .361 batting average. The other big hitters were outfielders Spike Shannon and Jim Jackson and shortstop Germany Schaefer, who went on to a lengthy career in the majors. The team's top hurler was Charley Chech, who had a record of 24–9.

After winning the league in 1903, the Saints played a pair of postseason benefit games in St. Paul against the Winnipeg Maroons of the Northern League. The two teams then continued on a barnstorming tour through Minnesota and the Dakotas.

The Saints lost three of their top players in 1904—Geier, Shannon, and Huggins all went to the major leagues—but the team still had some star talent. Jackson led the American Association in doubles, home runs, and stolen bases, and Chech led the league with 27 wins. Perry Sessions, who had pitched in the Northern League in 1903, also topped 20 victories for the 1904 team. (In modern record books, Sessions is listed with 27 wins in 1904, tying him with Chech for the league lead, although he was credited with 22 at the time. Statistics have been changed over the years with the discovery of recordkeeping mistakes; in the case of pitching victories, the criteria used to determine them in the early twentieth century varied, and modern corrections often involve attempts to retroactively apply uniform standards when determining the winning pitcher of a game from long ago.)

St. Paul easily finished first again in 1904, clinching the pennant on Monday, September 11, and then announcing a burlesque game for the coming Thursday, the day after the conclusion of its home schedule. The Saints, along with some outside participants, were divided into two teams. They played in various costumes, some of which illustrate the culturally insensitive attitudes of the time. The *St. Paul Pioneer Press* blithely reported the activities: "James Jackson, in the role of a Hebrew . . . played third base, went behind the bat, tried various other positions, always with true Hebrew walk and gesticulation." Manager Mike Kelley was "arrayed as a Chinese mandarin" and pitcher Charley Ferguson "attired as a white-haired Alabama negro."

The game itself was a farce, as neither runs scored nor innings were tracked. According to the *Pioneer Press,* "Players got tired and rushed to the bench from second or third when they felt like it."

A crowd of approximately 1,500 attended the event, and the newspaper reported that the fans "enjoyed themselves even more than at the regular games. Fun was announced as the order of the day, and was furnished without end." (Fun as the order of the day is a theme that would re-emerge with another St. Paul team ninety years later.)

The Saints concluded their regular season with a doubleheader in Kansas City, and the nightcap there was also described as a "burlesque" by the *Pioneer Press*. Players from both teams switched positions freely and clowned around during the game, which was called after five innings. In the final inning, umpire Bill Hart abandoned his post and pinch-hit for one of the Kansas City players (knocking a triple), and the team's owner and manager, Arthur Irwin, did the same. Despite its lighthearted nature, the game counted in the standings and was St. Paul's 95th win of the year.

The Saints barnstormed again in the 1904 offseason, this time heading east to play Columbus, the team that had finished second to them in the American Association.

THE PILLBOX

During their pennant-winning seasons of 1903 and 1904, and several years beyond that, the Saints played most of their games in a small ballpark on the edge of downtown St. Paul. Known as the "Pillbox" and sometimes referred to merely as the "Downtown Ball Park," this short-lived park was built in the shadow of the emerging state capitol building.

The team's regular home, Lexington Park, was more than two miles from downtown St. Paul, and Saints owner George Lennon wanted a more centrally located park. In late 1902 he announced plans for a new park between Robert, Minnesota, 12th, and 13th streets. Work began in early May 1903, and the first game was played there on July 20. The Saints beat Minneapolis 11–2 with more than 4,500 spectators on hand for the opener.

The article "The Downtown Ball Park" by the Junior Pioneer Association described the Pillbox as "not a thing of beauty." The stands were very close to the baselines, which "gave the spectators a good view of the players," according to local newspaper reports, although home plate was not visible from certain seating areas. When the umpire worked behind the plate, according to the Junior Pioneer Association article, his back would be against the screen in front of the stands, and "catching high fouls was impossible." The outfield wall, consisting of a high fence topped by a 20-foot-tall wire screen, was a mere 280 feet from home plate in left field and 210 feet in right field. With such short distances down the line, "The right fielder played with his back against the fence, and was only a few feet behind the second baseman even then. A 3-bagger was practically unknown, and would only result from a ball taking a freak bounce off a fence post or thru [*sic*] some other accident," according to the Junior Pioneer Association. Two-base hits, on the other hand, were quite common, given the park's special ground rules: balls hit over the short right- and left-field fences were counted as ground-rule doubles, and home runs were scored only if the ball cleared the fence in a limited area of center field.

Saints owner George Lennon presented his players with gold medals before the first game, which also featured a couple of competitions between Lefty Davis of Columbus and St. Paul's Charley Jones. The two tied in a foot race, both making it around the bases in 14.25 seconds, and Jones won a throwing contest with a toss of 131 yards, 3 more than Davis could muster. Chech pitched for St. Paul and shut out the Senators on five hits to give the Saints a game up in the best-of-three series. However, Columbus won the next two and took a $500 side bet made between the teams.

The Saints stayed in Ohio to play a team in Akron and then continued east for a three-game series against the Buffalo Bisons, pennant-winners of the Eastern League. The Bisons won the first two games, played in Buffalo. Although the series was clinched, the Bisons and Saints went to Columbus for the final game, which the Saints won.

Except for Sunday games, which were normally played at Lexington Park, the Pillbox was the regular home of the Saints through the 1909 season. One Sunday game was played at the Pillbox, on May 12, 1907. "It was perhaps the most orderly crowd that ever attended a Sunday baseball game in this city," reported the *St. Paul Pioneer Press* the next day. The team was hoping that the good conduct of the spectators would open the door to more Sunday games at the downtown ballpark. The *Pioneer Press* quoted Saints manager Ed Ashenbach as telling the fans, "We hope to play here again, and I hope you will not make any more noise than is necessary."

Although it was a close game—St. Paul defeated Indianapolis 6–5—the fans heeded Ashenbach's request and stayed reasonably quiet. Even so, this was the only Sunday game played at the downtown ballpark.

Lennon was vexed by the Sunday ban downtown and by his Lexington Park landlord, Edward Smith. Apparently the remoteness of Lexington Park was no longer an issue for Lennon, as he looked to build a new ballpark nearby. However, he fell short of the votes needed by the St. Paul Board of Alderman to vacate the land he wanted. Lennon hinted that it might mean the end of his team in the city (not the first, nor the last, time that a move of the Saints from St. Paul was rumored or threatened).

Lennon had filed a lawsuit to play Sunday games at the Pillbox, but in June of 1909 he dropped that suit, choosing to not antagonize the churches and residents in the area even though he was confident he could prevail in court. Instead, Lennon signed a ten-year lease for Lexington Park; the next year he purchased the ballpark from Smith.

The 1909 season was the last for the Pillbox. In its final summer, the ballpark hosted a series dubbed the "world's colored championship" between the St. Paul Colored Gophers and the Leland Giants of St. Paul. In the decisive fifth game, the Gophers trailed 2–0 and were without a hit until the eighth inning, when they rallied for 3 runs and held on to win the game and the championship.

The Eastern League became the International League in 1912, and for many years the champions of the American Association and the International League met in the Little World Series (which became the Junior World Series in 1932). The Saints-Bisons game of 1904 was the first postseason meeting between the league champions, and therefore this series is cited in record books as the initial Little World Series.

KELLEY'S CREW

Player-manager Mike Kelley first arrived in St. Paul in 1901 after a very brief career in the major leagues. He managed and played first base for the Saints in the Western League and stuck with the team when it joined the American Association the following season. He stayed in the Twin Cities, working on both sides of the Mississippi River, in a long and colorful baseball career in Minnesota.

Through the team's successes, Kelley's status was constantly changing. In addition to playing and managing, he was assuming some of the team's business duties from owner George Lennon. Rumors circulated over the final weeks of the 1904 season, and were confirmed by Lennon on the final day of the regular season: Kelley would be managing Toledo the following season. Michael Finn was rumored to be coming to St. Paul from Little Rock of the Southern Association to manage the Saints. When the 1905 season started, however, Kelley was back in St. Paul, where he even assumed the role of club president in addition to managing and playing. Finn became the manager in Toledo.

Reports of Kelley going to Toledo re-emerged in the summer of 1905, and by the end of the season the rumors extended to other teams, including the Minneapolis Millers. Fed up with the ongoing speculation and with the continuing disagreements with his manager, Lennon sold Kelley to the American League's St. Louis Browns.

Kelley disputed the sale, claiming he was a free agent. The National Commission, baseball's governing body, ruled against Kelley, who obtained a temporary restraining order delaying the sale. Donald Dunbar reported in *The Sporting News* that, in 1906, Kelley would be "at the head of the Minneapolis

Club of the American Association. He will acquire possession of the club no matter how the case between Owner Lennon and himself terminates." Dunbar was correct; by the end of 1905, Kelley was president and manager of the Minneapolis Millers.

Kelley's battle with Lennon wasn't over, however, and Kelley had to stay off the bench for the Millers' first game in 1906. That matter was soon settled, but during the season Kelley created his own problems. He accused umpire Brick Owens of dishonesty—twice—but was unable to back up his charges, and the American Association suspended Kelley indefinitely. He went to manage Des Moines in the Western League and Toronto in the Eastern League during the next two seasons.

The Saints had already started to slip in their final season with Kelley at the helm in 1905, and they kept dropping from there, finishing in last place in 1907 under manager Ed Aschenbach. Infielder Tim Flood joined the St. Paul roster during the 1907 season after being drummed out of the Eastern League for attacking an umpire, and the Saints named him manager the next year. Ironically, in 1908 the Saints had a manager who was banished from the Eastern League, and Toronto of the Eastern League had Kelley, who had been suspended by the American Association.

The situation soon changed again. Kelley left Toronto in August 1908, and the *St. Paul Dispatch* led the cheerleading to get him back in St. Paul. "No better manager could be secured than Mike Kelley," wrote the *Dispatch* on August 4.

The *Dispatch* acknowledged a snag in its drive: Kelley was still under suspension by the American Association. "There is only one thing that will lead the Association directors to raise Kelley's suspension," the *Dispatch* story continued. "And that is proof that the base ball public wants Kelley. The American association board will never reinstate Kelley just as a matter of sentiment or of convenience to Kelley. But this reinstatement will come if St. Paul gives evidence of the fact that Kelley is the man who can make money for the team here."

The league directors were scheduled to meet later in the week in Chicago. The *Dispatch* noted that some fans had started petitions for Kelley's reinstatement. Over the next two days the newspaper included its own "Kelley for Manager" form and reported, "Letters by the hundreds are pouring into the *Dispatch* office heartily endorsing the movement and urging it."

Although the *Dispatch* probably exaggerated its role and accelerated the hyperbole in its pages over the next couple of days, there was indeed a push from local fans in support of Kelley. Even Minnesota governor John Johnson got into the act, sending the directors a telegram that said, "I personally regard with favor the sentiment of Mr. Kelley and hope you may consistently see your way clear to do so for the best interests of base ball in our capital city."

Posing for a portrait in dapper street attire in 1904, Mike Kelley had a long career in baseball in Minnesota.

Only five of the eight league directors were present on the first day of meetings in Chicago on August 6, but four voted for reinstatement. The next day Minneapolis owner Mike Cantillon made it a majority, and Kelley was free to return to the Saints.

Amid the news from the Chicago meeting was a report that former league president Thomas Hickey planned to buy the Saints and move them to Chicago after the 1908 season. In addition, Toledo manager Bill Armour (referred to as "alleged manager" by the *Dispatch*) charged that the Saints were bankrupt, two years in arrears in American Association dues, and that the league directors were planning to "forcibly take the franchise away from St. Paul." The *Dispatch* responded with predictable indignation and inflated civic boosting, but the newspaper proved to be right in its assertion that the Saints would remain in St. Paul.

Kelley's return to the Saints drew a large crowd to the downtown ballpark on Monday, August 10, and the team responded with a 9–3 win over Minneapolis. St. Paul native Hank Gehring held the Millers to seven hits and also homered in the game. The Saints won 16 of 39 games under Kelley, which was not enough to lift them out of last place but was a winning percentage significantly better than in the year before he returned.

The team rose in the standings in 1909 and even came within a few games of a winning record. Louis LeRoy led the pitching corps, winning 20 games for the Saints that year. LeRoy, who attended Haskell Indian School in Lawrence,

THE RIVALRY BOILS OVER

The rivalry between the Minneapolis Millers and the St. Paul Saints was often more about the fans than the teams, whose rosters consisted of players from different places not caught up in bad blood between the cities. Sometimes, though, the spectators and the teams mixed it up. During a game at Lexington Park in May 1911, Minneapolis manager Joe Cantillon went into the stands with a bat to back up one of his players who was already in the stands and involved in an altercation with a fan.

The fan, William Crawdad, was black, and according to the *Minneapolis Tribune,* other fans had purchased a ticket for Crawdad, knowing

of his penchant for heckling. J. H. Ritchie of the *Minneapolis Journal* explained Crawdad's presence in the box seats as "the perverted sense of humor of a coterie of St. Paul adherents . . . who think it great sport to purchase the negro a ticket in the front box and have him turn loose his flow of wit and humor at the expense of visiting ball players in St. Paul."

Cantillon reportedly missed with his first swing of the bat but followed up with one that connected with Crawdad's head. Crawdad left his seat and got his head bandaged but later returned and was greeted with cheers from the St. Paul crowd.

BILL McKECHNIE

Bill McKechnie was an infielder for the Saints in 1912 and 1913 while spending some time in the majors. After finishing out his major-league playing career, he spent the 1921 season as the third baseman for the Minneapolis Millers and batted .321. A year later, he was managing in the majors, with the Pittsburgh Pirates. Over his twenty-five-year managerial career (including one as player-manager in the Federal League in 1915), McKechnie took three different teams to the World Series: Pittsburgh, the St. Louis Cardinals, and the Cincinnati Reds. He won the World Series with the Pirates and Reds and was inducted into the Hall of Fame in 1962. McKechnie is the only Hall of Famer to have played for both the Saints and the Millers.

Bill McKechnie, shown here during his time as a player for the Boston Braves in 1913, is one of nine former St. Paul Saints inducted into the Baseball Hall of Fame.

Kansas, and Carlisle Indian Industrial School in Pennsylvania, pitched for the Saints from 1907 into 1913 (when he split the year between St. Paul and Indianapolis) and had double-figure victories each year. (He also had at least 20 losses in three of those seasons.) LeRoy also pitched a no-hitter for the Saints in July 1910.

Charley "Sea Lion" Hall nearly preceded LeRoy in the no-hit department the year before. On June 18 he held Louisville hitless while striking out 14 batters through nine innings. However, his teammates couldn't get him a run, and Hall lost his no-hitter in the tenth inning and then the game in the twelfth. Hall had a tough-luck 4–13 record in 1909, but he was called back to the majors in 1910. He had several good years with the Boston Red Sox, including 15 wins for the 1912 world champions. Hall returned to St. Paul in 1914 and was a top pitcher for some dominant Saints teams over the next decade.

Hall was known to throw a spitball, which was then legal. Gehring was also a master of the pitch. Some reports claim a young Burleigh Grimes saw Gehring pitch in St. Paul and began imitating him. Grimes went on to a Hall of Fame career and is remembered as the last pitcher to have legally thrown a spitball. Gehring's best year was 1905, when he had 32 wins for Wichita of the Western Association. Although he died at the age of thirty-one in April 1912, he won nearly 140 games in the minors.

Near the end of the 1912 season Kelley accepted a deal to become part owner and manager of the Indianapolis Indians of the American Association. But the transfer didn't seem to work out for either team. Kelley couldn't raise the Indians from the cellar in 1913, and the next year the Saints, under Bill Friel, dropped to the bottom, winning only 56 of 167 games.

In addition to the team's poor performance on the field, owner Lennon was struggling financially, and fans again had to endure reports that the Saints might be on their way out. An attempt by a group of investors to buy the Saints from Lennon fell through. However, in early 1915, real-estate developer John Norton secured an option on the team and eventually purchased it. He was also able to lure Kelley back as manager.

In 1915, an unlikely pennant race developed between the Saints and Millers, who had finished in seventh place, ahead of only St. Paul, the previous season. Both teams started slowly in 1915 and, after splitting their Independence Day doubleheader (played on July 5 since the 4th fell on a Sunday), were far from the top. The Saints were in fourth place, eight games behind first-place Indianapolis; the Millers were another three and a half games back of St. Paul.

The Saints won their next 13 games to pass the three teams in front of them, including Indianapolis, which lost 9 in a row. Hall was in the midst of his own personal streak, winning 16 straight decisions.

Minneapolis also played well during this time and moved into second place but trailed St. Paul by seven games on August 13. The Millers then started their own 13-game winning streak and took over first place for good.

St. Paul crept as close as a half game of Minneapolis in the final week of the regular season, but the Millers hung on and finished with 92 wins and 62 losses, a game and a half ahead of the Saints. It was the closest pennant race ever between the Twin Cities rivals.

Hall finished the year with 24 wins. Three others were in double figures in wins: Bob Steele with 20, Albert "Lefty" Leifield with 17, and Rees "Steamboat" Williams with 15. On offense, center fielder Joe Riggert tied for the Association lead with 9 home runs and scored 102 runs.

Following their fight for first, St. Paul and Minneapolis fell a couple of notches in 1916. The following season, the Saints finished only two and a half games out of first, but they dropped to sixth place, one spot ahead of Minneapolis, during the war-shortened 1918 season.

Saints Dominate in a New Lexington Park

LEXINGTON PARK GETS A FACE-LIFT

Changes in ownership and in the Saints' fortunes on the field were accompanied by a new look for their ballpark in 1915. Lexington Park had already been transformed in a couple of renovations over the previous decade. First, the ballpark was repaired following a fire in 1908, and more changes came after George Lennon signed a new lease in 1909. At this time the stands were replaced and new outfield fences erected, cutting down on the spaciousness of the playing area.

However, Lexington Park remained a wooden structure, unlike Minneapolis's Nicollet Park, which made the transition to more permanent steel and concrete building materials after the 1911 season. In doing so, Nicollet Park was less at risk from devastating fires, which occurred with some degree of regularity at wooden ballparks around that time. National Park in Washington was destroyed by fire in March 1911, and the Polo Grounds in New York burned the following month. The same fate befell Lexington Park in November 1915.

The park was rebuilt with a reconfiguring of the field orientation. The diamond was turned 90 degrees, moving home plate from the southwest toward the northwest corner of the lot. "The principle reason for the radical change in the arrangement is that it will prove a great convenience for the fans," explained the *St. Paul Pioneer Press* on November 28, 1915. "The new plan would bring the fans into the grand stand almost as soon as they went through the gates, and the bleacherites would have less than half a block to walk." The article further stated that, in the park's original orientation, fans had to walk "two long blocks" from the streetcar stop to reach their seats, a particular nuisance in the rain.

Lexington Park was set back 100 feet from University Avenue, which was on the north side of the ballpark, and 100 feet back from Lexington Avenue to the east. The main entrance to the grounds was behind home plate, at the corner of University Avenue and Dunlap Street.

In a 2003 article for *Minnesota History* magazine, Kristin Anderson and Christopher Kimball wrote that the new Lexington Park emphasized function, in contrast to the remodeled Nicollet Park. Lexington Park was described as a baseball "plant," rather than a ballpark, and emphasized a utilitarian aesthetic. "Lexington Park's character and identity," Anderson and Kimball wrote, "were derived from the functional elements of the facility's interior spaces. The task was to speed fans—and more of them—to their seats. Baseball in St. Paul was amusement for the masses, without the elite imagery sought by more established clubs, including the Millers and many major-league teams."

On the other hand, Anderson characterized the construction of Lexington Park as "forward looking in terms of its design, its sense of the space around it, anticipating the 'City Beautiful' movement of the next decade—way ahead of the game." Careful consideration was given to the surrounding area and space, with which the designers had plenty to work.

Landmarks outside the stadium became familiar to fans, most notably the Coliseum Pavilion beyond the left-field fence along Lexington Parkway. To the

Fans are packed into the revamped Lexington Park for a game circa 1916.

south, behind right field, was Keys Well Drilling, which erected a sign bearing the company name that was visible to those inside. Keys Well Drilling occupied the site into the twenty-first century, its orange-and-black sign still prominent until the company moved to another part of St. Paul.

The Coliseum roof was the landing site for many home runs, an easier target than the Keys Well Drilling sign. In fact, for most of the life of the rebuilt Lexington Park, few balls cleared the right-field fence. The distance down the foul line in right field was 365 feet. A 12-foot-high wooden fence sat atop an embankment that led up to the fence.

RETURNING TO THE TOP

By the time they moved into the revamped Lexington Park, the Saints had established a relationship with the St. Louis Cardinals and, later, with the New York Yankees. The connection was Miller Huggins, who had played under Mike Kelley in St. Paul, and Huggins's chief scout, Bob Connery. Huggins

TAKING ON MAJOR LEAGUERS *from* THE WINDY CITY

On Good Friday in 1917, the same day that the United States formally entered the Great War in Europe with a declaration in Congress, the Saints were wrapping up spring training with a game in Fort Smith, Arkansas. The Saints still had two more exhibition games to play back in St. Paul, against the Chicago White Sox and Chicago Cubs. The White Sox had played exhibitions in Minneapolis the previous spring and found the territory "fertile" enough that they convinced the Cubs to join them for games against both Twin Cities teams in 1917.

On a cold Saturday, April 7, approximately 1,300 fans watched the Saints beat the Cubs 2–1 at Lexington Park. The Cubs had played a couple of their stars but sat out most of their regulars. The next day, even though the temperature was chilly again, more than 4,000 fans shivered through a game in which the White Sox used their regular roster and beat St. Paul 7–4.

Chicago's Claude "Lefty" Williams pitched the first three innings, and the White Sox starting lineup included Nemo Leibold, Swede Risberg, Eddie Collins, "Shoeless" Joe Jackson, Oscar "Happy" Felsch, Chick Gandil, Buck Weaver, and Ray Schalk—the same crew that led the White Sox to the world championship that fall. Collins and Schalk also ended up in the Hall of Fame. Williams, Risberg, Jackson, Felsch, Gandil, and Weaver were among those later banned from baseball for their roles in the 1919 Black Sox scandal, when some members of the team accepted money from gamblers to intentionally lose the World Series.

Over the coming decades, many other major-league teams visited the Twin Cities to play exhibition games, giving local fans the chance to see the top players in action before the area had a major-league team of its own in 1961.

managed the Cardinals from 1913 through 1917, and he and Connery moved to the Yankees in 1918. Huggins often sent his surplus talent to the Saints, and Connery frequently came to St. Paul to scout players for the majors. Prior to full-blown farm systems, informal pipelines between a minor- and major-league team were common, and the link between the Saints and Yankees remained strong over the next decade.

Among those who shuttled between St. Louis and St. Paul while Huggins was with the Cardinals were Joe Riggert, Charley Hall, Lee Dressen, Dick Niehaus, and Rees "Steamboat" Williams. These players were part of a core in St. Paul that launched a six-year run of success, bringing four pennants to the city following the end of World War I.

According to Jim Hinman, Kelley intended to retire after the 1918 season and become a livestock trader in Nashville, Tennessee, but Saints owner John Norton persuaded him to return for another year. Kelley stuck around for several seasons, and he was probably glad he did.

The Saints of 1919 featured many good players, including several who arrived through the team's connections with Huggins and Connery. Outfielder Elmer Miller was obtained from the Yankees prior to the season, and he led the Saints in home runs (15) and average (.314) in 1919. He maintained a .321 average over his three years in St. Paul.

During the 1919 season, the Saints received another outfielder from New York. George Halas, who had played in the 1919 Rose Bowl with the Great Lakes Navy team, was in his only season of professional baseball. At the end of the year, he turned his full attention to football. In 1920 Halas became

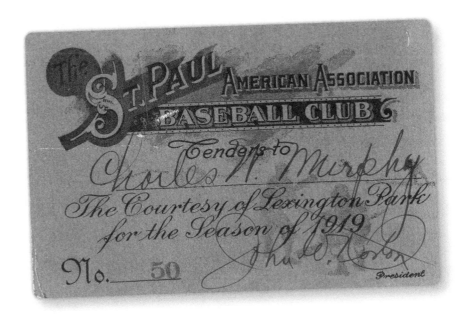

Season-ticket pass to Lexington Park for the 1919 Saints season.

coach of the Decatur (Illinois) Staleys, which became the Chicago Bears of the National Football League. "Papa Bear," as Halas was eventually known, was also a receiver for the Bears through the 1920s, became the owner, and coached the team off and on until 1967. He was a charter member of the Pro Football Hall of Fame in 1963.

Second baseman Marty Berghammer had played with the Pittsburgh Rebels in the short-lived Federal League, which lasted two years as a major league, and was acquired by the Saints after the Federal League folded following the 1915 season. Berghammer had a solid keystone partner in shortstop Lute "Danny" Boone, whom the Saints acquired from another Pittsburgh team, the Pirates of the National League. The two stayed together in St. Paul through 1925.

Left-hander Howard Merritt and catcher Bubbles Hargrave were back for their second seasons with the Saints in 1919. Hargrave became one of the top catchers in the National League during the 1920s before returning to the Saints as a player-manager in 1929.

The Saints returned to the top in 1919, fifteen years after winning their last American Association pennant. With a record of 94–60, St. Paul finished six and a half games ahead of second-place Louisville. Miller led the league with 15 home runs and tied for the lead with 16 triples. Lee Dressen was the league leader in stolen bases with 46. Niehaus led the mound corps with 23 wins, and Dan Griner had 21. Howard Merritt, Hall, and Williams won 19, 17, and 15 games, respectively.

At the time, the Little World Series was not yet a regular event. Two years before, the champions of the American Association and International League had met in a championship series for the first time since 1907 (when the International League was still known as the Eastern League). The minor leagues had ended their seasons prematurely in 1918 because of the war, eliminating the chance for postseason meetings, but there was hope for a resumption of the Little World Series in 1919.

However, the International League wrapped up its season two weeks before the American Association, and its champion, the Baltimore Orioles, decided not to hang around for a championship series. Instead, the Saints headed west to meet the Vernon (California) Tigers, winners of the Pacific Coast League title, playing games along the way.

Vernon, a small community outside the Los Angeles city limits, had its own ballpark, but the Tigers usually used Washington Park in Los Angeles. It was there that the Saints and Vernon played in a best-of-nine series. The Tigers roughed up Howard Merritt in the first game and won 7–1, but Griner pitched an eight-hit shutout in the second to even the series. The third game was tied 1–1 in the sixth when trouble occurred. Vernon had runners at first and third with two out when umpire Jim Murray called Hughie High out at first on the next play, ending the inning. Led by manager Bill Essick, the Tigers rushed Murray, who exchanged punches with Vernon's Zinn Beck. Although High was out on this play, he came up in the ninth and singled home the game-winning run for the Tigers.

Hard feelings continued through the series. The teams had disagreements ranging from the eligibility of players to which bench each team would use. The Saints accused Essick of having the infield watered excessively in an attempt to slow down their speedsters. Later in the series, Berghammer squared off with Vernon first baseman Stump Edington. After the final game, a Vernon fan came onto the field and assaulted Murray.

The Saints fell behind in the series but came back to tie it, with Niehaus pitching a six-hit shutout in Game Six. An eligibility issue came up before the next game when Vernon tried to bring in Jack Fournier, a veteran of the major leagues, to replace High, who had been injured. Kelley objected to the substitution, but the Vernon club refused to remove Fournier. As a result of the dispute, the Saints were awarded the game by forfeit. However, Kelley refused the forfeit, Vernon backed down and didn't use Fournier, and the teams played on. The Tigers won 6–2 to move ahead, four games to three. Kelley later explained his reason for turning down a forfeit victory. "I realized that if the game was not played, it would mean the finish of the series, not only for this season but for the future," he told Fane Norton of the *Los Angeles Times*.

The Saints stayed alive the next day with a 3–1 win behind a six-hitter by Griner, who won his third game of the series. St. Paul scored all its runs in the first inning. More trouble came up in the eighth when Murray saw Vernon right-hander Joe "Happy" Finneran rough up the ball and made him use a different one. Finneran fired the ball back at Murray, charged the umpire, and threw his glove at him. Murray's chest protector fell to the ground and Finneran stomped on it, ruining the protector and earning himself an ejection and $100 fine.

Niehaus took the mound for St. Paul in the decisive ninth game and had a pitching duel with Vernon's Wheezer Dell. The score was tied 1–1 in the last of the ninth. With two out and a runner on second, Dell jumped on a high curveball from Niehaus. He drilled it to left for a hit to bring in teammate Scotty Alcock with a run to win the game and the series.

Kelley was gracious about the loss and after the game went to the Tigers' locker room. "Congratulations, Bill," he told Essick. "The better team won. I have no alibis to offer. I hope I can come back next year and turn the tables on the Coast champions." However, American Association president Thomas Hickey declared that his league would never again play the Pacific Coast League in a postseason series in any year in which Vernon won the pennant.

The issue of another postseason series between the American Association and the Pacific Coast League didn't come up again. Instead, starting in 1920, the champions of the American Association began playing the champions of the International League in the Little World Series on an annual basis. That year's series matched a pair of teams ranked among the best in the history of the minor leagues.

The Baltimore Orioles were dominating the International League during this period. They were led on the mound by Robert "Lefty" Grove, who eventually won 300 games in the major leagues and was elected to the Hall of Fame. Another top pitcher was Jack Bentley, who also played first base and led the league with 161 runs batted in that year. The owner of the team was Jack Dunn, the man who had signed Babe Ruth to his first professional contract.

The Saints were good, too, and produced possibly the best team in the history of the American Association. St. Paul had a won-lost record of 115–49 in 1920 and finished 28 1/2 games ahead of second-place Louisville. In addition to holdovers Lee Dressen, Berghammer, Boone, Riggert, Miller, and Hargrave, the batting order was bolstered by a pair of newcomers. One was third baseman Joe "Goldie" Rapp, who led the Association with a .335 batting average.

In the outfield, Bruno Haas was starting a sterling eleven-year career with the Saints. He had made his major-league debut in 1915 with the Philadelphia Athletics. In his first game he gave up 11 hits, 3 wild pitches, and 16 walks. Although he pitched five more games and also played the outfield for the Athletics, he never played in the major leagues after 1915. In the minors, however, Haas was a player, manager, and/or owner for the next thirty years. He last played in 1946, the season he turned 55. Haas also played in the National Football League in 1921 and 1922.

Haas became well known in St. Paul for his acrobatic and daredevil plays in left field. Tony Salin, in *Baseball's Forgotten Heroes,* wrote of Haas's "belly catches": "Haas used a long narrow glove, a glove players back then called a 'motorman's glove,' and he was known for sliding on his belly, getting a mouthful of turf, and making the grab."

Salin quoted longtime Kansas City writer Ernie Mehl as calling Haas "perhaps the best-known player in the American Association. . . . If Bruno had not gone into the baseball business he would have been one of those men who leap into tanks of water or he would have been a motor car racer or a parachute jumper. Or a bigamist."

During the 1920 season the Saints averaged nearly 6 runs per game and won by scores of 27–5 over Louisville and 26–1 against Kansas City. Hall pitched a no-hitter during that season (his second with the Saints, the other had been in 1918) and led the American Association with 27 wins and a 2.06 earned-run average. Merritt and Williams also won at least 20 games, and southpaw Fritz Coumbe, with 19 wins, came close.

As good as the Saints were, their opponents in the Little World Series were on an amazing streak at the end of the year. The Orioles won their last 25 games of the regular season and held off the Toronto Maple Leafs, who had won 24 of their last 26 and finished two and a half games behind Baltimore for the International League title.

Bentley was outstanding for the Orioles in the series against St. Paul, winning three games on the mound while collecting 8 hits in 24 at-bats as a hitter. He was the winning pitcher in the first game and also hit 2 home runs. The Orioles won the next two as well before St. Paul, behind 8 shutout innings from Coumbe, won the fourth game of the series.

With the Orioles holding a three-games-to-one lead, the series moved from Baltimore to St. Paul. The first game at Lexington Park was a wild one. The Saints scored 4 off Bentley in the last of the seventh to tie the score 5–5. However, the Orioles scored in the top of the eighth after a controversial call at first base and after St. Paul's Griner was accused of throwing an emery ball (a doctored ball that had been outlawed). Angry fans responded by throwing seat cushions onto the field, and many attempted to attack the umpires after the game, which Baltimore won 6–5.

Behind Jack Ogden, who had won 27 games during the regular season, the Orioles won the next game 1–0 to finish the best-of-nine series. The game's only run came in the second inning when shortstop Joe Boley's liner to center got by the Saints' Miller, who slipped, and Boley came around for an inside-the-park home run.

The Saints dropped to sixth place in 1921. Third baseman Charley Dressen joined St. Paul that season and was a regular in the infield for the next few years. (Charley Dressen had a connection with former Saints outfielder Halas: he was the quarterback for Halas with the Decatur Staleys in the American Professional Football Association. During his first couple of years with the Saints, Charley Dressen played with the Racine, Wisconsin, team in the National Football League in the offseason.)

St. Paul had a number of new players in 1922, including catchers Miguel "Mike" Gonzalez and Nick Allen and acrobatic outfielder Walter "Sea Cap" Christensen. Tom Sheehan, in his first full season with the Saints, led the American Association with 26 wins. Hall and Rube Benton each had 22.

With a record of 107–60, the Saints finished 15 games ahead of Minneapolis and returned to the Little World Series to face Baltimore.

The series opened in Baltimore. The teams split the first two games, with Benton beating the Orioles' Grove in the second game. In the third game, the

The St. Paul Saints held spring training at Dawson Springs, Kentucky, in preparation for the 1921 season.

Saints knocked Bentley out of the game and built a five-run lead, only to blow it and lose 13–10. The next day, Benton faced Grove again and carried a 3–2 lead into the eighth inning, but Baltimore tied the game on a home run by Max Bishop. The Orioles then won the game in the last of the ninth when Wickey McAvoy hit a one-out grand slam off Hall. The series shifted to St. Paul with the Orioles holding a three-games-to-one lead.

In St. Paul, Baltimore won two of the next three games to win the Little World Series, five games to two. In the final game, a Saints runner was called out on a close play at the plate in the last of the eighth, setting off another shower of seat cushions at Lexington Park. After the game, fans attacked Charles Schmidt, an Orioles vice president, along with a Baltimore fan.

The Saints didn't repeat in 1923, even though they won 111 games and had four pitchers with at least 20 wins: Merritt (20), Hall (24), Cliff Markle (25), and Sheehan (31).

The team won its final 10 games in August and held first place through most of September. On the final day of the month, however, the power-laden

Kansas City Blues overtook them. After losing the first game of a doubleheader the next day, while St. Paul was losing its third straight game to seventh-place Indianapolis, the Blues won their final eight games of the season to finish two games in front of the Saints.

Sheehan's 31 victories that year matched the American Association record for pitching wins in a season, tying "Long Tom" Hughes, who had done it with the Millers in 1910. Sheehan already had a connection with Saints teammate Haas when he first arrived in St. Paul in 1921. They had been together on the 1915 Philadelphia Athletics, Sheehan joining the team after Haas's 16-walk debut. Both players experienced ignominy in Philadelphia. In 1916 Sheehan's

STALLING *on* SUNDAY

The Saints fell just short of the pennant in 1923, and one game in early July could have meant one more victory but instead got away from them—and resulted in a riot at Lexington Park. After losing the first game of a doubleheader with Milwaukee on July 1, St. Paul carried a lead into the top of the ninth in the nightcap. When Milwaukee rallied to tie the score, the Saints' strategy turned to stalling. By law, Sunday baseball games had to be stopped at 6:00 PM. If the Saints could draw the game out to that hour before the full inning was completed, the score would revert to that of the last full inning, which had the Saints leading 3–2, thus giving them the win.

Manager Mike Kelley did what he could to prolong the game, including bringing in a new pitcher, and the fans joined in by throwing cushions and bottles on the field. Milwaukee manager Harry Clark threatened to protest the game if the antics didn't cease. Milwaukee's Ivy Griffin was on first base when the game resumed, and he promptly took off for second. No one bothered to cover the base, and catcher Mike Gonzalez's throw sailed into center. Griffin continued to third and kept going, heading for home. Outfielder Walter Christensen threw to the plate, but Gonzalez made no effort to take the throw, preferring to let Griffin score a run that seemed sure to be wiped out when the curfew kicked in a few minutes later.

Instead of granting St. Paul the victory by the curfew rules, however, umpire John Mullen declared a forfeit win for the Brewers. Already unpopular with the fans for some of his other calls that day, Mullen became a target of more seat cushions tossed from the stands, and spectators swarmed onto the field. "One enraged fan aimed a right hand punch at the umpire," reported the *St. Paul Pioneer Press,* "but a vigilant policeman thrust him aside before he could strike again. Another slammed a leather cushion in Mullen's face, but the umpire was jammed through the dense throng with only slight injury." However, Milwaukee pitcher Chuck Palmer was taken to the hospital after being hit in the face with a soda bottle during the melee.

The Saints' failure to hold a ninth-inning lead or to run out the clock with more panache was costly. The Kansas City Blues won in Minneapolis on its way to a four-game sweep of the Millers, pulling closer to St. Paul in a memorable pennant race that ended in frustration for the Saints.

Tom Sheehan had a Jekyll-and-Hyde type of career in pro baseball. He won more than 62 percent of his decisions in the minor leagues and only 30 percent of his decisions in the majors.

PHOTO COURTESY JIM HINMAN

won-lost record was 1–16. He pitched again in the majors from 1924 to 1926, but he made his mark in the minors. Sheehan won 26 games with Atlanta in the Southern Association before coming to St. Paul and won 26 games with Kansas City in the American Association after his time with the Saints. In all, he won 250 games in his minor-league career; his lifetime major-league record was 17–39.

Sheehan put more than fifty years into baseball, coaching in the majors and managing in the minors with the Millers. He was a scout for the San Francisco Giants into the 1970s and also managed the team for more than half a season in 1960.

THE SAINTS WIN IT ALL

Even after dropping to 96 wins in 1924, the Saints made it back to first place and did so with a new manager. Kelley had once again moved to Minneapolis, purchasing the Millers and taking over as their manager. Under Allen, who had been promoted from catcher to manager (while still playing part time), St. Paul finished four games ahead of Indianapolis for the American Association pennant. The Indians held a half-game lead with less than a week left in the season when they came to St. Paul for a five-game series with the Saints. St. Paul won four of those games to open up a two-and-a-half game lead. The Saints then wrapped up their season by splitting four games with Louisville, while the Millers swept a three-game series against Indianapolis.

In the Little World Series, the Saints once again fell behind early to the Baltimore Orioles. The first game was tied 2–2 when Cliff Lee put St. Paul ahead with a home run off Grove in the top of the ninth. However, in the last of the ninth, the Orioles' Merwin Jacobson hit a two-run homer off Markle to give Baltimore a 4–3 win. The Saints tied the series the next day as Merritt pitched a three-hit shutout and Charley Dressen had 3 hits, including a home run. The third game ended in a 6–6 tie, called by darkness after thirteen innings. Behind Grove and George Earnshaw (later a three-time 20-game winner with the Philadelphia Athletics), the Orioles won the next two games to take a lead of three games to one as the series moved from Baltimore to St. Paul.

The Saints trailed 2–0 against Grove in the next game but came back with 4 runs in the last of the sixth before going on to win 5–3. St. Paul shortstop Mark Koenig, who had doubled earlier, started the comeback by leading off the sixth with a home run. After the Orioles won the next day to pull within one game of the championship, the Saints stayed alive with a 3–2 win, as Tony Faeth defeated Earnshaw and Koenig had three hits. Grove was on the mound the next afternoon, but Paul Fittery beat him 3–1 and the Saints had tied the series.

It all came down to a tenth and final game on Monday, October 13. The Saints got off to a 5–0 lead. Baltimore scored 3 runs against Merritt in the top of the seventh, but St. Paul got a run back in the bottom of the inning and won the game, 6–3. The Saints had won their first Little World Series championship.

After beating the Orioles, the Saints headed west to meet the Seattle Indians, champions of the Pacific Coast League. It was the first championship matchup between the leagues since the contentious series of 1919 between St. Paul and Vernon. A best-of-nine series was planned to determine the champion of the minors.

The Saints waited until the Pacific Coast League completed its schedule—with Seattle hanging on for the pennant on the season's final day—and left for the West Coast. When they arrived on Thursday, October 23, the weather in Seattle was described as "ideal." That didn't last. A downpour on Saturday postponed the first game. The weather cleared enough on Sunday, and St. Paul was able to beat Seattle 12–4. The Saints had 22 hits in the game, including a home run by Haas.

Another bout of heavy showers moved in an hour before the scheduled game on Monday, leaving the grounds unfit for play. Players on both teams talked about canceling the rest of the series. When the rain continued Tuesday, the teams agreed to give the weather one more chance. If they couldn't resume the series on Wednesday, the players would go home. (One didn't even wait that long: Seattle's Brick Eldred, who had homered in the Sunday game, took off for his home in Sacramento, California, after the Tuesday game.)

When the Wednesday game was rained out, the series was canceled. St. Paul claimed the title by winning the only game, and each of the Saints came away with $175.

The Little World Series of 1920 to 1924 matched two of the strongest clubs in the history of the minor leagues. In 2001, to commemorate the hundredth anniversary of the National Association, historians Bill Weiss and Marshall Wright rated the top 100 minor-league teams of the twentieth century. Three St. Paul Saints teams—1920, 1922, and 1923—made the list, with the 1920 team ranked as the sixth best. Five Baltimore Orioles teams—1919, 1920, 1921, 1923, and 1924—made the list, three of them in the top ten.

Dominance such as this was possible in part because the minor leagues withdrew from the National Agreement with the majors after World War I. The result was a short period during which major-league teams could no longer draft players from minor-league rosters for a set price. Some players got stuck in the minors as their owners held out for top prices from major-league clubs. One example was Grove of Baltimore, who remained in the minors longer than needed because his owner, Dunn, demanded a price that no major-league team would offer. When the draft resumed by the mid-1920s, minor-league operators could no longer employ such tactics.

CHAPTER 4

The St. Paul–New York Connection

THE SAINTS WON their first Little World Series in 1924 and by the end of the year were under new ownership. On New Year's Eve, John Norton sold the team to a group headed by Bob Connery. The previous owners had other primary interests, George Lennon with clothing and Norton with real estate.

Connery, on the other hand, was a baseball man. He played and managed in the minor leagues before becoming a scout. It was his recommendation that convinced the St. Louis Cardinals to purchase Rogers Hornsby, who became one of the greatest hitters ever, from Denison in the Texas Oklahoma League in 1915. Eight years later, Connery was called on for a second opinion before the Yankees signed Lou Gehrig.

Connery was a longtime friend of Mike Kelley, who had recommended him as a scout to Miller Huggins, Kelley's former second baseman with the Saints. Huggins and Connery were first connected with the Cardinals and stayed together when Huggins became manager of the Yankees.

Although it was originally believed that Huggins's sister, Myrtle, was an investor in the team, subsequent research by Jim Hinman and Steve Steinberg has revealed that Huggins himself, in fact, owned shares in the Saints. Following his death, Huggins's estate remained among the team's stockholders.

THE YANKEE-SAINTS PIPELINE

A player pipeline between the Saints and the major-league teams of Connery and Huggins had been in place for a number of years before Connery became a Saints owner. When he bought the team, Connery cut his ties with the Yankees and stated that St. Paul would not operate as a farm team. The *St. Paul Pioneer Press* quoted Connery as saying, "We shall not consider ourselves feeders to the big leagues."

That didn't mean he wouldn't use his connections to get players for the Saints. Three weeks after the purchase Connery was in New York forming an unofficial alliance with the Yankees. The *Pioneer Press* reported that Huggins would likely option his top prospects to St. Paul for seasoning. The *Washington Post* added that the Yankees' young talent would "be put to pasture on a Western farm," referring to St. Paul. In return, the Yankees often got a first look and chance to buy players off the Saints' roster. The connection between the Yankees and Saints was evident into the 1930s.

Connery didn't confine his dealings to the Yankees, however. Within a few days he sent catcher Leo Dixon to the St. Louis Browns in exchange for five players, including first baseman Pat Collins, outfielder Cedric Durst, and pitcher Ray Kolp, who all went on to have a good year for the Saints. After the 1925 season Connery then dealt Collins to the Yankees for $20,000 and several players, including shortstop Pee-Wee Wanninger. (During the 1925 season Wanninger had been involved in two consecutive-games streaks with the Yankees. He replaced Everett Scott at shortstop on May 6, ending Scott's record string of playing 1,307 straight games. On June 1, Gehrig pinch-hit for Wanninger, starting a streak of 2,130 consecutive games played.)

"Connery was a real trader," wrote Hinman in *Brief History of the St. Paul Saints*. "Only three members of the team he bought would be with the team after two years." The three players Hinman referred to were outfielder Bruno Haas, pitcher Herb McQuaid, and Oscar Roettger, who went from pitching to playing the outfield and first base.

Roster shuffling wasn't just a result of trades. Major-league teams could draft players from the minors, paying a set fee to the teams from whom they were obtained. Even during a period of independently owned minor-league teams, which controlled their own players, the nature of the system itself meant that players would be shuttled up and down the ladder. Those good enough to play in the majors couldn't have that chance denied. Savvy minor-league operators tried to make their own deals rather than have their players plucked away in the draft. The financial success of teams in the minors usually depended on making good deals. A minor-league club was still more focused on winning a championship than teams today, but sales of players to the majors was also a necessary component of a team's operation.

The ability of major-league teams to draft players from minor-league rosters again meant the Saints would have trouble continuing the dominance they had displayed over the past six years. However, Connery's ownership and resulting deals allowed the Saints to continue to have good teams.

After spending most or part of five seasons with the Saints, Koenig was sold to New York during the 1925 season. Huggins and Yankees general manager Ed Barrow had come to St. Paul in May to scout Koenig, according to author

Steinberg. Two weeks later New York worked out a deal to send several players and $50,000 to the Saints in exchange for Koenig.

In 1926 Koenig became the starting shortstop for the Yankees. He was never the star Huggins and Barrow had hoped for, but he was a regular on three Yankees World Series teams. Years later, when Koenig was with the Chicago Cubs, his Yankee connection made him a part of one of the team's legendary moments. The Cubs were the Yankees' opponents in that year's World Series and had drawn Ruth's wrath by voting Koenig only a partial World Series share. Speaking up for his former teammate, Ruth called the Cubs cheapskates. Chicago fans responded strongly, and Ruth answered their insults with a long home run to center field at Wrigley Field, one he had allegedly "called" by pointing to the bleachers before hitting it.

Another shortstop, Leo Durocher, was owned by the Yankees and assigned to St. Paul in 1927. Durocher later had a long career as a manager, which earned him a plaque in the Hall of Fame. The Yankees sent right-handed pitcher George Pipgras to St. Paul, where he won 22 games in 1926, before bringing him back to the majors. Pipgras won 24 games for the Yankees in 1928. In 1930 Vernon "Lefty" Gomez started the season with New York before being sent to St. Paul for further development. Gomez was back in the major leagues for good in 1931, continuing an outstanding career with the Yankees that put him in the Hall of Fame.

Others in the New York–St. Paul pipeline were a pair of stars on the 1929 Saints, Dusty Cooke and Ben Chapman. Cooke had a .362 batting average and led the American Association with 33 home runs, 148 runs, 105 walks,

MOBSTERS

The Bob Connery era of St. Paul Saints ownership corresponded with the peak of a gangster period in St. Paul. The O'Connor System, named after Chief of Police John O'Connor, made St. Paul a safe haven for criminals as long as they met certain conditions, the primary one being not to commit crimes in the city. Bootlegging was big in the 1920s but declined greatly at the end of Prohibition, so many gangsters turned to armed robbery and kidnapping to make money. Banker Edward Bremer and

brewmaster William Hamm Jr. were snatched and held for ransom in the 1930s. This was the time period when famous gangsters Alvin Karpis, Homer Van Meter, Baby Face Nelson, John Dillinger, and Ma, Doc, and Freddie Barker were connected with St. Paul. Dillinger lived in St. Paul only briefly, but it was long enough for him to be involved in a shootout at the Lincoln Court Apartments, a short distance from the Saints' home, in March 1934. Dillinger escaped, only to end up dead a few months later, shot by police and federal agents in Chicago.

and 120 runs batted in. His major-league career was hampered by injuries, however, and he never came close to those numbers with the Yankees.

Chapman also had a great year in St. Paul in 1929. He led the league with 162 runs and hit 31 home runs while driving in 137 runs. Chapman went on to some solid seasons as a player in New York. He is most remembered, however, for his abusive treatment of Jackie Robinson in 1947, when Robinson was breaking baseball's color barrier and Chapman was manager of the Philadelphia Phillies.

The 1929 Saints won 102 games but finished eight and a half games behind the Kansas City Blues, who won 111. Bubbles Hargrave, who had been the best catcher in the National League in the 1920s, was back with the Saints as a player and manager, succeeding Nick Allen in the latter role. Catching part time, Hargrave produced a .369 batting average. Roettger played first base and drove in 132 runs to go with 13 home runs and a .326 batting average. An aging Haas was a regular in the outfield and hit .296. Billy Rogell split time between shortstop and second base while producing a .336 batting average.

The hardest hitting of the 1929 season came in the morning game of the Independence Day twin bill with the Millers. Huck Betts was on the mound for St. Paul in the last of the third when Minneapolis's Hughie McMullen hit

George Pipgras (far left) and Oscar Roettger (far right) both spent time in St. Paul on their way to the New York Yankees. They are shown here with Yankee teammates Carl Mays and Harvey Hendrick in 1923.

a grounder to Roettger. Betts covered first and took Roettger's throw. As Betts crossed the base, McMullen stepped on his foot. McMullen later admitted that the spiking was intentional in retaliation for a pitch Betts had thrown behind his head.

Betts also indicated he was aware of McMullen's motives; he took the ball from his glove and fired it at his antagonist. Sammy Bohne, coaching at first base for the Millers, rushed at Betts with his fists swinging. "The human thing was to sock and sock Bohne did," wrote Halsey Hall in the *Minneapolis Journal*, "and we'll say, as socks go, it was a good one. The Millers had been riding Betts hard all day, but that's in the game and if Mr. Betts can't take a riding like the good pitcher which he sometimes is, it's just too bad for him."

BATTING-AVERAGE BATTLES

Record books tracking yearly leaders in the American Association don't agree on the rightful recipients of batting-title crowns. Disagreements about the minimums needed to qualify for percentage titles, such as batting average, led to changes in the record books.

In 1929 the American Association required a minimum of 100 games played to qualify for a percentage title. Bubbles Hargrave of St. Paul was originally crowned the 1929 batting champion, with a .369 average. He played in 104 games that year. A few years later, the league officially changed the leader to Toledo's Art Ruble, who had a .376 average in 1929 but played in only 89 games. Ruble had more hits, at-bats, and plate appearances than Hargrave, and the American Association decided he was more deserving of the league batting title.

Many years later, researchers compiling a minor-league encyclopedia established a minimum standard of 2.6 at-bats per game and applied this to all leagues for all time, regardless of what a league used as its minimum at the time. As a result, both Ruble and Hargrave were removed as 1929 qualifiers, leaving St. Paul's Dusty Cooke (.358) as the batting champion. Since Cooke also led the league in home runs and RBIs that season, he retroactively became the American Association's first Triple Crown winner.

Researchers used similar gyrations in other years as well. Vern Washington of St. Paul was removed as the batting-average leader for 1936 in place of Jack Winsett of Columbus, who then became the American Association's second Triple Crown recipient.

Regardless of what the revisionists have tried to do by anointing different leaders in percentage categories, the official American Association record book—first compiled by Lou McKenna in the 1930s and continued by the American Association through its various incarnations through 1997—continued to list Ruble as the batting leader in 1929 and Washington in 1936. Thus, the only two official Triple Crown winners in the American Association are Ted Williams of Minneapolis in 1938 and Ab Wright of Minneapolis in 1940.

As Betts and Bohne battled, Roettger came to the defense of his pitcher, and the dugouts emptied. According to McMullen, "You hit anyone near you."

Roettger may have gotten the worst of the brawl, having to leave the game because his eyes were too swollen to see. It was Roettger who characterized the Minneapolis–St. Paul rivalry as "pay days. . . . Even during the Depression, fans would come to see the Millers-Saints games." Despite the bad blood at Nicollet Park that day in 1929, Roettger said the players on both teams were good friends off the field. The teams barnstormed together across the state after the season to "have some fun and get a little pheasant hunting done," he recalled.

A lifelong baseball and sports man, Roettger went to work for Rawlings Sporting Goods in 1939 and continued with the company into the 1980s. He also attended the annual minor-league meetings for more than fifty years. At the 1983 meetings in Nashville, Tennessee, Roettger received the King of Baseball title, an award in recognition of longtime service to professional baseball.

Hargrave lasted only one year as Saints manager, but not because he wasn't able to capture the pennant in 1929. Rather, his play had been so good that he

ANGELO GIULIANI

Angelo Giuliani grew up within a few blocks of the center-field gate of St. Paul's Lexington Park, close enough to hear the cheers from the ballpark. While still in high school, he served as the bullpen catcher for the Saints and joined the team as a player in 1932. Between 1936 and 1943 Giuliani caught for the St. Louis Browns, Washington Senators, and Brooklyn Dodgers at the major-league level.

In 1930 he had the chance to warm up Lefty Gomez in the bullpen, when the future Hall of Famer was getting a final tune-up in the minors. "He used to knock me back a few feet," Giuliani recalled. He had the chance to catch for Gomez again thirteen years later when Lefty was pitching his final game in the majors while with the Senators.

Giuliani had other Hall of Fame brushes during his career as well. While with the Browns in 1936, he played for manager Rogers Hornsby and roomed with "Sunny Jim" Bottomley. That same year, he was in the lineup when Bob Feller of Cleveland made his first start in the majors. Feller struck out 15 batters, including Giuliani once, but Giuliani also had 1 of the only 6 hits St. Louis got that day. Catching for Washington on July 4, 1939, Giuliani was present at Yankee Stadium when Lou Gehrig made his famous farewell speech.

Giuliani returned to the Twin Cities in 1941 and 1942 to play for Minneapolis. In 1949, he came out of retirement to play one game for the Millers when injuries left the team short on catchers.

After his playing career, Giuliani became a scout for the New York Giants and later the Washington Senators, remaining with the team after it moved to Minnesota. He said one of his proudest moments was seeing four of the players

earned a promotion to the Yankees in 1930. Connery tapped longtime friend and former St. Paul pitcher Albert "Lefty" Leifield to manage the team.

LEFTY'S CHAMPS

Under Leifield, the Saints had another second-place finish in 1930, but the next year St. Paul won 104 games and the American Association pennant. Roettger came through with another big year, hitting .357 and driving in 123 runs. The rest of the infield was also productive. Second baseman Jack Saltzgaver had a .340 batting average, hit 19 home runs, and led the league with 26 stolen bases. On the left side, shortstop Joe Morrissey hit 22 home runs and third baseman Marty Hopkins 23. Two other players—outfielders George "Kiddo" Davis and Hal Anderson—also hit more than 20 homers. Betts led the pitchers with 22 wins, and Slim Harriss had 20.

The 1931 Little World Series (renamed the Junior World Series the following year) opened in St. Paul, and the Saints got off to a good start against the

St. Paul native Angelo Giuliani (his name misspelled on this baseball card) played four seasons with the Saints in the 1930s before getting called up to the big leagues.

he signed—Tim Laudner, Kent Hrbek, John Castino, and Jim Eisenreich—in the opening-day lineup for the Twins in 1983. Giuliani also interacted with hundreds of thousands of kids through the baseball clinics he led for many years throughout the state and beyond.

Nearly as important as baseball to Giuliani were his homing pigeons, which he started raising when he was a teenager. He says he once gave Halsey Hall an assist in relaying his account of a Minneapolis Millers game in Kansas City, Missouri. "The Western Union operators were on strike," Giuliani recalled, "and Halsey was worried how his story would get back in time for the next day's edition. I put one of my birds in a crate for Halsey, and he hauled it down to Kansas City. When he finished his story, he put it into the capsule attached to the bird's leg and let it go. As I recall, the pigeon delivered Halsey's story on time and he made his deadline."

THE SAINTS' $100,000 INFIELD

The "$100,000 Infield" of third baseman Marty Hopkins, shortstop Joe Morrissey, second baseman Jack Saltzgaver, and first baseman Oscar Roettger helped lead the Saints to the American Association pennant in 1931.

COURTESY JIM HINMAN

Connie Mack's Philadelphia Athletics teams of the early 1910s had the "$100,000 infield" of Stuffy McInnis, Eddie Collins, Jack Barry, and Frank "Home Run" Baker. The 1931 Saints infield of Oscar Roettger, Jack Saltzgaver, Joe Morrissey, and Marty Hopkins was dubbed with the same label. Owner Bob Connery was offering the players to major-league teams with an asking price of $50,000 for Saltzgaver and another $50,000 for the other three. Three big-league scouts were reportedly on the trail of the players. Connery eventually sold Saltzgaver to his regular trading partner, the Yankees, for an amount slightly less than what he had been seeking.

International League champion Rochester (New York) Red Wings. The first game was scoreless until Roettger hit a grand slam in the eighth. Betts finished off a six-hitter for a 4–0 win, giving him a third straight shutout after pitching scoreless games in his final two starts of the regular season.

However, the Red Wings took the next four games. In Rochester, the Saints stayed alive with a 9–3 win. They were victorious again the next night 9–5, behind Betts, who won the game on the mound and also hit a double and a triple. But that was as close as they came, as Rochester won the eighth game to take the series, five games to three.

During the season the Saints and Yankees consummated another deal. Huggins's successor as New York manager, Joe McCarthy, scouted Saltzgaver. The Yankees purchased Saltzgaver from St. Paul for $40,000, along with right-handed pitcher Johnny Murphy for $10,000. While Saltzgaver produced little in New York, Murphy became a useful relief specialist for the Yankees for eleven seasons.

Other major transactions included the Yankees paying St. Paul $40,000 for Julian Wera (a native of Winona, Minnesota) before the 1927 season and $25,000 for Eugene Robertson that midseason. Neither had a significant career in New York.

In his book *Ed Barrow: The Bulldog Who Built the Yankees' First Dynasty*, a biography of the longtime Yankees general manager, Dan Levitt noted that the relationship between the clubs benefited Connery and the Saints much more than it did the Yankees. "New York paid him [Connery] huge prices for his players," Levitt writes, "and none became stars." According to Levitt, Yankees owner Jacob Ruppert complained that he had spent as much as $300,000 for players from St. Paul—a figure supported by his team's financial records—yet had little to show for it. "Barrow and his scouts did not distinguish themselves when buying players from the Saints," Levitt continues, "and one can only wonder at Huggins's influence in these acquisitions. He had an obvious conflict of interest, and Barrow must have known of his ownership stake."

On the other hand, author Steinberg notes that Huggins tried to mitigate the conflict. An example was the Yankees' 1928 purchase of pitcher Fred Heimach from the Saints for $20,000. According to Steinberg, Huggins urged Ruppert and Barrow to send their own scouts to St. Paul to see Heimach themselves, rather than just take his recommendation, to ensure that the decision was made in the best interests of the Yankees, not for Huggins's financial benefit.

The pipeline between the teams stopped after the 1931 season. It wasn't because Barrow finally realized how poor the purchases from St. Paul had been nor that Huggins was no longer alive. It was because the Yankees decided to follow the lead of the St. Louis Cardinals and build their own farm system. One of the minor-league clubs the Yankees took control of was the Newark (New

Jersey) Bears, which became one of the most powerful teams in the history of the minors and helped stock the ongoing New York dynasty.

St. Paul was left out of the mix and no longer had an East Coast sugar daddy to keep it solvent. Connery may have foreseen this shift and began looking at offers to sell the Saints. Only a week after St. Paul lost to Rochester in the 1931 Little World Series, Connery announced that a pair of wealthy Canadian sportsmen were about to pay him a "lavish" price for the team. Such a transaction would have resulted in the Saints being moved to Winnipeg. Although this deal didn't happen, it became clear that Connery's reign with the Saints was winding down. The bigger question for local fans was if the team would remain in St. Paul.

CHAPTER 5

Ownership Drama and the Road to the Farm

A "NEW DEAL" FOR THE SAINTS

After winning the American Association pennant in 1931, the Saints dropped in the standings. Attendance at Lexington Park also plummeted. Once again St. Paul fans faced unsettling news about the team's future in the city. When the Saints drew fewer than 75,000 fans in 1934, the word was that the team would be moved to Peoria, Illinois.

The St. Paul newspapers reporting the dire details also got involved with civic leaders and the business community to keep the Saints, leading efforts to raise money to buy the team. The November 15, 1934, *St. Paul Dispatch* had a cheerier headline: "St. Paul to Keep Baseball Franchise: Group Gets Club from Old Owners."

The *Dispatch–Pioneer Press* (the two papers had the same owner at this time) and the *St. Paul Daily News* were listed among those participating in the purchase of the Saints, and *Dispatch–Pioneer Press* sports editor Lou McKenna became the team's business manager. Walter Seeger, a local refrigerator magnate, was named president, and he later bought a controlling interest in the Saints. Former owner John Norton once again had a stake in the team, and outgoing owner Bob Connery stayed on as a stockholder and investor.

St. Paul mayor Mark Gehan said, "I congratulate the new owners of the St. Paul baseball team. A baseball club is a matter of substantial advertising to St. Paul, and it furnishes not only recreation and amusement to our people, but it is a very valuable asset in attracting visitors. The civic pride displayed by the new owners deserves support of the community."

Frank Delaney, who chaired the St. Paul Association of Commerce's baseball committee, echoed the chirpy spirit of the mayor. "Organized baseball is a distinct asset to the community," he said. "St. Paul in the past has had its share

of winning teams, and I feel confident that the public will do its part to back up the new owners and maintain our reputation as a good baseball town."

Jim Hinman, in *Brief History of the St. Paul Saints,* writes that the owners declared a "New Deal" for the fans and explained some of the components: "A public-address system was installed at Lexington, replacing grounds-keeper Emil Bossard and his megaphone. Reserved seats were numbered so particular seats could be bought. Lexington was also repainted and the restrooms enlarged. The team was outfitted in new black-and-green uniforms and given warm-up jackets modeled after those of the Detroit Tigers. Radio broadcasts of all games were transferred to the *Pioneer Press* and *Dispatch* radio station WTCN."

An item in the June 30, 1935, *St. Paul Dispatch* noted that the broadcasts would be sponsored by Minneapolis-based General Mills, makers of Wheaties. George Higgins, who had broadcast Minneapolis Millers games at Nicollet Park the year before, was to do the announcing. "Higgins," according to the *Dispatch*, "will present descriptive play of the games with the inside knowledge of baseball through his rating as a prominent umpire for eleven years and [is] considered a leading authority in all sports. . . . The baseball broadcast is another step in the 'new deal' for the St. Paul club."

UNOFFICIAL WHITE SOX FARM CLUB

A former major-league catcher and skipper, Gabby Street managed the St. Paul Saints in 1936 and 1937.

The new deal lived up to its name in transactions, in the dugout, and on the field. The Saints had Marty McManus and Charles "Gabby" Street as managers in 1935 and 1936. Street had been a catcher in the majors in the early 1900s and managed the St. Louis Cardinals to two pennants and one world championship in 1930 and 1931. He also caught Walter Johnson in Washington, between 1908 and 1911, although he is better remembered for a 1908 stunt in that city, when he caught a ball dropped from the Washington Monument.

Under Street the Saints rose to second place in 1936 and made the postseason in a new playoff scheme called the Governor's Cup. Replicating the system used in the International League, the Governor's Cup series featured the top four teams from the regular season playing for the league title and a spot in the Junior World Series (formerly the Little World Series). The Saints lost in the first round of the 1936 playoffs. After a drop-off in 1937, Street was replaced as manager by Phil Todt.

A slick-fielding first baseman, Todt had been a popular figure at Lexington Park through much of the 1930s. Good with the glove and the bat, he topped 90 runs batted in for the Saints in four seasons. In 1935 he got 6 hits in one game.

A number of other Saints distinguished themselves during these years as well. Outfielder Ivey Shiver hit 31 home runs, scored 107 runs, and drove in

125 runs in 1935. Also that year, Angelo Giuliani became the Saints' regular catcher. Giuliani had grown up near Lexington Park and, while still in high school, was the team's bullpen catcher.

Another St. Paul native, Larry Rosenthal, did an outstanding job in center field from 1933 until he was sent to the White Sox during the 1936 season in exchange for Vern "George" Washington. Despite playing only 73 games with St. Paul that season, Washington was credited with the American Association batting championship, having hit .390. Hank Steinbacher had a .353 batting average and led the league with 49 doubles in 1936 while producing a 35-game hitting streak.

The pitching staff included Monty Stratton, who won 17 games for the Saints in 1935 before going back to the Chicago White Sox. He produced a pair of 15-win seasons for Chicago before he shot himself in the knee in a hunting

LARRY ROSENTHAL

Larry Rosenthal grew up in St. Paul and played baseball at St. Agnes High School, less than two miles from Lexington Park. Within a few years, he was playing there as a member of the St. Paul Saints.

Rosenthal could pitch as well as hit, but it was his ability to cover ground in the outfield that attracted the Saints. He worked out with the team in 1933, along with other local standouts, including Angelo Giuliani. Rosenthal made it onto the Saints and three years later debuted with the Chicago White Sox in the majors.

In 1941 Cleveland purchased Rosenthal from Chicago. That year he not only played in the game in which Joe DiMaggio's 56-game hitting streak was stopped but he played a part in nearly getting DiMaggio one more chance to get a hit. The Yankees held a 4–1 lead in the last of the ninth when Rosenthal pinch-hit for Ray Mack and drilled a two-run triple to pull the Indians within a run. If Rosenthal could score and send the game into extra innings, DiMaggio would have been the fourth batter up for the Yankees in the tenth and might have gotten another shot at extending his

streak. However, Clarence "Soup" Campbell hit a comebacker to the pitcher, and Rosenthal, trying to come home, was caught in a rundown and tagged out. Roy Weatherly then grounded out to end the game as well as DiMaggio's hitting streak.

Rosenthal had another opportunity to vex the Yankees in 1944 when he was playing for the Philadelphia Athletics. After a loss in the opener of a three-game series, New York faced the Athletics in a doubleheader before more than 55,000 fans at Yankee Stadium on September 17. The teams were tied for second place, a half game out of first. Bob Evans, in a biography of Rosenthal for the book *Minnesotans in Baseball,* explained that Rosenthal, sitting on the bench, noticed Yankees hurler Ernie Bonham was tipping off his pitches with something in his delivery. Although most of the inexperienced Athletics hitters were unable to take advantage, Rosenthal would get a chance to exploit Bonham, who held a 4–3 lead going into the ninth inning. As Evans described it,

The first A's batter in the ninth singled, and as fate would have it, Connie Mack looked down

mishap. The accident required the amputation of his right leg, ending his major-league career, although he continued to pitch in the minor leagues. He was the subject of a 1949 movie, *The Stratton Story,* in which he was portrayed by James Stewart.

Right-hander Lou Fette had a won-lost record of 25–8 with the Saints in 1937. The following year he was with Boston in the National League and won 20 games as a thirty-year-old major-league rookie.

Art Herring was a mound mainstay, pitching nine seasons for the Saints starting in 1936. Herring reached double-figures in victories during seven of those years.

In 1937 the Saints finally installed lights at Lexington Park, and the Millers did the same at Nicollet Park. The teams scheduled their initial night games

Larry Rosenthal played nearly 600 games at the major-league level and more than 1,000 in the minors during a baseball career lasting fifteen years.

the bench to Rosenthal, and called him over. Rosenthal recalled, "Mr. Mack said to me 'Now Mr. Roosevelt, we don't want these Yankees winning any more pennants, so I want you to go up there and hit a home run.'" Mack sometimes did a whimsical play on players' last names, so Rosenthal became Roosevelt. . . . Mack had Rosenthal hit for George Kell, and Rosenthal selected one of Bonham's fastballs and lined it into the right-field stands. The two-run homer gave Philadelphia a 5–4 win.

The Athletics won the second game of the doubleheader as well, and the sweep of the Yankees squelched New York's hopes for a pennant in 1944.

Rosenthal played with the Athletics into June 1945 and in the minors with several teams, including the Saints again, until 1948. He continued playing amateur baseball in the state and, at the age of thirty-nine, had a .379 batting average for the Winona Chiefs in the highly regarded Southern Minnesota League.

on back-to-back evenings in July. The event in St. Paul drew more than 9,000 people, including American Association president George Trautman and former president Thomas Hickey. To allow for the full effect of the lights, the game was scheduled for 8:45 PM, leaving time for the skies to darken. All the ballparks in the league now had lights, and night baseball was becoming a staple in the minor leagues.

Although the Saints were still a few years away from becoming a full-fledged farm team of a major-league organization, from 1935 through 1940 they had a working relationship with the Chicago White Sox. The degree of formality of working agreements between major- and minor-league teams at this time varied; often it meant that a major-league team would option players to a specific minor-league team, which was still free to make deals with other major-league teams.

In the late 1930s the Millers had a similar arrangement with the Boston Red Sox, which led to Ted Williams spending a season in Minneapolis. Nineteen-year-old Williams, finishing a minor-league tune-up, was the most exciting and intriguing player in the American Association in 1938. He led the league in

MORE BRUSHES *with* BASEBALL LEGENDS

The American Association was a minor league only a step from the majors. Fans got to watch many players who had been major-league stars as well as players who were on their way to becoming big names. Once in a while, they even had the chance to see these great players in their prime.

In 1927 the Yankees Murderers' Row team played an exhibition game against the Saints at Lexington Park. Babe Ruth and Lou Gehrig were in the lineup for New York, and, prior to the game, the pair "spilled nearly a quart of ink autographing baseballs and score cards for small boys," according to the *St. Paul Pioneer Press*.

In July 1935 the world-champion St. Louis Cardinals also came to St. Paul for an exhibition. It was clear that Dizzy Dean, who had won 30 games the previous year, wouldn't be in the game for the Cardinals since he had pitched the day before. However, St. Paul fans were angered

when Dean and his brother, Paul Dean (a former American Association hurler who won 19 games for the Cardinals in 1934), would not even come out of the dugout when introduced. Dizzy Dean was unhappy about his team taking a detour for a game in St. Paul rather than going directly from Chicago to St. Louis, and he took it out on the fans. Blasted by the local press as well as by Cardinals manager Frank Frisch, the Deans sent a letter of apology that appeared in the *St. Paul Dispatch*. Dizzy Dean said he hoped he would have a chance to pitch should the Cardinals play in St. Paul again. He got his chance on August 14, 1936, when the Cardinals returned to St. Paul and Dean started the game. Before he took the mound, he had a turn at the plate as the Cardinals scored 7 runs in the top of the first inning. Dean capped the rally with a home run to left. He then retired the Saints in order in the last of the first.

numerous offensive categories, including the three that gave him the Triple Crown: batting average, home runs, and runs batted in.

However, St. Paul had the best team in the league that year, along with the league's co–Most Valuable Player. Minneapolis's Williams finished third in the balloting.

THE "BAM" TRIO

Foster "Babe" Ganzel became the Saints' manager in 1938. He had played third base on the powerful Minneapolis teams of the early 1930s. His father, Charley Ganzel, named his son after his best friend and teammate on the 1884 St. Paul team, Elmer Foster.

Six pitchers had at least 10 wins for the 1938 Saints: Vic Frasier with 17; Herring with 16; Ray "Babe" Phelps, Lloyd Brown, and Merritt "Sugar" Cain with 12; and Italo Chelini with 10.

On offense, St. Paul had the "BAM trio" of Bejma, Anton, and McCullough—second baseman Ollie Bejma, first baseman Leroy Anton, and outfielder Malin "Bit" McCullough—although over the first part of the season the initial letter was better filled by Bob Boken, who played all infield positions as well as the outfield before settling in at third base. All contributed to the team's success in 1938, as did catcher Ken Silvestri, outfielders George Stumpf and Fred Berger, and shortstop Tony York. But the leader that year was Bejma, who did an outstanding job in the field while producing a .326 batting average with 25 home runs and 114 runs batted in. Bejma also walked 60 times, meaning that he reached base safely nearly 40 percent of the time in 1938.

Bejma had spent the previous five seasons shuttling between San Antonio of the Class A Texas League and the St. Louis Browns of the American League. When he was unable to make the major-league squad in the spring of 1938, the Browns released Bejma, who ended up in St. Paul. Bejma started slowly in 1938, as did the Saints.

At the end of May the Saints were 15–17 and in fifth place; Bejma was hitting .227 with just one home run and had been pulled from the lineup. He got his chance again in early June when Boken, playing second base, ran into right fielder Washington while chasing a short fly ball in a game against Toledo. Washington, who was hitting .426 at the time, broke two bones in his shoulder, ending his season; Boken suffered lacerations and bruises and missed four games. When Boken returned, it was at third base in place of Jesse Landrum, while Bejma stayed in the lineup as the second baseman.

Following a rainy month of May that led to numerous rainouts, the weather improved in June, and so did the Saints. An 11-game winning streak from June

8 to June 18 lifted St. Paul from sixth to second place, just two games behind Indianapolis. Bejma had raised his batting average by 50 percentage points by the time the Saints' streak ended, and he kept climbing.

The Saints finished June with a great pitchers' duel between Phelps and Marvin Breuer of Kansas City. The game was scoreless with two out in the last of the twelfth, and Breuer had retired the last 25 batters to this point. He then gave up singles to York and Anton. Bejma, on a 3–2 pitch, hit a three-run homer to win the game. The win moved the Saints into first place, a half game ahead of Indianapolis.

By the latter half of July, Bejma had taken the league lead in batting average, hitting .342. He had another big hit to end July, breaking a 3–3 tie with a two-run homer in the seventh against Minneapolis. The 5–3 win pushed the Saints to a five-game lead over second-place Kansas City.

St. Paul held its lead through the end of the season to win the pennant. The Saints also drew more than 250,000 fans for the season, setting a new team record. In the balloting for the league's Most Valuable Player, Bejma tied for the award with Milwaukee Brewers pitcher Whitlow Wyatt, who won 23 games. Ted Williams of Minneapolis was third.

LOCAL CELEBS *and* THE SAINTS

Baseball in St. Paul has helped shape the careers of several iconic local artists. Charles Schulz, creator of the famous comic strip *Peanuts,* was an avid fan of his hometown Saints. His love of baseball carried into his comic strip, featuring the forlorn team led by Charlie Brown. Schulz worked the 1938 Saints—including the team's star that year, Ollie Bejma—into a *Peanuts* strip in 1974.

Another St. Paul native, Dave Frishberg was also a big fan and even got to assist on Saints radio broadcasts as a thirteen-year-old in 1946. Frishberg became a renowned jazz musician and songwriter. He wrote many baseball-themed compositions, notably "Van Lingle Mungo," a bossa nova named after the one-time Millers pitcher of the same name and with lyrics consisting of baseball names Frishberg remembered from his youth. In the lyrics, he also includes Eddie Basinski, whom Frishberg saw play with the Saints.

A lesser luminary, Jim Lange grew up in St. Paul and worked in the visitors' clubhouse at Lexington Park before finding fame as the host of *The Dating Game* from 1965 to 1980.

The connection between *Peanuts* creator Charles Schulz and local baseball is recognized with this statue of Snoopy dressed in a Saints uniform.

PHOTO COURTESY OF THE ST. PAUL SAINTS

The Saints faced the Brewers in the first round of the 1938 playoffs and lost three of the first four games. In the fifth game, Herring faced Wyatt, a rematch of the series opener in which Wyatt had shut out St. Paul on 4 hits. This time, facing elimination, St. Paul jumped on Wyatt for 3 runs in the first inning and went on to a 5–4 win. The Saints won again, on a shutout by Phelps, to tie the series. Wyatt was back on the mound for Milwaukee in the seventh game and took a 1–0 lead into the fourth, when Bejma tied the game with a home run off the roof of the Coliseum beyond the left-field fence at Lexington Park. McCullough followed with a long drive to center and circled the bases with an inside-the-park home run. The Saints held the lead and won the game to capture the series.

The Saints then played for the league championship against Kansas City, by this time a farm club of the Yankees. After St. Paul took a three-games-to-one lead in the series, the Blues won Game Five. In the sixth game, the Saints led 11–8 after seven innings, but the Blues scored 2 in the eighth and 2 in the top of the ninth to win the game and stay alive. Breuer then pitched a shutout against the Saints in the final game, capping the Kansas City comeback and ending the season for the Saints.

Under manager Babe Ganzel, the St. Paul Saints won the American Association pennant in 1938 but lost in the playoffs.

FRONT ROW LEFT TO RIGHT: GEORGE STUMPF, ART HERRING, LLOYD BROWN, BABE GANZEL, MGR., TONY YORK, OLLIE BEJMA, BIT McCULLOCH, KEN SILVESTRI.
SECOND ROW LEFT TO RIGHT: BABE PHELPS, FRED BERGER, LEROY ANTON, BOB BOKEN, JOHN PASEK, HUGO KLAERNER, ITALO CHELINI, BOOTUS CHAPMAN.
BACK ROW LEFT TO RIGHT: SUGAR CAIN, ART WEIS, VIC FRASIER, JACK PEERSON, HARRY TAYLOR.   INSET: GEORGE HIGGINS.

THE VEECKS *in* ST. PAUL

The Veeck name has a long history in St. Paul. It goes back a half century, before Mike Veeck made himself a popular man in town by spearheading the formation of the new St. Paul Saints in the 1990s. Mike's father, Bill Veeck, took a while to get on the good side of the St. Paul fans following an initial, self-induced stormy relationship.

While operating the Milwaukee Brewers of the American Association in the 1940s, Bill Veeck became somewhat of a villain among Saints fans, which he claimed was by design. In the chapter "Mention My Name in St. Paul" in his 1965 *Hustler's Handbook,* Veeck writes that, while his Milwaukee club was winning American Association pennants, "St. Paul was deep in the cellar and suffering badly at the box office. Naturally, I wanted to help them." Helping St. Paul was really about helping himself, he acknowledged, since, with attendance so poor, his team wasn't able to earn back its expenses for trips to St. Paul. By building himself up as a villain and thus creating a rivalry between the Brewers and Saints, Veeck could ensure that fans would show up to the games. He accomplished that by preying on and exploiting the most highly charged issue for St. Paul citizens: the "blood rivalry" with St. Paul's twin city of Minneapolis.

"I went on the radio in Minneapolis and blasted the city of St. Paul," Veeck writes. "I blasted their fans and their park and their bridges and their hotels and I expressed grave misgivings about their sewer system. I would never again, I announced—working myself up into a fury— submit my fine, upstanding young players to the atmosphere of such a backward, jerkwater town." He even went so far as to say that he would have his team stay at a hotel in the "fine, progressive metropolis of Minneapolis."

St. Paul, perhaps not surprisingly, took offense. Bill Veeck was attacked in the city's newspaper, on the radio, and by its mayor "most bitterly of all."

Veeck made sure to travel with the team on the next visit to St. Paul to "give the paying customers a chance to hiss the villain." He sat in a box seat near the Milwaukee dugout for a Sunday doubleheader on July 20, 1942, with a nearly sold-out crowd on hand at Lexington Park. After the Brewers came from behind to win the first game, they again rallied in the second game with 9 runs in the second inning. As Veeck shouted words of encouragement to his players, a Coke bottle flew past, "just ticking my cheek," he writes, and shattered on the dugout roof. "Well," Veeck states, "fun is fun and a crowd is a crowd but a Coke bottle is a lethal weapon." He leaped from the boxes into the grandstand whence the projectile came and confronted the young fellow who threw it. As Veeck tells it, "I slapped him back and forth across the face, first with the palm of my hand and then with the back. . . . Holy smoke! The fans came rushing at me from everywhere and, within seconds, the Milwaukee players were racing up from the dugout, bats in hand. Fights broke out all around me, and the sound of falling bodies filled the air. Attorneys were racing up and down the aisles, briefcases swinging and pens at the ready, to bring legal aid and succor to any citizen with a cut, a bruise or a vivid imagination."

Bill Veeck embellished the yarn a bit and had a few details wrong, but the essence of his story checks out with news accounts of the time. Gordon Gilmore of the *Pioneer Press* described Veeck leaping into the stands after the bottle sailed by and giving the thrower a "left-handed slap on the cheek. Customers and police milled around, all shouting, some applauding and some challenging Veeck to further action. Order was restored when the fan disappeared and police escorted Veeck to the radio booth for the remainder of the game."

Whether or not it had really been his plan to boost attendance in St. Paul, Veeck and the Saints had been at each other from the start in 1942. The American Association would present an award to the team with the highest attendance at its home opener. Milwaukee, with more than 15,000 people packed into Borchert Field on April 16, seemed assured of winning the prize, but its opener was called by rain in the second inning. The league declared that the Brewers' attendance figure would count toward the award, but Saints business manager Lou McKenna objected. That objection brought the fury of Veeck on the team and the city of St. Paul. "There aren't enough people with sporting blood in that jerk town to try to win an attendance trophy," he told Gilmore of the *Pioneer Press*. When Gilmore asked if Veeck had any preferences in lampposts from which to be hanged in effigy, he said, "Heck NO,

if the people of that town haven't any more fight than the St. Paul ball club, I can lick the whole population single-handed."

By chance, the Saints' home opener on April 23 was against Milwaukee. Veeck attended, and though St. Paul management made him pay his way into Lexington Park, the Milwaukee owner encountered few problems with the Saints or the 6,800 fans at the game. He did have a few more comments for publication, including, "I'll say the weather up here is magnificent, the crowd poor, and the team—it stinks, yes, stinks."

Veeck returned to the self-described "jerk town" the following January as the featured speaker at the St. Paul Hot Stove League Old-Timers banquet and, though not backing down from his earlier remarks, managed to charm the nearly 400 people in attendance. Gilmore wrote the next day that Veeck left "an impression that there is something beneath his kinky dome besides a born love for playing the clown."

Although all was patched up, Veeck continued to house his team in Minneapolis when the Brewers came to town. It made sense to keep them in one place, since visiting teams usually played a series against both Minneapolis and St. Paul when they came to the Twin Cities. However, a league resolution in November 1943 required "teams to make their quarters at a hotel in the cities where they play." It passed almost unanimously, Veeck the only dissenter.

Years later, Mike Veeck laughed about his dad's dealings with St. Paul. "He was never averse to a good rivalry," he said of Bill Veeck.

After the loss in the 1938 league championship game, the Saints didn't produce a winning record again for another six years and went through a series of managerial changes. Ganzel resigned after the 1940 season, and the next week Saints business manager McKenna received a letter from Roy Doan, a friend of and advisor to Babe Ruth. Ruth wanted to manage in the major leagues and knew he would need an apprenticeship in the minors. Doan told McKenna that Ruth might be interested in managing the Saints.

McKenna said he would give the Ruth offer "careful consideration." Instead, he hired Ralph "Red" Kress, who had led the American Association in RBIs as a member of the Millers in 1937. He started the 1940 season as a player-coach with the Detroit Tigers but quit playing at the end of July, staying on as a coach for the rest of the year. He was then given his release to become a player-manager for St. Paul. Under Kress, the Saints finished seventh in 1941.

Next at the helm was Virgil "Truck" Hannah. Hannah had been a catcher for three seasons with the Yankees before the team started winning pennants. His brief major-league career was flanked by twenty years in the Pacific Coast League, and he was later inducted into the league's Hall of Fame. Hannah had managed two years with Memphis in the Southern Association before being hired by the Saints at the minor-league meetings in late 1941.

By this time, the United States was fully involved in World War II. As more players and fans enlisted or were inducted into military service during the war years, fielding teams and drawing people to the games was a challenge, but baseball leagues managed to keep going.

The Saints' 1942 attendance of 73,990 was the lowest ever recorded by the club. (Attendance figures for 1918, a season stopped at midseason because of World War I, are not available, nor are numbers prior to 1908.)

Despite the lower attendance, the rivalry with the Minneapolis Millers remained strong. Once again, fists—or, in this case, a fist— flew during the Independence Day doubleheader. In the afternoon game at Nicollet Park, Saints first baseman Phil Weintraub "took righteous exception to the insulting remarks of a heckler in the first-base box seats," according to Gordon Gilmore in the *St. Paul Pioneer Press*. "After twice warning the customer and starting back to his position at first base only to hear the abusive language repeated behind his back, Phil returned to the boxes and let fly a punch."

A top hitter with the Millers only a few years before, Weintraub was thrown out of the game. Gilmore added that the

The St. Paul Saints appealed to the nation's patriotic fervor during World War II, as seen on this game program from 1944.

BASEBALL DURING WORLD WAR II

Milwaukee Brewers owner Bill Veeck was never shy about his promotions. He was especially active with his shenanigans during the lean World War II years, providing entertainment to people working long hours in support of the national war effort. The Brewers scheduled many morning games to accommodate the night shift, including a "Rosie the Riveter" game that started at 9:00 AM. All women who wore welding caps or riveting masks were admitted free. The ushers, dressed in nightgowns and nightcaps, served breakfast to the patrons. (The promotion foretold the predawn game at Midway Stadium by Mike Veeck's Saints team in 2005.)

Milwaukee manager Charlie Grimm came up with a hilarious Hitler imitation, which he performed for fans throughout the American Association. Bill Veeck formed a band, of which he and Grimm were a part. According to Veeck in his autobiography, the Brewer band had an excellent violin player, who was also a terrible pitcher. Veeck kept him on the roster the entire season just to play the violin but rarely let him near the mound.

Sometimes the Saints got into the musical act as well, although it was with a prison band during their annual game against a team of inmates at the state prison in Stillwater, Minnesota. St. Paul pitcher George "Slick" Coffman once left the diamond, grabbed a clarinet, and joined the music-making prisoners. The yearly get-together inside prison walls included the inmates hosting the Saints to a postgame dinner.

For the most part, St. Paul business manager Lou McKenna eschewed the antics that have since become a staple of the minor leagues. "Although a believer in modern progressive ideas of showmanship, McKenna sold baseball to St. Paul strictly on its merits as an entertaining, healthful outdoor pastime, shunning as poison the more obnoxious drums of ballyhoo," wrote *The Sporting News* in McKenna's 1943 obituary.

Still, the Saints followed the practice of other teams in the majors and minors by hosting special event nights. They also played exhibition games against service teams. A strong Great Lakes Naval Station team, the Sailors, came to Lexington Park in July 1942. The Saints played one of their better games of the season with a 5–0 win over the Sailors. Former Detroit Tigers star Mickey Cochrane managed the Great Lakes team. The losing pitcher for Great Lakes was Johnny Rigney, who had attended St. Thomas College in St. Paul and pitched for the Saints before moving up to the Chicago White Sox in the 1930s. The game and event included a ceremony in which thirty-eight men were sworn in to the navy.

Curfews, another staple of wartime baseball, created a strange scene and dramatic ending to a 1942 game at Lexington Park. The contest crept into extra innings, drawing near the time designated to end the game prior to a scheduled blackout in the city. The visiting Kansas City Blues seemed content to go away with a tie and stalled in the top of the tenth, employing delaying tactics that caused umpire Frosty Peters to clear the Kansas City bench. With two out in the bottom of the inning and the game about to be halted, Dave Philley doubled to drive in the game-winning run. The Saints had secured a victory, instead of a tie, and still allowed the fans to get home before the blackout.

Minneapolis fans "joined the Saint supporters in a chorus of boos over the ejection." However, the *Pioneer Press* reported that the abusive fan later left his seat and "sought out Weintraub to make apologies."

The next day the Saints swept the Millers in a doubleheader at Lexington Park. Even with the wins, St. Paul was still in last place, and Hannah resigned as manager. "My conscience would bother me if I continued to take money as manager of a losing club," he said. "Maybe it will be better for all concerned if I step out."

Bob Tarleton, McKenna's assistant general manager, took over for Hannah and was a dugout-only manager. Tarleton worked in his street clothes instead of a uniform and sometimes resembled the venerable Philadelphia Athletics' manager Connie Mack, standing on the step of the dugout and waving a scorecard to direct his players.

BLACK BASEBALL *in* MINNESOTA

Minnesota was never on the main circuit of the organized Negro Leagues. But the state has a rich, if often hidden, history of great African American players and teams in the decades prior to the integration of organized baseball in 1947. More than 100 years ago, a team called the St. Paul Colored Gophers had a collection of stars that took on the St. Paul Saints of the American Association in a three-game exhibition in 1907. Both teams beefed up their rosters for the series, with the Colored Gophers bringing in Rube Foster of Chicago, one of the top pitchers in the game. After the teams split the first two games, the Colored Gophers had Foster on the mound and won the rubber game of the series. Two years later, the Colored Gophers won a best-of-five series against the Chicago Leland Giants in what was billed as the "World's Colored Championship."

Among the individual stars cultivated in St. Paul was Marcenia Lyle Stone. Better known as Toni, Stone pitched for the semiprofessional Twin Cities Colored Giants in the 1930s. Stone was also a sixteen-year-old girl. As Jimmy Lee wrote in the July 30, 1937, *Minneapolis Spokesman,* "The team has the distinction of having a girl pitcher on its roster. . . . Miss Marcenia Stone, 16-year-old girl athlete, has been doing much to amuse the fans with her great catcher [*sic*] and wonder hitting power." In 1953 Stone became the first woman to play in the Negro American League.

The 1942 Twin Cities Colored Gophers roster included Reece "Goose" Tatum, who later became a main attraction on the Harlem Globetrotters basketball team. That year, the Colored Gophers played several games at Lexington Park in St. Paul against Negro League and other noteworthy all-black teams. According to historian Todd Peterson, the Colored Gophers were a barnstorming team operated by Abe Saperstein, founder of the Harlem Globetrotters and owner of a number of black baseball teams, particularly in the Upper Midwest.

Frank White, an outstanding athlete at Mechanic Arts High School in St. Paul and later

The Saints remained in last place and finished in the cellar for the first time since 1914. Before the 1942 season was over, Gilmore reported on another threat to the team's future in St. Paul. "The St. Paul Baseball club, plagued by mounting debt and lack of attendance, will sell all its players piecemeal and then let the franchise revert to the American Association," Gilmore wrote, citing McKenna as the source. He added that the league would determine the disposition of the team itself, "whether it will remain in St. Paul or be moved to some other city."

McKenna, who had been named the outstanding minor-league executive by *The Sporting News* in 1938, was trying to get a major-league team to buy the Saints or at least work out a partnership with the club. Seeger, who had become the team's majority stockholder, made it clear he no longer wanted to operate the club. The Brooklyn Dodgers and Philadelphia Athletics indicated interest

a sports official and manager of parks and recreation programs, grew up watching teams of all colors and sports. He often accompanied his father, Louis "Pud" White, on sports trips and was shocked at some of the attitudes and discriminatory practices he witnessed, which his dad's generation was already accustomed to.

Frank White has delved into the history of black baseball in St. Paul and the surrounding area through an exhibit called *They Played for the Love of the Game: Adding to the Legacy of Minnesota Black Baseball,* which has appeared throughout the Twin Cities.

White has worked to restore and keep alive the significant stories of teams and people who played the game they loved while encountering racial discrimination from subtle to blatant. Many of the sandlots where they played—the Hollow Field, Welcome Hall Field—have been abandoned, renamed, or in other ways forgotten.

"What continues to amaze me," White notes, "is that this untold story of Minnesota black baseball is only beginning to be shared."

St. Paul native Toni Stone—shown here meeting boxer Joe Louis when she played for the New Orleans Creoles circa 1949—was a pioneer as a woman playing professional baseball.

MINNESOTA HISTORICAL SOCIETY COLLECTIONS

in affiliating with the Saints, but the uncertain conditions of the ongoing war made both teams reluctant to make commitments.

Minneapolis, St. Paul, and Indianapolis were the only teams in the American Association that were not affiliated with a major-league team. Gilmore did not find it a coincidence that they had finished in the bottom three spots in the standings in 1942.

As it had fewer than ten years before, the city of St. Paul became involved in the team's future, especially after a bid came in from Nebraska investors, who planned to move the Saints to Omaha. Mayor John McDonough and representatives of the St. Paul Association of Commerce pitched a purchase of the Saints to major-league owners as well as to potential local investors.

By early 1943 news concerning the Saints became more positive. With a civic group in St. Paul preparing to buy the team, Seeger announced he had bought all the players on the roster of the Shreveport Sports, which had just won the Texas League title.

The transaction came after the Texas League disbanded, a casualty of the loss of players and fans during wartime. Among those acquired by St. Paul was player-manager Salty Parker, who would assume the same role with the Saints. The twenty-nine-year-old Parker had not only been the youngest manager in the Texas League; he had played every inning of every game for the Sports in 1942. With the Saints, he became the regular shortstop in addition to managing.

Perhaps revived by the influx of new talent, Seeger soon changed his mind and decided to keep the Saints. McKenna had also been on his way out, planning to get back into the newspaper business, but he decided to return as well. Unfortunately, McKenna died of pneumonia at the age of fifty only a few months later. (Among McKenna's contributions to baseball was the development of an annual *Record Makers of the American Association* guide, which the league continued as its official record book after his death.)

Seeger carried on. The Saints did marginally better at the gate in 1943, and Parker got 10 more wins out of the team than they had the year before, although St. Paul still finished tied for last in the Association. Parker, awaiting induction into the army, resigned as manager after the season, and the Saints hired Ray Blades to succeed him.

Blades had played ten seasons for the St. Louis Cardinals and produced a lifetime batting average of .301. He later managed the Cardinals and managed in their minor-league system before coming to St. Paul.

The biggest news for the Saints was reaching a working agreement with the Brooklyn Dodgers, one that eventually resulted in the purchase of the Saints by the Dodgers. Seeger and St. Paul fans looked ahead to greater stability with a major-league affiliation. Better times were on the way.

Dodger Blue Comes to St. Paul

"STRETCH" SCHULTZ STARTS A TREND

The original working agreement between the Saints and Brooklyn Dodgers was prompted by the sale of a St. Paul native to Brooklyn. Howie "Stretch" Schultz had attended Central High School in St. Paul and went on to become a basketball star at the city's Hamline University. While in college, Schultz also began his professional baseball career. He joined the Saints in 1942 and became their regular first baseman the following year. In August 1943 the Dodgers acquired Schultz from St. Paul in exchange for four players and $40,000.

The Dodgers were happy with the deal, and by the following spring they were sending more players St. Paul's way. Brooklyn president and general manager Branch Rickey, along with members of the scouting staff, visited the Saints' spring-training camp in Springfield, Missouri, in late March 1944. While with the St. Louis Cardinals in the 1920s, Rickey had developed the concept of a farm system that gave a major-league team command of players through the ownership or control of a group of minor-league teams. By 1940, the Cardinals had thirty minor-league teams in their system. After Rickey went to Brooklyn prior to the 1943 season, he began building another stable of farm teams that included St. Paul.

The working relationship between Brooklyn and St. Paul culminated with the Dodgers' purchase of the Saints from Walter Seeger after the 1947 season. Even before this, fans had the opportunity to watch up-and-coming stars who were under contract with the Dodgers play in St. Paul. One was outfielder Duke Snider, who started the 1947 season in Brooklyn and was sent to St. Paul in early July. He hit 12 home runs in 66 games with the Saints before being recalled to Brooklyn in September. Snider went on to hit more than 400 home runs in his major-league career and was elected to the Hall of Fame in 1980.

St. Paul became a full-fledged Brooklyn farm team in 1948. It was a memorable season for the Saints. However, local scribes didn't predict great heights for the team that year. Covering the Saints at spring training in Abilene, Texas, *St. Paul Pioneer Press* columnist Joe Hennessy wrote, "Deep in the heart of wind-swept Texas, an eight-hour round-trip bus ride from Fort Worth, the Saints' chances in the American Association race seem dismal indeed."

But Saints fans sensed excitement as the regular season opened. The "Welcome Home Saints" party in the theater section of the St. Paul Auditorium drew thousands of fans, with many more turned away. On the eve of the home opener, the festivities included a nine-act vaudeville show and the crowning of the "King of Fans," who received a lifetime pass to Saints games.

The next day, more than 11,000 fans filled Lexington Park as Danny Ozark and Eric Tipton homered to lead the Saints past the Columbus Red Birds 9–6. The number of fans attending games had picked up since the end of World War II, and in 1948 the Saints went on to top 300,000 in attendance for the first time.

HOWIE SCHULTZ

Lanky Howie "Stretch" Schultz combined a pro baseball career with stardom on the basketball court at Hamline University, near where he had grown up in St. Paul. After graduating from Central High School, the six-foot-six Schultz signed a baseball contract, starting with the Grand Forks Chiefs in 1941 and working his way to the St. Paul Saints the following year. He became the team's regular first baseman in 1943 and did well enough to have his contract purchased by the Brooklyn Dodgers.

As he played baseball from the spring and into the fall, Schultz also starred on the hardwood for the Hamline Pipers under coach Joe Hutton. In Schultz's sophomore season, the Pipers won the National Association of Intercollegiate Basketball title, the first of three small-college championships the team won under Hutton.

Too tall for the military, Schultz was exempted from the draft, but his classification changed in early 1945, and he was told to stay in Minnesota until his status was determined. The Dodgers optioned him to the Saints. Schultz was able to play only home games and games in Minneapolis until his draft papers were recalled. He then played the rest of the year with Brooklyn as well as for another Dodgers' farm team in Montreal, Quebec.

Schultz stayed in the majors in 1946 as the Dodgers tied for first place with the St. Louis Cardinals, forcing a best-of-three playoff to determine the pennant. In the first game Schultz connected for the first home run ever hit in a tiebreaker game, and he later had a run-scoring single. The Cardinals, however, won the game and eventually the playoff series to advance to the World Series.

Schultz was also playing professional basketball by this time, causing him to report late to spring training in 1947. A bigger issue was the presence of Jackie Robinson, who broke the longtime color barrier in the majors and also took Schultz's first-base position. Schultz got into only two games for

CAMPANELLA STARS IN ST. PAUL

Despite his innovative work in expanding and refining baseball's system of minor-league farm teams, Dodgers president Rickey may be better remembered for his role in integrating organized baseball. The Dodgers' farm club in Montreal, Quebec, had three black players during the 1946 season, including Jackie Robinson. The following season Robinson integrated the major leagues.

Another star African American player signed by the Dodger organization in 1946 was catcher Roy Campanella, who began his career as a teenager in the Negro Leagues in 1937. After two seasons in the Dodgers' farm system, Campanella opened the 1948 season in Brooklyn but was sent to the minors after appearing in just three games. He joined the Saints on May 18 to become the first black player in the American Association.

Campanella's debut with the Saints was in Columbus on May 22. He went hitless in 4 at-bats, striking out twice, while also making an error at catcher. Over the Dodgers over the next month before being traded to the Philadelphia Phillies, a team that became notorious for its maltreatment of Robinson.

"It was embarrassing," said Schultz. "I was playing first [for the Phillies in a game against the Dodgers] and Jack got on. The abuse was almost continuous. And I said, 'Jack, how can you handle this crap?' And he said, 'Oh, I'll have my day.' That's all he said. And, of course, he did."

Schultz played in the majors through 1948, but by this time he was focusing on basketball. In the early 1950s he played for the Minneapolis Lakers basketball team, which was in the midst of winning six league titles in seven years.

Schultz then began a teaching and coaching career that lasted for more than thirty years. He continued to play baseball on town teams through the 1950s.

HOME-RUN BONANZA *on* INDEPENDENCE DAY

The Independence Day twin bills between the Millers and Saints frequently brought pre-dusk fireworks. The brawl of 1929 and Phil Weintraub's clocking of a Minneapolis fan in 1942 occurred on July 4. But sometimes the game highlights were produced by bats, rather than fists or fireworks.

In the morning game on July 4, 1940, Ab Wright of the Millers hit 4 home runs and a triple against the Saints. In the 1945 matchup, St. Paul shortstop Bill Hart duplicated Wright's home-run feat in the morning game played at Lexington Park. Hart hit 4 home runs and drove in 9 runs in a 16–1 Saints win over the Millers. Right-hander Otho Nitcholas held Minneapolis to 7 hits in the game and nearly matched that total himself with the bat, hitting 4 singles and a double in the game. Saints third baseman Bud Kimball had 3 home runs during the holiday games, although he split them between the two games, with 1 in the morning game and 2 in the afternoon contest at Nicollet Park.

the following week, as the Saints completed an eastern road trip, Campanella had only 4 hits, all singles. Meanwhile, the Saints dropped from first to fourth place.

Although the Saints barely climbed in the standings following their return home, Campanella found his stroke. His first Twin Cities appearance was in Minneapolis on May 30. Campanella hit 2 home runs and drove in 3 runs, although the Millers won the game 17–9. The next morning, before a crowd of 11,000 in his first game at Lexington Park, Campanella gave the Saints a 2–0 lead in the last of the first with a triple to right-center with two runners on base. In the fourth inning, he hit a solo home run to left.

ERIC THE RED

Despite the team's beneficial arrangement with the Dodgers, the star who defined Saints baseball in the 1940s wasn't part of the Brooklyn connection. Eric "The Red" Tipton had been a star football player at Duke University in the 1930s but chose a baseball career, signing with the Philadelphia Athletics in 1939. His best years in the majors were with the Cincinnati Reds during World War II. As the veterans returned from the war, however, Tipton lost his spot on the major-league roster and returned to the minors. The Reds sold Tipton to the Saints after the 1945 season.

"His charisma, shirted in flannel with a large '7' on his back, spread like the scent of sweet clover in a spring Zephyr," wrote Ken Haag of Tipton in a 1990 *Sports Collectors Digest* article. "His bat spoke a needed language; longball, base hits, and RBI in a city that had long since reminisced the likes of Miller Huggins, Chuck Dressen, Bruno Haas, and Gabby Street. The time for a new hero was at hand."

Playing for St. Paul in 1946, Tipton had 19 home runs and 100 runs batted in, the first of four years that he reached the century mark in RBIs. His best year in St. Paul was 1948, when he had a .313 batting average while also walking 115 times. He hit 28 home runs, scored 111 runs, and drove in 126.

Eric Tipton averaged nearly 17 home runs and 103 runs batted in per season during his six-year stint with the Saints. He was the team's top star during the late 1940s.

MINNESOTA HISTORICAL SOCIETY COLLECTIONS

Campanella hit only 1 home run during the Saints' road trip the following week, but he caught fire after the team returned to St. Paul. Against the Louisville Colonels on June 8, Campanella had a three-run homer and a bases-loaded triple for a total of 6 runs batted in. In the next game, against Columbus, he hit a pair of home runs and collected 5 RBIs—giving him 11 in 2 games.

Campanella hit another home run against Columbus on June 10 and added one more in the first game of a doubleheader against the Toledo Mud Hens the next day. He did not play in the second game, but he continued his streak the next night with another home run against the Mud Hens. His home run in the opening game of a doubleheader with Indianapolis on June 13 was his sixth straight game with a homer and his eleventh overall with the Saints.

Campanella did not start the second game of the doubleheader, but he entered the game as a pinch hitter in the seventh and final inning. (In the minor leagues at that time, one game of a doubleheader was usually scheduled for seven innings. It was typically the second game, but this could vary.) The Saints trailed Indianapolis 7–0 when Campanella drew a walk to start the seventh. St. Paul rallied for 4 runs and had the bases loaded with 2 out when Campanella came up again. He hit a deep drive to right-center. It was long enough to be a game-winning grand slam in some ballparks, but in cavernous Lexington Park, Indianapolis center fielder Tom Saffell had room to catch it, ending the game.

Campanella's home-run streak also came to an end. But he had another chance at heroics later in the week. He missed a couple of games with bruised fingers but was back in the lineup in the first game of a doubleheader against Milwaukee on June 19. This time, the first game was scheduled for seven innings, and the Saints again trailed 7–0 going into the last of the seventh. St. Paul rallied and got within a run on Tipton's two-out, three-run homer. Campanella was the next batter, and he homered to tie the game. St. Paul then won in the last of the eighth.

Following a doubleheader against Kansas City on June 20, Campanella's wife, Ruthe, gave birth to a son at St. Joseph's Hospital in St. Paul. The next day, the Saints left on a road trip, but Campanella stayed back to be with his family; by the time the team returned, Campanella was gone. He was recalled to the big-league club at the end of June.

Over the next ten years with the Dodgers, Campanella won three National League Most Valuable Player awards, in 1951, 1953, and 1955. His major-league career was curtailed at both ends, the beginning by baseball's color line and the end by an auto accident that left him paralyzed at the age of thirty-six. However, during his career he hit 242 home runs in ten major-league seasons and was elected to the Baseball Hall of Fame in 1969.

ONE LAST RUN AT A CHAMPIONSHIP

Campanella was not the only future Hall of Famer with the Saints in 1948, nor was he the team's only black player. In August, Dan Bankhead moved up from the Dodgers' farm team in Nashua to join the Saints. He had been with Brooklyn briefly in 1947, becoming the first black pitcher in the majors. Bankhead won 20 games for Nashua in 1948 before being promoted to St. Paul. With the Saints, he won 4 more games, without a loss, during the regular season, but he struggled in the playoffs that year.

Walter Alston had taken over as St. Paul manager that year. He managed the Saints for two years and later managed the Dodgers, in both Brooklyn and Los Angeles, from 1954 to 1976. Alston was elected to the Hall of Fame in 1983.

Despite a strong start to the season, the Saints finished third in 1948, but they got hot again in the playoffs. Their first-round opponent was the Indianapolis Indians, which, under manager Al Lopez, had won 100 games to take the pennant. The Indians and Saints split the first four games of the

Roy Campanella gets a handshake from manager Walter Alston as he rounds third base after hitting a home run against the Minneapolis Millers at Nicollet Park in May 1948. Campanella was with the Saints for only 35 games before rejoining the Dodgers in Brooklyn.

series, leading to an entertaining fifth game at Lexington Park. The Saints were trailing 2–1 in the last of the eighth when Tipton tied the game with a home run. In the top of the ninth, center fielder Bob Addis threw out two Indianapolis runners at the plate to keep the game deadlocked. Indianapolis scored in the eleventh, but the Saints tied it in the bottom of the inning. In the twelfth, the Indians again took the lead, but St. Paul's Al Brancato drove home the tying run with 2 outs in the Saints' half. Finally, in the last of the thirteenth, Johnny "Spider" Jorgensen won the game for the Saints with a long home run over the right-field fence.

JACK VERBY

Pitcher Jack Verby initially passed on a chance to play professional baseball so he could pursue a very different career, in medicine. A two-sport star at Johnson High School in St. Paul, Verby continued in basketball and baseball at Carleton College in Northfield, Minnesota, and also played a season of baseball for the Minnesota Gophers while attending medical school at the University of Minnesota. He received his bachelor's degree at Carleton in 1944 and graduated from medical school at the University of Minnesota three years later.

During this time, according to Joe Hennessy of the *St. Paul Pioneer Press,* the New York Yankees, Boston Red Sox, Chicago White Sox, and St. Louis Cardinals tried to sign Verby, with the top bid for his services at $7,500—an impressive sum at the time. Although he stuck with medicine, Verby continued to play baseball as well, and he stood out in both areas. "Jack Verby, who won 12 games as a high school pitcher one season with St. Paul Johnson, set a record in attaining his M. D.," wrote Hennessy in 1948. "By attending school twelve months a year he crammed eight years of study into six."

Verby played on various Minnesota town teams that were part amateur, part semipro. As one of the top pitchers in the state, Verby was paid enough to finance much of his tuition. After graduating, he began practicing medicine in rural Minnesota, finding himself in Litchfield in 1949, providing the community with a doctor as well as bringing new life to the local baseball team. A sore arm limited his pitching, but Verby remained "one of the most feared hitters in the state," according to Armand Peterson and Tom Tomashek in the book *Town Ball: The Glory Days of Minnesota Amateur Baseball.* His popularity in Litchfield was noted in the town's newspaper with a story of two boys going to the park to play baseball. Said one of the boys to the other, "You can be Joe DiMaggio. I'll be Jack Verby."

During his medical career, Verby did much to improve and promote health care throughout the state, and he has received numerous honors in recognition of his work. In 1972 he was inducted into the Johnson High School Hall of Fame, which includes among its members Chief Justice Warren Burger, golfer Bev Vanstrom, hockey Olympians Herb Brooks and Wendell Anderson (the latter also governor of Minnesota and member of the US Senate), sports artists Terry Fogarty and Ken Haag, and Bruce Vento, a member of Congress.

The win gave the Saints a three-games-to-two lead. In the sixth game, Indianapolis led 3–2 in the last of the eighth, but Jorgensen came through again. His two-run single put St. Paul ahead, and the Saints held on to win the game and the series.

St. Paul went on to face the Columbus Red Birds for the league championship. Trailing three games to two, St. Paul stayed alive with a 3–1 win in the sixth game on Jorgensen's two-run homer in the top of the fourteenth at Columbus. The Saints won the final game 5–3 to advance to the Junior World Series for the first time since 1931.

VOICES OF THE SAINTS

The Saints went on the air for the first time in 1926 with WCCO Radio broadcasting Saturday games from Lexington Park. Herbert Paul was the announcer, and many others followed.

Marty O'Neill was one of the best and most remembered. An outstanding athlete, O'Neill had a long career broadcasting different sports, including the Saints. After the Twins came to Minnesota in 1961, O'Neill shifted sports and did the ring announcing and television commentary for *All Star Wrestling* for many years.

One of the greatest sportscasters in Minnesota history, Ray Christensen, called Saints games on WLOL Radio in the team's final year at Lexington Park and first year at Midway Stadium. A master of painting a word picture for listeners, Christensen carried the skill into a studio when he re-created games from a Western Union wire while the Saints were on the road. In his 1993 autobiography, *Golden Memories,* Christensen explains how he would get detailed descriptions of the action over the wires. "B1 meant ball one, S1C was strike-one called. How about FOGS? No, this didn't refer to low clouds descending on the stadium. FOGS stood for Foul over Grand Stand. Not all the operators gave that much detail on a foul ball. If they didn't, I could put it anywhere I wanted. I could have it sail back over the grandstand, or have it land in the first row behind the dugout, just out of the third baseman's reach." He described communicating with his engineer to let him know what sound effects were needed to accompany the play-by-play, including crowd noise ranging from loud cheers to boos.

Christensen also discovered a way to re-create another important baseball sound. "One sound effect that is needed constantly is the one of the bat meeting the ball," he writes. "Broadcasters around the world have tried to re-create the crack of the bat. I found it by accident. I was attending a symphony concert when I heard the drummer's box—a small wooden box that is part of the percussion section—and I thought, 'Gee, that sounds like a bat.' I bought a drummer's box and tapped it with my pencil. It was a great sound."

As for familiar voices, many fans still recall the distinctive tones of public-address announcer Don Dix booming throughout Lexington Park and Midway Stadium. As a youth, Dix played baseball at Central High School in St. Paul, and he got a job as an usher at Lexington Park so that he could get into the games free. After serving in the army during World War II, Dix became the in-stadium voice of the Saints, working in that job through the remainder of the team's history in St. Paul.

St. Paul's opponents in the minor-league championship were the Montreal Royals, the other top farm team of the Brooklyn Dodgers. The Royals' pitchers were led by 17-game winner Don Newcombe, and the team had a hard-hitting infield that included shortstop Bob Morgan, second baseman Jimmy Bloodworth, and first baseman Kevin "Chuck" Connors, who went on to greater fame as an actor, most notably in television's *Branded* and *The Rifleman*. Connors had also already played professional basketball with the Rochester Royals and Boston Celtics and later played briefly in the baseball major leagues with Brooklyn and the Chicago Cubs.

The Saints won the first game of the Junior World Series. Pat McGlothin shut out the Royals on 5 hits and beat Newcombe. However, the Royals won the next four games to win the championship.

In 1949 the Saints went to spring training at Dodgertown in Vero Beach, Florida. The expansive facility at Dodgertown was the vision of Rickey, who brought the Dodgers' farm teams together in one spot. Jim Hinman described Rickey's hope of "an intensive spring training [that] would cut two years off the average five years spent in on-the-job training in the minor leagues."

One of the Brooklyn prospects at Dodgertown was a St. Paul native, Walt "Moose" Moryn. Moryn grew up in the Dayton's Bluff area of St. Paul and attended Harding High School. He served in the US Navy as a gunner's mate on an ammunition ship in the South Pacific during World War II, according to biographer Art Mugalian, and he returned to play amateur baseball in his hometown after the war. Moryn was invited to a Dodgers tryout camp in St. Paul in the summer of 1947 and signed with the team. As for Dodgertown, Moryn recalled, "We slept five or six to a room and many a night killed spiders and snakes in our bunks. . . . Seven hundred players were in camp."

Sifting one's way through the throngs of young players in camp was a competitive process. At the top of the ladder was a Brooklyn team loaded with stars, particularly in the outfield, which was Moryn's position.

Another St. Paul native to star for his hometown team, Walt "Moose" Moryn was first signed by the Dodgers organization in 1948 and made his way to the Saints by 1953. He belted 25 homers and drove in a team-high 88 runs during a full season with St. Paul in 1955.

PHOTO COURTESY JOE O'CONNELL

Moryn worked his way up, playing with Montreal and St. Paul in 1953 and then splitting time between the Saints and the Dodgers the next two years. Although he made the majors for portions of two seasons, it was apparent he would not become a regular in Brooklyn. After the 1955 season Moryn received a hoped-for trade, going from the Dodgers to the Chicago Cubs. He became a favorite in the Windy City and is still remembered for his shoestring catch to preserve and end Don Cardwell's no-hitter for the Cubs in 1960.

The Saints had another good start in 1949, winning their first 12 games. After a 2–1 loss to Indianapolis on May 4, the Saints won their next four games, giving them a 16–1 record and a five-game lead in the American Association. Phil Haugstad topped the pitching staff with 22 wins that year. Clem Labine led the league with 64 pitching appearances, all but one in relief. On offense, Tipton and third baseman Danny O'Connell each had more than 100 runs batted in. Addis produced a batting average of .346 and, with 68 walks, had an on-base percentage of .427.

ST. PAUL SAINTS *in* THE HALL OF FAME

Charles Comiskey (player-manager 1895, manager 1896–99, Western League)

Miller Huggins (1901–03)

Bill McKechnie (1912–13)

Leo Durocher (1927)

Lefty Gomez (1930)

Duke Snider (1947)

Roy Campanella (1948)

Dick Williams (1954)

Walter Alston (manager 1948–49)

After a 20–16 win at Minneapolis on September 3, St. Paul was in first place, five and a half games ahead of Indianapolis, with just eight days left in the season. However, the Saints lost their next six games, and Indianapolis got hot.

St. Paul's lead over Indianapolis had shrunk to half a game by September 11, as both teams were wrapping up their 1949 seasons with doubleheaders, the Saints in Milwaukee and the Indians against Toledo. Indianapolis swept the Mud Hens to close their regular season with eight straight wins. St. Paul came out of its slump to win the first game against Milwaukee. In the second game, Haugstad, who had pitched seven innings in a loss the night before, started and went into the seventh before being relieved. St. Paul hung on to win the game and the pennant.

In the first game of the playoffs, twenty-year-old Norman Roy of Milwaukee shut out the Saints on 4 hits. St. Paul won the next two but again couldn't solve Roy in the fourth game. The Milwaukee righty carried a perfect game into the top of the ninth. After retiring the first batter of the inning, Roy walked Buddy Hicks, who became St. Paul's first base runner of the game. Roy then retired pinch hitter Lou Welaj for the second out, but he lost his no-hitter when Earl Naylor singled to center. Roy hung on to complete his second straight shutout and even the series. Milwaukee then won the next two games, to win the series four-games-to-two and eliminate the Saints. Never again would St. Paul finish first in either the regular season or postseason in the American Association.

CHAPTER 7

The Final Years

LAST SEASONS IN LEXINGTON PARK

In the early 1950s, the Saints boasted one of the American Association's top middle-infield combinations with Jack Cassini at second base and Jim Pendleton at shortstop. Pendleton was the shortstop for the Chicago American Giants of the Negro American League in 1948, but he played the outfield upon joining the Saints in 1949. He moved back to shortstop the following year and led the league with 19 triples while hitting 10 home runs and driving in 105 runs in 1950. The next year he hit 21 home runs and scored 116 runs. By 1952 Pendleton joined the Montreal Royals of the International League and then was traded to the Braves of the National League, for whom he made his major-league debut in 1953.

Cassini, meanwhile, averaged 33 stolen bases per season in his four years with the Saints (1950–53) and twice led the American Association in that category. He too was promoted to Montreal, in 1954, but never made it back to the majors after a brief stop with the Pittsburgh Pirates in 1949.

Earl Naylor was in his third season as a Saints outfielder in 1950 when he hit 13 home runs. He made the occasional appearance as a pitcher as well. Naylor played more than 1,500 games in the minors but just 112 in the big leagues. He settled in St. Paul after his playing career was over.

The Brooklyn-born Bill Antonello was another former Saints player who stuck around St. Paul after playing for the Saints. He first arrived in 1950 after beginning the year with the Dodgers' Pacific Coast League affiliate, the Hollywood Stars. Antonello then hit 15 homers in a full season with the Saints in 1951. He played 40 games for the Dodgers in 1953 but spent most of his career in the minors.

The Saints' top slugger in 1950 was first baseman Lou Limmer, who belted a league-high 29 home runs, only one of them in his home park. The lefty Limmer's home-run power was held back by Lexington Park's spacious right-field dimensions.

In late July 1951, a gale swept through the Twin Cities, tearing apart Lexington's right-field fence with winds reportedly reaching 100 miles per hour. The Saints management took the opportunity to rebuild and reposition the damaged fence while the team was on a road trip. When the Saints returned home in August, Lexington Park had a new right-field fence, one that was much closer to home plate. The distance down the line had been shortened to 330 feet. To make home runs a bit more challenging, a twenty-five-foot-high, double-decked fence was erected, although the embankment on which the previous fence had rested was gone.

Building new fences was not all that kept Saints management busy, as the team remained an active trading partner with its big-league owner. In the late 1940s and early 1950s, the Brooklyn Dodgers had two Class AAA farm clubs, Montreal and St. Paul, and Dodgers vice president Buzzie Bavasi said neither outranked the other. Players in the Brooklyn system could get sent to either city, and over the years many prospects were shuttled to both the Royals and the Saints. The same was true with managers. After the 1949 season, Walter Alston went from St. Paul to Montreal while Royals manager Clay Hopper made the reverse journey.

Hopper managed the Saints for two seasons before Clay Bryant, a former Cubs pitcher in the late 1930s, took over in 1952. That year, the Saints had one of the association's best outfields, with Sandy Amoros, Gino Cimoli, and Bill Sharman. Amoros and Cimoli went on to play for the Dodgers in Brooklyn and Los Angeles, as well as other major-league teams. Sharman, who played with the Saints again in 1955, was already pursuing a career in basketball with the Boston Celtics. He played eleven seasons in the National Basketball Association and is in the Basketball Hall of Fame.

Shortstop Don Zimmer was one of the top players for the 1953 Saints. That year, his fifth season of professional baseball and his first at the Class AAA level, Zimmer was leading the league in home runs, with 23. In the first inning of a game at Columbus, Ohio, on July 7, he was struck in the head by a pitched ball. Knocked unconscious, Zimmer was taken to the hospital. He was diagnosed with a fracture in his upper forehead. Two days later, after completing their series, his teammates stopped by his room, but Zimmer did not recognize them.

Zimmer didn't play the rest of the season, but he eventually recovered and returned to the Saints in 1954. That July he was called up to the big-league club and went on to play for the world champion Dodgers of 1955 and 1959.

In all, Zimmer remained in the game as a player, manager, and coach for more than fifty years.

Another notable Saints player at the time was Ray Moore. He was a right-handed starter for St. Paul from 1952 to 1954, but he worked primarily as a reliever during his major-league career. Known as "Old Blue" (after his hunting dog), Moore returned to Minnesota and spent his final three seasons as a reliever for the Twins.

This era also was notable for changes in the makeup of the American Association. Prior to the early 1950s, the league had been stable in terms of membership for its first half century. Other than a two-year shift of Toledo to Cleveland in 1914 and 1915, the teams and cities in the association remained unchanged until 1952, when Toledo, hurting financially, moved to Charleston, West Virginia, during the season.

More shifts came rapidly in the following years, mainly the result of movement among major-league teams for the first time in fifty years. Just prior to the 1953 season, the Boston Braves of the National League moved to Milwaukee, displacing the minor-league Brewers. The 1955 move by the Philadelphia Athletics to Kansas City, Missouri, caused that city's Blues to move to Denver, where they were renamed the Bears. In the International League, the Class AAA Baltimore Orioles gave way to the relocated St. Louis Browns, who assumed the Orioles name for the American League franchise, in 1954.

In the Twin Cities, news of other cities getting big-league teams fostered hope that Minnesota would get a team of its own. The Minneapolis Chamber of Commerce formed a committee to lure a major-league team to the area, but it became apparent that a new stadium would first be needed.

The aging Lexington Park and Nicollet Park weren't suitable for the majors, even on a short-term basis, and their days as minor-league ballparks were numbered as well. St. Paul and Minneapolis looked at building new ballparks for their teams and hoped these facilities would also become home to a major-league club.

In 1954 the Minneapolis City Council approved the issuance of revenue bonds to finance a new stadium in the suburb of Bloomington, Minnesota. St. Paul declined to participate in this project; instead, it included $2 million for a stadium in its city as part of a $39 million bond issue for municipal improvements. Several St. Paul locations were considered, and a gravel-pit site to the southeast of the state fairgrounds was selected. It was on the east side of Snelling Avenue and was bounded on the north and south by railroad tracks. Like the new stadium for the Millers in Bloomington, the St. Paul facility was not confined by city blocks and had space for a parking lot outside the stadium.

Brooklyn Dodgers president Walter O'Malley came to St. Paul for the ground breaking in April of 1956, as the Saints wrapped up their sixty-year

history at Lexington Park that season. On June 13, the Brooklyn Dodgers came to St. Paul for an exhibition game. Duke Snider, Roy Campanella, and Gil Hodges homered for Brooklyn. Don Drysdale, pitching five innings in relief, was the winning pitcher in the 7–2 Dodgers victory.

On the night of Wednesday, September 5, in front of just over 2,000 fans, St. Paul concluded its home schedule against the Minneapolis Millers. Stan Williams pitched the Saints to a 4–0 shutout win, and Roy Hartsfield capped the scoring with a home run in the last of the eighth. The Saints fell short of the playoffs that year, finishing in fifth place with a 75–78 record, making the September 5 game the last one ever played at Lexington Park.

BUILDING A MAJOR-LEAGUE BALLPARK

The Saints opened their brand-new Midway Stadium with a day-night double-header against the Wichita Braves on Thursday, April 25, 1957. The Saints

The powerful bats in the St. Paul lineup helped the Saints score the fourth-most runs in the American Association in 1956. The pitching staff gave up the third-most runs in the league, however, and the team finished under .500 in the final season at Lexington Park.

PHOTO COURTESY JOE O'CONNELL

lost both games, but a crowd of 10,169—slightly below the stadium's capacity—showed up for the opener. Another 5,800 fans attended the second game that night.

The distances down the line to both left and right field at Midway Stadium were 320 feet, and it was 410 feet to center. The outfield fence was 18 feet high. Joe Koppe of Wichita was the first player to clear the fence when he hit a home run in the seventh inning of the first game.

The stadium was built with a single deck, but it was designed to allow for expansion with additional decks to accommodate more seating for major-league baseball. "It will be very easy to expand this park to seat from 30 to 40,000 fans," St. Paul city architect Alfred Schroeder told the *St. Paul Pioneer Press*. "We could go up either one or two levels, depending upon the number of seats we need. Before we put on another level, however, we would probably extend the present grandstands all the way out to the fences."

JERRY KINDALL

An all-around talented athlete in St. Paul, Jerry Kindall led Washington High School to the state baseball title in 1953 and three years later was a key player on the Minnesota Gophers team that won its first College World Series title. Kindall signed a pro contract with the Chicago Cubs for a reported $50,000, an amount that designated him as a bonus player. Under rules of the time, designed to curb high payouts for young stars, bonus players were required to spend two seasons on the major-league roster before being allowed to develop in the minors. As was the case with many others in his category, Kindall's initial experience with the Cubs included a lot of pinch-running appearances. However, he had the chance to start at shortstop for a few weeks in August of 1956 when regular shortstop Ernie Banks was out with a hand infection.

Although Kindall had been a powerful hitter at Washington and the University of Minnesota, it was his glove that kept him in the major leagues for nine seasons. His final year was back home, with the Twins, in 1965. He was released the following spring and went to his alma mater, the University of Minnesota, to work in the athletics department. In addition to fundraising, Kindall became the freshman coach for the university's basketball team and an assistant coach under Dick Siebert on the baseball team.

Recognized as a savvy baseball man, Kindall gained valuable experience working under Siebert and took many of those lessons with him when he was offered the head coaching job at the University of Arizona in the early 1970s. Kindall's teams at Arizona won the College World Series in 1976, 1980, and 1986. He was the first man to win a college title as a player and as a coach.

Kindall remained in Arizona after retiring from his coaching career in 1996 with an overall record of 861 wins and 580 losses. He has stayed active in the game and has been an announcer for the Big Ten Network since 2009.

Saints president Mel Jones touted the new stadium in the March 1957 issue of the St. Paul Athletic Club magazine *ACE: Athletic Club Events,* calling it "a structure well worth seeing and talking about." Jones noted the large entrances and wide concourse area, which "leads you to any one of eight, extra-wide ramps extending into the Stadium proper." The seats were color coded to match the ticket color: green for the box seat near the field, grayish white for the loge seats (which Jones called an "upper level box seat"), red for reserved seats, and blue for general admission. "Even a trip through the public restrooms proves inviting," wrote Jones. "Completely tiled with face brick tiling from top to bottom, they offer the finest in comfort and sanitation."

With the Twin Cities now home to two stadiums worthy of the majors, the drive to lure a team increased. Having already missed out on three franchises that had moved—the Browns (now Orioles), the Braves, and the Athletics—the Twin Cities looked elsewhere.

The New York Giants had owned the Minneapolis Millers since 1946, and the Giants indicated interest in moving into Metropolitan Stadium in suburban Bloomington. The Giants played in an aging New York stadium, the Polo Grounds, and the team wanted a new ballpark, even if it meant leaving the city. The Brooklyn Dodgers were in the same situation, wanting to get out of Ebbets Field and looking for a new home. If they couldn't get one in New York, they were willing to move across the continent.

In the end, both the Giants and Dodgers moved to California, to San Francisco and Los Angeles, respectively, following the 1957 season. Minnesota missed out again.

But the Twin Cities were recognized as a desirable market, and many baseball experts had no doubt the region would, one way or another, get a club. The city of St. Paul made it clear that it wanted Midway Stadium to be home to a major-league team. As early as July 1954, St. Paul mayor Joseph Dillon said that "under no circumstances" would St. Paul support the Bloomington site then under consideration.

In August 1959, barely one week after news broke that Minneapolis–St. Paul would get a team in the Continental League (a proposed third major league that never materialized), a group of St. Paul fans began a petition stating they would not support major-league baseball unless half the games were played at Midway Stadium.

Bloomington's new Metropolitan Stadium eventually became the home of the Minnesota Twins in 1961. Despite the city's efforts, no major-league games were ever played in St. Paul.

LEXINGTON PARK LEGACY

The original Midway Stadium site has no vestige of its baseball history. As for the Lexington Park site, it was replaced by a Red Owl grocery store. In 1958 Red Owl imbedded a plaque in the floor of the store to mark the site of home plate for Lexington Park (even though it was not the exact spot). Red Owl eventually moved out, but the property remained a supermarket. In the course of changing management, however, the home-plate plaque disappeared. In the summer of 1994, the Halsey Hall Chapter of the Society for American Baseball Research began raising money to erect

another marker. In April 1994 a new plaque was mounted on the outside of the structure. However, the building was abandoned, and this plaque went into storage, awaiting an appropriate site where it could be remounted. In 2007 a TCF Bank opened on Lexington Parkway, on the site of the Coliseum that was just beyond the left-field fence. Bank officials accepted the plaque and mounted it on a footstone amid other Lexington Park photos on a plaza outside the front door, marking the rich baseball heritage of the site.

THE FINAL SEASONS OF THE SAINTS

During the 1950s, players and managers from the Dodgers organization continued to play for the Saints in front of St. Paul fans. Many of them went on to the majors.

Twenty-year-old Stan Williams was a 19-game winner for the Saints in 1957, his second of three seasons with the team. Williams was primarily a starter for the Dodgers from 1958 to 1962, but he pitched mostly out of the bullpen for subsequent teams, including the Minnesota Twins in 1970, when he had a 10–1 record with 15 saves. Williams later worked as a scout for many years and was often back in Minnesota. Whenever asked about his time with the Saints, he proudly pointed out that he threw the last pitch at Lexington Park.

Roger Craig spent nearly three seasons with the Brooklyn Dodgers before getting shipped to St. Paul early in 1958. He had a 5–17 won-lost record for the Saints that year—preparing him for what was to come a few years later as a member of the New York Mets. Taken in the expansion draft by the Mets from the Dodgers, Craig lost 24 and 22 games in the first two years of the Mets franchise (1962 and 1963).

In four years with the Dodgers, in Brooklyn and Los Angeles, from 1955 to 1958, pitcher Ed Roebuck appeared in 166 games, all but one in relief. With the Saints in 1959, he started all 28 games he pitched, completing 14 of them, and posted a 13–10 record with a 2.98 ERA. He returned to Los Angeles the following season and remained in the majors until 1966, pitching a total of 459 games as a reliever and 1 as a starter in his eleven-year career. Roebuck later helped future major-league pitcher Bert Blyleven develop his curve ball while Blyleven was still in high school.

Larry Sherry, like Roebuck, was a starting pitcher with the Saints in 1959, although his major-league career was defined as a reliever. He was called up to the Dodgers in July 1959 and went on to win 2 games in relief during the 1959 World Series. His brother, catcher Norm Sherry, served as his battery mate from 1959 to 1962, during their years together with the Los Angeles Dodgers.

Reliever Ron Perranoski split time between St. Paul and Montreal in 1960, and after becoming a member of the Dodgers' bullpen in 1961, he established himself as one of the best relievers in the game. Perranoski had a 16–3 record and 1.67 ERA with the world champion Dodgers of 1963. He returned to Minnesota to become the Twins' "relief ace" later in the decade, and he led the American League in saves in back-to-back seasons (1969 and 1970).

Norm Larker played first base for the Saints from 1955 to 1957 on his way to the majors. He joined the Los Angeles Dodgers in 1958 and made the National League All-Star team in 1960, when he posted a .323 batting average, which was second-best in the league.

Pictured here in 1957, Bob Lillis, Don Demeter, Dick Gray, and Stan Williams (left to right) all starred for the Saints in the late 1950s and eventually made their way to the major leagues. All four spent time on the Los Angeles Dodgers team that won the World Series in 1959.

MINNESOTA HISTORICAL SOCIETY COLLECTIONS

Bob Lillis, St. Paul's shortstop from 1956 to 1958, first went to the majors with the Dodgers late in the 1958 season. Along with Larker, Pendleton, and several other former Saints, Lillis ended up on the expansion Houston team in the National League in 1962.

Dick Gray was the Saints' top RBI man in the team's first season at Midway Stadium, driving in 111 runs in 1957, a performance that earned him a promotion to the majors. Playing third base, he debuted with the Los Angeles Dodgers on April 15, 1958, against the San Francisco Giants, in the first major-league game played on the West Coast.

Outfielder Don Demeter led St. Paul with 28 home runs in 1957 and batted .309. His 14 homers in 1958 again were the most by a Saints player, and he hit 5 more in 43 games for the big-league club that year. He became a regular outfielder for Los Angeles in 1959 and remained in the majors through 1967, five times hitting 20 or more homers in a season.

Jim Gentile hit 27 home runs for the Saints in 1959. Two years later he hit 46 home runs for the American League's Baltimore Orioles, who had acquired him after the 1959 season. A solid hitter for many years, Gentile was named to the American League All-Star team every year from 1960 to 1962 and finished his career with 179 home runs. He later played for the Kintetsu Buffaloes in the Japan Pacific League.

Solomon "Solly" Drake from Little Rock, Arkansas, first came to Minnesota when he was recruited to play for the Twin City Colored Giants, according to black-baseball historian Frank White. Drake played 55 games for the Saints in 1956 and hit 9 home runs with a .333 batting average. He played briefly in the majors in the late 1950s with the Cubs, Dodgers, and Phillies. When his brother, Sammy Drake, debuted with the Cubs in 1960, the pair became the first black brother combination to reach the major leagues in the twentieth century.

Lacey Curry was a fine-fielding second baseman who spent ten seasons in the minors but never made the majors. He played for the Kansas City Monarchs traveling team (not the same team that played in the Negro American League) as well as in Cuba in the winter. With the Saints, Curry played the outfield in addition to spending time at shortstop and second base from 1956 to 1960.

Outfielder John Glenn played for the Saints franchise in its final years, from 1957 to 1960, before he was traded to the St. Louis Cardinals organization. He hit 15 home runs for St. Paul in 1959.

Carl Warwick was one of the top hitters for the Saints in 1960, hitting .292 with 19 home runs and 104 runs scored in 1960. He broke in with the Dodgers in 1961 but moved around over the next few years. Warwick won a World Series ring with the St. Louis Cardinals in 1964.

Bob Aspromonte was part of a talented crew of brothers who played on Brooklyn's Parade Ground, a set of fields that showcased some of the best

The Saints players gather for a clubhouse celebration before kicking off the team's final season in 1960.

young ballplayers in the area. Aspromonte signed with the Dodgers in 1956, one month after his eighteenth birthday. He made it to St. Paul in 1960, where he hit .323 in 102 games. He spent thirteen seasons in the National League, playing for the Dodgers, Houston, Atlanta, and the New York Mets. One of Aspromonte's brothers, Ken, also played in the major leagues, and another, Charles, played in the minors.

After three seasons under Bryant, the Saints hired Max Macon as the new manager in 1955. Macon had managed the Dodgers' Montreal farm team (which included the legendary Roberto Clemente) in 1954. Macon stayed with the Saints through 1959. Danny Ozark, who had played for the Saints in the early 1950s, took over in 1960. He later managed the Philadelphia Phillies and the San Francisco Giants in the National League.

As the rotation of players and managers continued, St. Paul missed making it to the playoffs from 1953 through 1956. In their first year at Midway Stadium, 1957, the Saints finished fourth and defeated the Wichita Braves in the opening round of the playoffs before losing to Denver in the league championship series.

St. Paul dropped to seventh place in 1958. The American Association expanded to ten teams in 1959 and split into two divisions, with the Saints in the East Division. The top two finishers in each division made the playoffs. St. Paul finished in fourth place with an 81–81 record, and so again did not make the postseason.

The Minneapolis Millers were also placed in the East Division, and the rivalry with the Saints remained spirited. In the morning game of the Independence Day doubleheader in 1959, Millers manager Gene Mauch went into the Midway Stadium stands and got into an altercation with a fan. Mauch was upset with the heckling of his team by the St. Paul fan—boxing announcer and gadfly Chuck Van Avery—who was well known for his ability to irritate opposing teams. Minneapolis general manager George Brophy, who was at the game and helped to break up the altercation, said Mauch was already in a bad mood. The day before, the Boston Red Sox (then the parent club of the Millers) had fired their manager, Pinky Higgins, and Mauch was hoping to get the job. Instead, the Red Sox went outside the organization and hired Washington Senators coach Billy Jurges to succeed Higgins. St. Paul's Jim Gentile had a pair of doubles and later added 2 home runs, which also couldn't have helped Mauch's mood. The Saints went on to win the game, 8–4.

In 1960 the league was back to eight teams as Dallas and Fort Worth merged and Charleston dropped out. Jim Golden won 20 games for St. Paul and became the last 20-game winner ever in the American Association. He also led the league with a 2.32 earned-run average. The Saints finished with an 83–71 record, one game in front of Minneapolis for fourth place—and the final playoff spot.

LITTLE/JUNIOR WORLD SERIES APPEARANCES *by* THE SAINTS

1904: Buffalo Bisons 2, St. Paul Saints 1

1920: Baltimore Orioles 5, St. Paul Saints 1

1922: Baltimore Orioles 5, St. Paul Saints 2

1924: St. Paul Saints 5, Baltimore Orioles 4 (1 tie)

1931: Rochester Red Wings 5, St. Paul Saints 3

1948: Montreal Royals 4, St. Paul Saints 1

Although not an official championship series, the Saints played the Vernon (California) Tigers, winners of the Pacific Coast League, in 1919 and lost five games to four. In 1924, after beating the Orioles in the Little World Series, the Saints went to Seattle for a best-of-nine series against the Pacific Coast League champions. However, because of rain, they played only one game against the Seattle Indians, winning 12–4.

The Saints faced the Louisville Colonels in the opening playoff round and fell behind, three games to two. In the sixth game, held in Louisville, the Saints had a 4–1 lead after six innings, but the Colonels tied the game with 2 in the seventh and 1 in the eighth. Then, with 2 out in the last of the ninth inning, Louisville's Mack Jones singled home Frank Torre to end the game and the season for the Saints.

It would prove to be the final game in the history of the St. Paul Saints franchise. In the fall of 1960, the American League voted to expand by two teams for the following season. One of the new teams was placed in Washington, DC, allowing Senators owner Calvin Griffith to move his team to Minnesota. Both the Saints and Millers closed up shop.

The Saints and Millers had been the best two teams during their fifty-nine years in the American Association. Their departure left the league with only six teams. The association carried on for two more years before folding.

However, in 1969, with further expansion of the major leagues and the need for more farm teams, the American Association reorganized and was back in business. It operated for twenty-nine years before once again disbanding after the 1997 season. Another American Association emerged in 2006, this one an independent league and one that, once again, contained the St. Paul Saints.

ST. PAUL SAINTS *in* THE AMERICAN ASSOCIATION, 1902–1960

YEAR	WON	LOST	PLACE	MANAGER	ATTENDANCE
1902	72	66	Third	Mike Kelley	—
1903	88	46	First	Mike Kelley	—
1904	95	52	First	Mike Kelley	—
1905	73	77	Fifth	Mike Kelley	—
1906	66	80	Seventh	Dick Padden	—
1907	59	95	Eighth	Ed Ashenbach	—
1908	48	104	Eighth	Tim Flood/Mike Kelley	90,510
1909	80	83	Fifth	Mike Kelley	146,691
1910	88	80	Fourth	Mike Kelley	165,619
1911	79	85	Fourth	Mike Kelley	153,240
1912	77	90	Sixth	Mike Kelley	106,149
1913	77	90	Fifth	Bill Friel	123,568
1914	56	111	Eighth	Bill Friel	75,621
1915	90	63	Second	Mike Kelley	137,295
1916	86	79	Fourth	Mike Kelley	126,372
1917	88	66	Second	Mike Kelley	99,254
1918	39	38	Sixth	Mike Kelley	
1919	94	60	First	Mike Kelley	139,915
1920	115	49	First	Mike Kelley	229,285
1921	80	87	Sixth	Mike Kelley	179,527
1922	107	60	First	Mike Kelley	213,029
1923	111	57	Second	Mike Kelley	219,979
1924	96	70	First	Nick Allen	242,268
1925	91	75	Third	Nick Allen	195,236
1926	82	81	Sixth	Nick Allen	166,197
1927	90	78	Fourth	Nick Allen	163,423
1928	88	80	Fourth (tie)	Nick Allen	175,638
1929	102	64	Second	Bubbles Hargrave	197,099
1930	91	63	Second	Lefty Leifield	180,685
1931	104	63	First	Lefty Leifield	176,512

YEAR	WON	LOST	PLACE	MANAGER	ATTENDANCE
1932	70	97	Seventh	Lefty Leifield	85,487
1933	78	75	Fourth	Emmett McCann/Phil Todt	89,562
1934	67	84	Seventh	Bob Coleman	74,801
1935	75	78	Fifth	Marty McManus	120,954
1936	84	68	Second	Gabby Street	168,734
1937	67	87	Seventh	Gabby Street/Phil Todt	144,395
1938	90	61	First	Foster "Babe" Ganzel	251,308
1939	73	81	Fifth	Foster "Babe" Ganzel	169,168
1940	69	79	Fifth	Foster "Babe" Ganzel	112,278
1941	61	92	Seventh	Ralph "Red" Kress	75,178
1942	57	97	Eighth	Virgil "Truck" Hannah/Bob Tarleton	73,990
1943	67	85	Seventh (tie)	Francis "Salty" Parker	82,116
1944	85	66	Fourth	Ray Blades	116,315
1945	75	76	Fourth	Ray Blades	187,780
1946	80	71	Third	Ray Blades	289,544
1947	69	85	Seventh	Herman Franks/Curt Davis	222,331
1948	86	68	Third	Walter Alston	320,483
1949	93	60	First	Walter Alston	352,911
1950	83	69	Fourth	Clay Hopper	200,149
1951	85	66	Second	Clay Hopper	171,999
1952	80	74	Third	Clay Bryant	125,769
1953	72	82	Sixth	Clay Bryant	139,348
1954	75	78	Fifth	Clay Bryant	134,006
1955	75	78	Sixth	Max Macon	118,318
1956	75	78	Fifth	Max Macon	102,004
1957	82	72	Fourth	Max Macon	202,260
1958	70	84	Seventh	Max Macon	132,120
1959	81	81	Fourth (East)	Max Macon	116,574
1960	83	71	Fourth	Danny Ozark	119,926

JOURNEY TO
INDEPENDENCE

CHAPTER 8

Transformation of the Minor Leagues

NORTHERN LEAGUE FOREFATHERS

The first Northern League was formed in 1902 with a composition true to its name, having no team south of Fargo, North Dakota. The original six-team league was based in cities mostly in a line from Fargo to Winnipeg, Manitoba. In between were the North Dakota cities of Cavalier, Grand Forks, and Devils Lake, and to the east was Crookston, Minnesota. In 1913 the league added teams from St. Paul and Minneapolis, even though both cities already had clubs in the higher-level American Association. St. Paul didn't last long in the Northern League, and the team moved to La Crosse, Wisconsin, during the season; Minneapolis folded after the season.

All minor-league teams of that period were independent, not affiliated with any major-league parent. Some leagues, including the Northern League, were also independent, but most functioned under the umbrella of the National Association, which dictated operating procedures and assigned minor leagues to various classifications.

The Northern League operated off and on through July 1917, when World War I brought the season and the league to a premature end. It was revived in 1933, in many of the same cities, and lasted for nine years before again folding due to strained resources from World War II. While the reformed league was up and running, though, a couple of former St. Paul Saints stars played a big part in it. Lute "Danny" Boone, who had been a star player for the Saints from 1919 to 1925, was a player-manager for the Crookston Pirates and also served as the Northern League president during the 1933 season. Former Saints outfielder Bruno Haas was one of the league's main organizers and president of the Winnipeg Maroons, in addition to playing for them.

When the Northern League came alive again following World War II, it featured eight teams from Minnesota, Wisconsin, and the Dakotas. The St. Cloud Rox, a farm team of the New York Giants, won the league in 1946; the Duluth Dukes, a St. Louis Cardinals affiliate, finished at the bottom of the standings. In between were the Fargo-Moorhead Twins, Superior Blues, Eau Claire Bears, Aberdeen Pheasants, Grand Forks Chiefs, and Sioux Falls Canaries.

This incarnation of the Northern League operated until 1971, although Aberdeen and St. Cloud were the only franchises to survive the full quarter century. The league ranked toward the lower end of the minor-league ladder, but it nevertheless developed many memorable players.

Frank Gravino of the Fargo-Moorhead Twins was the league's greatest slugger for a time in the 1950s. He led the league with 32 home runs in 1952 despite playing in only 94 of the team's 124 games. He hit 52 and 56 homers in the following seasons. Gravino started his pro career in 1940 at the age of seventeen but then missed several seasons because of military service during the war. His declining eyesight contributed to his early retirement at age thirty-one after the 1954 season. Although he never reached the majors, Gravino has been called the greatest slugger in Northern League history.

One of Gravino's teammates in 1953 did go on to make a name for himself in the major leagues. Roger Maras, a graduate of Fargo's Shanley High School, was a strong left-handed hitter who made his pro debut with Fargo-Moorhead in 1953 and was voted the league's top rookie. After changing the spelling of his last name, Roger Maris reached the majors with the Cleveland Indians in 1957. A few years later, then with the New York Yankees, he was named the American League Most Valuable Player in back-to-back seasons. In the second of those, 1961, he set a single-season record with 61 home runs.

Jim "Mudcat" Grant broke into pro ball a year after Maris and was one of the Northern League's top pitchers. He won 21 games for the Fargo-Moorhead Twins in 1954, a total he matched eleven years later as he helped lead the Minnesota Twins to the American League pennant.

The Eau Claire Bears were a farm team of the Boston and then Milwaukee Braves and produced several key players for the Braves' pennant-winning teams of 1957 and 1958. One was Henry Aaron, who hit 9 home runs in 87 games for the Bears in 1952. Aaron's outfield mates on the champion Milwaukee Braves of 1957 were Bill Bruton and Wes Covington, who had also played in Eau Claire. Joe Torre batted .344 for Eau Claire in 1960 before going on to an all-star playing and managerial career in the majors that led to his induction into the Hall of Fame.

The Duluth Dukes merged with Superior in 1956, and the team maintained the affiliation the Blues had with the Chicago White Sox. Although it represented both cities in the bi-state Twin Ports region, the Duluth-Superior White

Sox played their games at Wade Stadium in Duluth. In 1956 and 1957, Duluth-Superior, managed by former Minneapolis Millers slugger Joe Hauser, featured Jack Kralick and Don Mincher, who later played for the Minnesota Twins. When Duluth-Superior became a farm team for the Detroit Tigers in 1960 (after taking back the Dukes name), local fans got to watch a number of future Tigers stars play, including Bill Freehan, Gates Brown, Jim Northrup, Mickey Stanley, Willie Horton, and Denny McLain.

Through their Northern League years, the Aberdeen Pheasants were a farm club of the St. Louis Browns, who became the Baltimore Orioles in 1954. Hall of Famer Earl Weaver managed the Pheasants in 1959, and several players who helped the Orioles to four World Series between 1966 and 1971 passed through Aberdeen on their way to the majors.

An eighteen-year-old Jim Palmer won 11 games for Aberdeen in 1964, when the team won the Northern League title with an 80–37 record. Now a member of the Baseball Hall of Fame, Palmer pitched for Baltimore for nearly two decades, during which time he won three American League Cy Young Awards (1973, 1975, and 1976) and was an eight-time 20-game winner.

Steve Dalkowski never reached the big leagues even though some considered him to be the fastest pitcher in baseball history up to that time. With the

JIM RANTZ

An all-around athlete who played on championship teams at Washington High School in St. Paul and the University of Minnesota, Jim Rantz devoted his life to baseball.

Rantz played hockey, football, and baseball at Washington and was a member of two state-champion baseball teams. He received a hockey scholarship at the University of Minnesota but really made his mark on the diamond for the Gophers. Primarily a reliever, Rantz was called on to start the championship game of the 1960 College World Series. He had a shutout until two out in the ninth inning, when the University of Southern California Trojans scored the tying run that sent the game into extra innings. Rantz retired the Trojans in the top of the tenth inning and became the winning pitcher as his team scored in the bottom of the inning to give the Gophers the national title.

Rantz signed a contract with the Washington Senators, which became the Minnesota Twins the following year. He pitched in the minors through 1964; managed a Twins farm club in St. Cloud, Minnesota, in 1965; and then helped out Tom Mee in the public relations department as the Twins prepared to play in the World Series. Rantz stayed with the Twins, working in public relations and as the assistant farm director. He became the team's director of minor-league operations in 1986 and remained with the team until retiring after the 2012 season.

Rantz received the first Sheldon "Chief" Bender Award for distinguished service to the minor leagues. In 2007 he was inducted into the Minnesota Twins Hall of Fame.

1959 Aberdeen Pheasants, he struck out 99 batters in 59 innings; the next year, with the Stockton Ports of the California League, he struck out 262 batters in 170 innings—but he also walked as many as he fanned that season. Wildness on the mound, along with alcoholism, doomed his career, but he remains a minor-league legend. Reportedly, the character of Ebby "Nuke" LaLoosh in the movie *Bull Durham* is loosely based on Dalkowski.

St. Cloud was a farm team of the New York/San Francisco Giants, Chicago Cubs, and Minnesota Twins during its quarter century in the Northern League from 1946 to 1971. Future Hall of Famers Gaylord Perry and Lou Brock had their first professional experience with the Rox. Another member of the Hall of Fame, Orlando Cepeda, played in St. Cloud in 1956 and won the Northern League Triple Crown, leading the league in batting average, home runs, and runs batted in, as well as hits and total bases.

Charlie Fox was the Rox's player-manager in the late 1940s and early 1950s. He spent more than thirty years in the Giants organization as a player, manager, coach, and scout. He was the manager when San Francisco won the National League West Division in 1971.

The Rox became affiliated with the Minnesota Twins in 1965, and St. Cloud fans got to watch a number of players who were on their way to the big-league team that was based only seventy miles away. Future Twins George Mitterwald, Jim Hughes, Craig Kusick, Charley Walters, Steve Brye, Danny Thompson, and Dave Goltz played for the Rox.

Though near the bottom of the minor-league hierarchy, the Northern League produced its share of big names. In addition to those already noted, the list includes Vada Pinson, Ken Griffey Sr., Don Gullett, Donn Clendenon, Greg Luzinski, Manny Trillo, Rick Reuschel, Rico Carty, Bob Uecker, Gene Michael, Matty Alou, Dave Nicholson, Max Alvis, Horace Clarke, Darold Knowles, Rudy May, Bob Turley, Willie Kirkland, Cookie Rojas, Tony Taylor, and Leon Wagner. Dallas Green and Cal Ripken Sr. managed in the league.

The Northern League that restarted in 1946 was part of a postwar boom in minor-league baseball that began to bust in the 1950s. In 1949, the Duluth Dukes drew more than 100,000 fans for the season. By 1961, the Minnesota Twins' first year, the Northern League was down to six teams. Only two of them attracted more than 45,000 fans. The league shuffled its membership, new cities popping in and out, as it struggled to keep enough teams to continue operating.

Duluth-Superior dropped out following the 1970 season after losing its affiliation with the Chicago White Sox. Only four teams remained in 1971: St. Cloud, Sioux Falls (South Dakota), Aberdeen, and Watertown (Minnesota), which withdrew at the end of the year. When an attempt to get a team back in Duluth failed, the Northern League shut down.

With the Northern League's demise, baseball in Minnesota belonged to the Twins. Town ball carried on, as did college ball. The University of Minnesota Gophers went to the College World Series in 1973 and 1977 under coach Dick Siebert, featuring such big-name local heroes as Dave Winfield and Paul Molitor. But the Twins were the baseball cynosure in the state, and it was not a good time for them.

Mirroring a national trend, baseball was falling behind football in popularity in Minnesota. After an initial decade fielding competitive teams, including a World Series trip in 1965 and back-to-back division titles in 1969 and 1970, the Twins began slipping. In 1971, they finished in fifth place with a 71–91 record and drew fewer than 1 million fans for the first time. Attendance surpassed 1 million in only two seasons between 1971 and 1981, the final years at Met Stadium.

On the gridiron, the Minnesota Vikings were heading in the other direction. They made it to four Super Bowls in an eight-year period, and although they lost all four, the Vikings were kings of the Minnesota sports pages during this time.

The Twins rarely stirred the passions of the masses during the decade, but even so, the team received more attention than minor-league Minnesota teams. The closest minor-league teams to Minneapolis and St. Paul—Wisconsin Rapids, Wisconsin; and Waterloo, Iowa—were nearly 200 miles away. But even when Minnesota hosted its own minor-league teams, Twin Cities residents weren't likely to venture to their games following the arrival of major-league baseball to the state. Even the people in Duluth and St. Cloud were more focused on the Twins than their local teams.

Years later many fans, even those in cities with major-league baseball, have become attached to the charm of the minors and make pilgrimages to more-distant places to watch games. But in the 1970s, attending minor-league games just wasn't considered "cool" among professional baseball fans in Minnesota.

NORTHERN LEAGUERS *in* THE HALL OF FAME

Rube Waddell, Minneapolis and Virginia, 1913

Dizzy Dean, Fargo-Moorhead, 1941, and Superior, 1942

Dave Bancroft, St. Cloud, 1947 (manager)

Henry Aaron, Eau Claire, 1952

Orlando Cepeda, St. Cloud, 1956

Gaylord Perry, St. Cloud, 1958

Earl Weaver, Aberdeen, 1959 (player-manager)

Travis Jackson, Eau Claire, 1959 (manager)

Joe Torre, Eau Claire, 1960

Willie Stargell, Grand Forks, 1960

Lou Brock, St. Cloud, 1961

Jim Palmer, Aberdeen, 1964

Steve Carlton, Winnipeg, 1964

THE CHANGING FACE OF THE MINOR LEAGUES

The folding of the Northern League in 1971 was an indication of the overall state of the minor leagues during the preceding two decades. A boom in everything, from babies to baseball, included expansion of the minor leagues to nearly sixty leagues and more than 400 cities in 1949. Then the 1950s and 1960s happened: wars, superhighways, air conditioning, television, hippies—all have been cited in the decline of fans attending minor-league games.

In addition, the number of cities that had major-league teams more than doubled between 1952 and 1970. In 1953, the first geographic shifting of the majors in fifty years saw clubs leaving multi-team cities to set up shop in Milwaukee, Baltimore, Kansas City, Los Angeles, and San Francisco. The 1960s brought two waves of expansion and more franchise transfers that introduced major-league baseball to Houston, Minneapolis–St. Paul, Atlanta, Oakland, San Diego, Montreal, and Seattle.

The minor leagues continued to dwindle as the major leagues expanded. Fewer than 20 minor leagues existed in 1971, the last year of the Northern League.

Another change in the minors that had been in process for decades was the growing influence of the farm system. Although the leagues had long been affiliated with the majors within the purview of organized baseball, the teams operated as entities unto themselves for a significant portion of the early twentieth century. For example, the Minneapolis Millers and St. Paul Saints, competing in the top-flight American Association, had many of the same players coming back year after year. That meant fans wouldn't find themselves cheering for a local favorite only to realize his success was bringing the player closer to being plucked away by a major-league parent.

But in the 1940s both Twin Cities teams became full-fledged affiliates of big-league clubs, the Millers of the New York Giants and the Saints of the Brooklyn Dodgers. In a way, the connections intensified the local feud between the Minneapolis and St. Paul teams, as it was fueled by the intense rivalry of their major-league partners. But the affiliations also meant that long-term attachments to players were no longer possible.

Duke Snider played for the Saints in 1947, but it was clear that his time in St. Paul was limited. He was soon launching his Hall of Fame career in the majors. Minneapolis fans experienced the same thing, such as when the popular Willie Mays was called up to the majors after only 35 games with the Millers.

After Milwaukee got a major-league team in 1953, the quest for a team in Minnesota intensified and dominated the rest of the decade. Minor-league teams were no longer enough.

Even cities that weren't necessarily looking to upgrade to major-league status were affected by the changing nature of the minors. Eugene, Oregon, had a team in the Pacific Coast League starting in 1969. The next year Eugene fans watched a young slugger, Joe Lis, hit 36 home runs for the Emeralds, but he was soon called up to finish the year with the Philadelphia Phillies.

After a season of mostly sitting on the bench with Philadelphia, Lis was back in Eugene to start 1972, and he was even hotter with the bat than he had been two years before. Though he was hitting home runs at a record pace, it was clear he would not have the chance to approach the Pacific Coast League single-season mark of 60 set by Tony Lazzeri of Salt Lake City in 1925. Each time Emeralds fans cheered another blast by Lis, they knew he was one step closer to being called away. Sure enough, the Phillies summoned Lis back to the big leagues in June, after he had hit 26 home runs. (Lis would hit a total of 32 home runs in a major-league career that spanned eight years. His single-season high was 9, for the 1973 Minnesota Twins.)

About 100 miles to the north of Eugene, the Portland Beavers were completing a long run in the Pacific Coast League, which had stood out among minor leagues for many years. The Pacific Coast League held on to many stars who chose to stay close to home rather than play in the majors in faraway midwestern and eastern locales. For most of its history, the core Pacific Coast League cities were Seattle, Portland, San Francisco, Oakland, Sacramento, Los Angeles, and Portland. By 1969 the major leagues had reached each of these cities, with the exception of Sacramento, which had already left the league after the 1960 season, and Portland, which in 1972 was the last of the original Pacific Coast League teams still operating in the league.

The Beavers drew fewer than 100,000 fans to their home games in 1972. Last in the league in attendance, the Portland franchise was moved after the season to Spokane, Washington, which had had a Pacific Coast League team from 1958 through 1971.

INDEPENDENT REVIVAL

"You know what killed Coast League baseball in this town?" asked Neil "Bing" Russell, regarding Portland. "Every time we got somebody the fans loved, that guy was called up to the major leagues by the parent club."

Bing Russell was an actor, known for his roles in *Bonanza* and *The Magnificent Seven,* who became a minor-league entrepreneur. In 1973 Russell was president and part owner of the El Paso Diablos of the Class AA Texas League. On the team was Bing Russell's son, Kurt Russell, who had an acting career already behind and still in front of him.

Later that season Kurt Russell moved to the Portland Mavericks, an independent team his dad had started in the Class A Northwest League. The Mavericks were the first unaffiliated team in organized baseball since Quincy,

Illinois, had an entry in the Midwest League in 1964. Acting on his sentiments about farm systems, Bing Russell decided to start a team that would have no affiliation with a major-league team.

Bing Russell had played in the Class D Georgia-Alabama League in the late 1940s before moving into television and movies. His Mavericks were a reflection of his baseball and Hollywood background. Several players and managers were a part of both worlds. Hank Robinson, the team's manager in 1973, had an ongoing career as a stunt man and actor. He had also played and managed in the minor leagues in the 1940s and 1950s and managed in collegiate winter leagues in California. Hank Robinson's son, Henry "Robbie" Robinson, played on the team and was an actor, as were Mavericks Jason "Jay" Tatar and Ken Medlock. Even Todd Field, a batboy in the early years of the team, achieved prominence on screen and as a director.

Baseball, however, was Bing Russell's main focus in the mid-1970s. He built a team of his own and refused to accept players on option from other organizations. "There's no plan to produce players for the major leagues," he said. "All we want are some players who will be playing for Portland for a long time. I don't care about developing athletes for folks in Minneapolis or Cleveland or Cincinnati to enjoy. That's stupid."

Bing Russell recruited primarily from semipro leagues in California. In early June 1973, just before the opening of the Northwest League season, he held a tryout camp to fill out the roster. The camp drew more than 100 players. Some were just out of college. Others had been released from pro ball and came at their own expense, for what would probably be their last chance at playing baseball for money.

After a trip to Alaska and exhibition games against a semipro team in Anchorage, the Mavericks opened their 1973 schedule. The team drew more than 31,000 fans in its first fourteen home games, which was nearly double the average attendance of the Portland Pacific Coast League team the year before. "I didn't come up here to lose money," Bing Russell had said before the season.

Nor had he come to Portland to lose games. Showcasing speed and daring play, the Mavericks won the league's South Division with a record of 45–35. With more than 80,000 fans turning out for only thirty-six home gate openings (which included doubleheaders), Bing Russell's Mavericks set a short-season Class A attendance record. (Short-season Class A leagues are a notch below full-season Class A and play half the number of games.)

In an article for *The Sporting News* by Nick Bertram, Bing Russell stressed three traits needed by every organization in professional baseball: know-how in the front office (which he termed "accountability"), an understanding of the game, and a knowledge of dramaturgy, the art of producing drama, which was a byproduct of Russell's career in television and movies. His formula was one that would be followed by independent operators years later.

Following the success of the Mavericks, Bing Russell looked for other cities in the area to join his independent movement. "Russell wants Vancouver [British Columbia], Seattle, Spokane, Sacramento, and Victoria [British Columbia]—all the Coast League dropouts—to join with Portland next summer in this grand experiment," wrote Wells Twombly in *The Sporting News*.

Seattle was the only one of the group cited by Twombly that fielded an independent team in the Northwest League, and that folded when the city got a major-league franchise in 1977. A number of smaller cities—Pasco and Grays Harbor (in Aberdeen), Washington; and Eugene and Salem, Oregon—joined, and eventually the league had a division made up entirely of independents. (The Grays Harbor Loggers got some attention during the summer of 1978 when comedian Bill Murray came to Aberdeen to "try out" for the team as part of a segment being developed for NBC's *Saturday Night Live*. Murray spent a few days auditioning for a part on the team, one that was assured. On July 26, he coached first base for the Loggers in a game against the Victoria Mussels. In the eighth inning he pinch-hit and singled. With an NBC television crew on hand, Murray had one more plate appearance in another game.)

The Mavericks continued with winning records and broke their own attendance records in 1974 and 1975. Portland got a boost at the gate the latter year with the addition of former major-league pitcher Jim Bouton, who had achieved greater fame with *Ball Four*, his book chronicling his experiences with the Seattle Pilots and Houston Astros in 1969.

Bouton had retired as a player and was a sportscaster in New York, but he never lost the urge to get back in the game. The Mavericks gave him a chance, and Bouton shuttled between the coasts to pitch for Portland during the second half of the 1975 season. Nearly 10,000 fans showed up at Portland's Civic Stadium for Bouton's first appearance, on August 8. He pitched a complete game and beat Walla Walla (Washington). He pitched for them again in 1977.

In an updated edition to *Ball Four*, Bouton characterized the Mavericks as the "dirty dozen of baseball" and shared entertaining stories of playing for Bing Russell's independent team:

> The soul of the Mavericks was an old red school bus which was used for transportation. In addition to a seatless interior with mattresses on the floor, it featured a loudspeaker on the roof from which important announcements could be made via a microphone inside the bus.
>
> The Mavs had a unique way of attracting crowds to the ballparks. The afternoon before a game, we'd drive through the streets of whatever town we were playing in and insult the citizens over the loudspeaker. "You there,

in the blue shirt," one of the players would broadcast while the bus stopped at a light. "Pull in that gut, it looks disgusting." No insult was too outrageous. "Hey, Lady, that sure is an ugly baby you got there." And so on. Needless to say, that night the stands would be filled with hundreds of irate fans rooting passionately for our defeat.

The renegade spirit of the Mavericks was also captured in a 2014 documentary, *The Battered Bastards of Baseball,* directed by Bing Russell's grandsons, Maclain and Chapman Way.

In 1977 the Mavericks peaked in attendance at more than 125,000. It was enough to make the Pacific Coast League pay attention to Portland again. A new Beavers team in the league returned to the city the next season, driving out Bing Russell and the Mavericks. Even with a winning record, playing at the highest level of the minors in a season twice as long as that of the Northwest League, the Portland Beavers drew barely 96,000 fans in 1978, nearly 30,000 fewer than the Mavericks had in their final year.

Others followed but few approached the Mavericks' success as independents, and some reached an opposite extreme. The Bakersfield Outlaws of the California League began in 1978 by losing 10 of their first 11 games, many by

DENNIS DENNING

Dennis Denning was one of the most successful coaches in Minnesota history, leading championship teams in high school and college for more than thirty years while also managing summer youth leagues.

In Minnesota, Denning was on the state champion Cretin (now Cretin–Derham Hall) High School team in 1962 and played at St. Thomas College (now the University of St. Thomas). Drafted by Baltimore after his junior season, he was an infielder in the Orioles organization for three years before a serious wrist injury ended his playing career.

Denning was already teaching and coaching back in St. Paul at this time. At St. Luke's grade school, he coached Paul Molitor in sixth-grade basketball. He moved from St. Luke's to Nativity grade school, and then became the head baseball coach at Cretin High School in 1979. There Denning led the Raiders to state titles in 1981, 1982, 1986, 1989, 1990, and 1992.

While coaching the Raiders, Denning also scouted for the Orioles, the Phillies, and the Major League Scouting Bureau, but he had to give that up in 1994 when he left Cretin-Derham Hall to coach at St. Thomas.

None of the schools in St. Thomas's conference, the Minnesota Intercollegiate Athletic Conference, had ever reached the Division III College World Series. Under Denning, the St. Thomas Tommies not only made it four times in ten years; they won titles in 2001 and 2009 and finished second in 1999 and 2000.

lopsided scores. In one game against the Reno Silver Sox, Bakersfield pitcher Ray Gault threw eight wild pitches in one and two-thirds innings. A couple of months later four Outlaws pitchers combined to walk 20 Silver Sox batters in a game.

The Outlaws played in Sam Lynn Park, which had a capacity of 888, well more than was needed on most nights. George Culver, who had pitched in the majors between 1966 and 1974, managed Bakersfield and discovered how tight the team's budget was. The Outlaws had purchased its uniforms from a previous Bakersfield team that had been in the Los Angeles Dodgers farm system. One day Culver noticed his name stenciled on the beltline of a pair of pants; it turned out they had belonged to him when he had pitched for Los Angeles five years before!

Bakersfield finished at the bottom of the league standings and near the bottom in attendance in 1978. The Outlaws made improvements to their ballpark and increased their attendance as well as their winning percentage in 1979. It wasn't enough to keep the team afloat, though, and it folded after only two years.

A few years later another independent team based farther up the coast fared even worse on the field. The San Jose Bees, an independent team in the

Another highlight of 2000 was a historic trip to Cuba for the team to play games against the University of Havana, which was a sister school of St. Thomas. The Tommies won the games in Havana and then hosted a game at St. Thomas that spring. The Cuban team brought fireballing pitcher Jonder Martinez, who was not on the Havana squad in the earlier games. On May 9, Martinez shut out St. Thomas. Jake Mauer got the only hit for the Tommies. Adding drama to the trip was the defection of Cuba's second baseman, Mario Miguel Chaoul, soon after the team arrived in Minnesota.

Denning was named the Division III Coach of the Year in both championship years of 2001 and 2009. He retired after the 2009 season with a career record at St. Thomas of 522–157. Four of the Tommies he coached were drafted by major-league teams, including Jake Mauer, who became a manager in the Minnesota Twins organization, and Leonard "Buzz" Hannahan, who later became an assistant to Denning at St. Thomas, and Chris Olean, who succeeded Denning as the Tommies' head coach.

Beyond his wins, titles, and players developed at Cretin–Derham Hall and St. Thomas, Denning spent more than thirty years coaching youth teams. Future Twins player Joe Mauer attended one of his summer camps at Cretin–Derham Hall. Denning recalls the great control Joe Mauer had as a pitcher. "He even threw a knuckleball," Denning said, "and got it over the plate."

As of 2015, Denning continued to live in St. Paul and enjoyed baseball as much as ever, regularly attending Twins games at Target Field.

California League from 1983 through 1987, posted a won-lost record of 33–109 in its final season.

Harry Stavrenos, using the name Harry Steve, took over operation of the Bees in 1986. Serving as president, general manager, and field manager, he stocked the roster with former big leaguers who had been drummed out of the majors for drugs and other problems. The team became known as the Bad News Bees. The roster included Steve Howe, the 1980 National League Rookie of the Year who was later suspended because of his cocaine addiction (with many suspensions to follow); Ken Reitz, a fine-fielding third baseman in the National League through the 1970s but who had abused amphetamines; and Mike Norris, who won 22 games for Oakland in 1980 and was runner-up for the Cy Young Award before having arm problems and drug struggles. Derrel Thomas, an infielder in the National League for fifteen seasons, didn't even make it to opening day; he was fired after trying to organize a coup to overthrow Stavrenos as the manager during spring training.

Troubled players didn't make up the entire Bees team. It had also established a relationship with the Seibu Lions of the Japan Pacific League during this period, and several Japanese players played for San Jose.

The California League fielded several independent teams during the 1970s, and a few leagues were composed entirely of independents, though without much success. The Gulf States League was an all-independent organization in 1976; it became the Lone Star League in 1977 but didn't continue after that. The Inter-American League of 1979 consisted of six independent teams based in Florida, Puerto Rico, the Dominican Republic, Panama, and Venezuela, but it didn't even make it through a full season, folding on June 30.

FROM REVIVAL TO RESURGENCE

While few independent teams of the time were able to duplicate the success of the Portland Mavericks, the Mavericks' impact on the baseball landscape produced a seed that bloomed a number of years later.

During Portland's five-season run, Northwest League president Bob Freitas sold a rising baseball entrepreneur on the merits of independence. Miles Wolff, the general manager of the Class AA Savannah Braves and the 1971 Executive of the Year in the league, met Freitas and left with a longing for an independent team of his own.

"Bob Freitas was the lone voice saying independent baseball can make it," recalled Wolff. He also said Freitas's philosophy was, "Playing to win is a lot more fun than playing to develop."

Wolff entered the ownership realm, though not with an independent team, in 1980 when he purchased a franchise in the Carolina League and revived the

Durham Bulls. (The team later became the focus of the movie *Bull Durham,* directed by former Baltimore Orioles farmhand Ron Shelton.) During this time Wolff also purchased a publication, *All-American Baseball News,* which he renamed *Baseball America* and which became the premier publication covering minor-league baseball.

Also in 1980, the Utica (New York) Blue Jays, a Class A affiliate of the Toronto Blue Jays in the New York–Penn League, suffered through a losing season while drawing fewer than 500 fans per game. Toronto cut ties with the Utica team, and Wolff stepped in. He couldn't get the team, renamed the Utica Blue Sox, a working agreement with a big-league team, so it operated independently. Wolff drew on the expertise of Van Schley to bring in quality players.

Schley first got into baseball with a team in the Lone Star League in 1977. The next year he was director of player personnel for the Grays Harbor Loggers and was responsible for bringing actor Murray there for his brief appearance.

Along with Wolff and Schley, Murray became involved with the Blue Sox. Marvin Goldklang, a New York lawyer with a hankering for baseball, later joined them as another investor.

A New Jersey native, Goldklang had grown up a fan of the New York Yankees and Joe DiMaggio. In the late 1970s he purchased a stake in the Yankees with his Livingston, New Jersey, neighbor Barry Halper, who was a noted collector of baseball memorabilia.

A few years later Goldklang got involved in a less-famous team through Schley, who was a client of his law firm. Schley was looking for help to arrange a small loan to finance the purchase of concessions equipment for the Utica ballpark. "I told him he would pay more in legal fees than he was looking to borrow," Goldklang recalled, "and I asked him how much of the team I would get if I simply wrote him a check." It was about six percent.

Goldklang had another reason for his investment in the Blue Sox. A pitcher at the University of Pennsylvania twenty years earlier, he said he bought the team with a handshake agreement that he would be allowed to pitch a game, "But I wound up on firm business in Tokyo and Guam most of the summer and never got to pitch."

Although he was connected with Utica for only a year, Goldklang established a relationship with Wolff and Schley. This troika stayed involved in the minors, lifting independent baseball to greater heights a decade later.

Utica's attendance in 1981 was only 19,000—barely more than the team had when it was an affiliate of the Toronto Blue Jays the year before—but the Blue Sox picked up at the gate as they improved their winning percentage. Even with a losing record in its final season as an independent in 1985, Utica brought in more than 56,000 fans. By this time, author Roger Kahn was president of the Blue Sox, and he used the experience to write the 1985 book *Good Enough to Dream*.

The biggest year for the Blue Sox had been 1983, when the team won the league title under manager Jim Gattis. Two years later Gattis was the manager of another independent team, the Salt Lake City Trappers of the Pioneer League, which had a Summer A classification (a rookie league). The Trappers were established in 1985 in a city that had a long on-and-off history in the Pacific Coast League.

Schley secured the franchise rights to Salt Lake City in 1985. Other investors in the Trappers included actor Murray and Arte Moreno, who

BILL PETERSON

A prominent local athlete and sports official, Bill Peterson may be better known as a coach and mentor to many St. Paul athletes and for his contributions to youth athletics for more than five decades. Peterson took over the Oxford playground, at the corner of Oxford Street and Rondo Avenue, in the early 1960s. In his 1988 autobiography, Dave Winfield wrote that he learned a lot on the Oxford field and that the "really heavy-duty lessons came when Bill Peterson, a young white man fresh out of the University of Minnesota, took the job of supervisor at the playground—a job no one else in St. Paul's all-white Parks Department wanted." With Dave and Steve Winfield on the team, Peterson later coached the St. Paul's Attucks-Brooks American Legion team to the state championship in 1967 and 1968.

Peterson coached Attucks-Brooks to another state title with Paul Molitor in 1974. Peterson also mentored Molitor on the Oxford playground and coached him at Cretin High School.

Peterson became the supervisor of St. Paul municipal athletics and continues to lead efforts to upgrade and maintain fields and diamonds in the city. In recognition of his efforts, a youth athletic field at Dunning Recreation Center, just to the west of the Oxford playground, was named Billy Peterson Field in 2010.

In 2006, at the age of sixty-five, Peterson returned to coaching, taking over as head baseball coach at Central High School. Under Peterson, the Minutemen won the city conference title for the first time since the 1960s and the first outright title in baseball for the school in more than seventy years. Kevin Khottavongsa, one of the players on the team, told columnist Patrick Reusse, "I've learned more about hitting, about playing baseball, than I ever knew. Bill Peterson is the reason for that."

Peterson also had a long career in sports officiating, working as an umpire and referee in baseball, softball, and basketball. He has been inducted into the Minnesota and American Softball Association Halls of Fame, the Mancini's Sports Hall of Fame, and the St. Paul Central High School Sports Hall of Fame.

In his honor, the St. Paul Saints created the "Billy P. Friend of the Game" award. In 2007 Peterson received the Play Ball! Minnesota Terry Ryan Award, which honors those who have supported youth baseball and softball in the state.

later became owner of the Anaheim/Los Angeles Angels. Salt Lake City drew 57,000 fans in 1985, the second most in the league. Building a strong season-ticket base, the Trappers attracted more than 100,000 fans the next season and eventually topped out in attendance at 217,263, an average of more than 6,000 per home game.

The Trappers were just as impressive on the field, winning four Pioneer League titles in their eight years in the league, including in each of their first three seasons, 1985 to 1987. The team generated national attention in 1987 with a 29-game winning streak.

In a rookie league that emphasized developing players coming out of high school, the Trappers were loaded with college players and others who hadn't been drafted or had been released by major-league organizations. The 1987 team featured catcher Frank Colston and designated hitter Mathis "Matt" Huff, both of whom had on-base percentages greater than .470. Normally performances like that earn a fast promotion out of a rookie league, but Huff and Colston spent the entire season with Salt Lake City. This hoarding of young talent was widely criticized, including by longtime and respected baseball people. Joe Baird of the *Salt Lake Tribune* brushed off the complaints as sour grapes. "The major league organizations just don't like a bunch of undrafted guys beating up their teams," he wrote.

The Trappers were adhering to league rules regarding how many years a player could be with a team and a limit on how many could return from the previous season, but the nature of Salt Lake City's operation was in some ways a return to the glory years of the minor leagues—a stocked roster free of encumbrances of a parent team. Local fans could enjoy the exploits of its top stars from start to finish, rather than watching the best players getting promoted midyear.

Wolff said that most independent teams bore that status "out of necessity" because they were unable to get an affiliation with a major-league organization. But, he added, the success of teams in Portland and Salt Lake City demonstrated that independents could thrive: "When it was done in a big market, it worked."

By this time Goldklang was getting what he called his "first real involvement" in baseball after buying the Miami Miracle team in the Class A Florida State League in late 1989. Goldklang wanted an affiliation with a major-league team, but the Miracle wasn't seen as a desirable farm club by most organizations.

The Miracle had been playing at a college field Goldklang characterized as "shabby." In addition to a new place to play, Goldklang needed to stock his roster. He partially solved the latter problem by spotting a loophole that allowed minor-league teams to participate in the amateur draft. Affiliated

minor-league teams normally delegated the picks to the parent club, but the Miracle, as an independent, didn't have that option. "We didn't have an affiliation, so I called Major League Baseball and said I would be participating in the draft commencing with round 4 [when Class A teams could begin drafting]," Goldklang recalled. "After a month of them figuring out if I was a practical joke, they found out that's what the rules provided."

Though new, Goldklang impressed some of the veteran executives with his picks in the 1990 draft, including a sixth-round selection of Mike Lansing, who went on to a nine-year career in the major leagues. Midway through the draft, one of the teams (thought to be the Montreal Expos) neglected to hit the mute button on the phone after making its selection, and a few comments not intended for other ears made their way to the entire group. At one point, a voice was heard to say, "The Miracle is having a better f***ing draft than the Mets."

Around this same time, the major leagues were looking to drastically change the agreement they had with the minors, which had been in place for decades. Some minor-league operators viewed Major League Baseball's desire for a new agreement as a move toward further domination of the minors. Without much

Municipal Stadium was built in the 1980s to replace the original Midway Stadium, and it became a perfect home for the new St. Paul Saints. The adjacent parking lot provided ample opportunity for pregame tailgating. The stadium was eventually renamed Midway Stadium.

leverage, the minor leagues agreed to stipulations that included giving up control of logos, paying a percentage of their gate receipts to the parent clubs, and upgrading stadiums to standards specified by Major League Baseball. Wolff recalled, "We signed the agreement reluctantly but also wondered, 'Why do we want to be in business with these guys?' Let's call their bluff."

Calling their bluff meant expanding independent baseball—not just teams but leagues that would have no connection to organized baseball. Wolff, who had just sold the Durham Bulls and was still the publisher of *Baseball America,* was seen as a leader in minor-league baseball and an expert on the topic. He began getting calls from city leaders interested in bringing baseball to their area.

Wolff started looking at regions where independent baseball could thrive. He visited Wade Stadium in Duluth in 1991. In the book *Wild and Outside: How a Renegade Minor League Revived the Spirit of Baseball in America's Heartland,* Stefan Fatsis wrote that the stadium and city reminded Wolff of what he had in Durham. "You could just feel baseball in it," said Wolff of Wade Stadium.

The Upper Midwest region had other cities looking for baseball, from Thunder Bay, Ontario, in the north to Sioux Falls, South Dakota, in the south. In between was St. Paul, which wasn't even on Wolff's radar. He wasn't aware that the city had built a new ballpark near the former site of Midway Stadium, which had been torn down in 1980. Municipal Stadium, as it was then known, had plenty of dates open, especially in the summer between the high school baseball and football seasons. Although the Twin Cities had a major-league team, St. Paul was a city with its own identity and a stadium that could use more events.

In 1992 Wolff gathered representatives from interested cities in the Upper Midwest, and a new league began to take shape.

THE NEW SAINTS

CHAPTER 9

The New Face of Baseball in St. Paul

VEECK FAMILY LEGACY

Marv Goldklang was at the organizational meetings for what became the Northern League. With him were Van Schley and a man Goldklang had hired to operate his team in the Florida State League, Mike Veeck.

Mike Veeck had a name that was familiar in baseball circles—for better or worse. His dad was Bill Veeck, who had owned the Cleveland Indians, St. Louis Browns, and, on two occasions, the Chicago White Sox. Bill Veeck was associated with offbeat promotions, usually loved by the fans and scorned by his staid baseball brethren. Among his most famous stunts was signing Eddie Gaedel, who was only three feet seven inches tall, and sending him to the plate for the St. Louis Browns in 1951. Bill Veeck also introduced an exploding scoreboard in Chicago. He devoted his career in baseball to injecting fun into the game.

Born in 1951, Mike Veeck grew up moving around the country as his dad worked his way in and out of baseball. Mike lived the usual life of a young man, including playing in a rock band, before moving into baseball after his dad bought the White Sox for a second time in 1975 (he had earlier owned the team from 1959 to 1961).

Working in the White Sox front office, Mike Veeck said, he "learned from my old man by osmosis." But it was Rudie Schaffer, Bill Veeck's longtime business manager, who took Mike under his wing.

Within a few years came a meeting of two promoters that resulted in a memorable, if infamous, event involving the Veecks.

Steve Dahl was a Chicago radio personality who had launched a string of on-air off-the-wall stunts. In 1977, while working for WWWW Radio in Detroit, Dahl told his audience he was despondent and about to "end it all."

Prompted by emergency calls from listeners, the police came to the radio station only to find the suicide threat was nothing more than a prank. In 1978 Dahl moved to Chicago and worked at WDAI-FM until the station switched its format to disco music later in the year. Dahl got a job at WLUP-FM in Chicago and began an "Insane Coho Lips Anti-Disco Army," a pushback against the growing popularity of disco music and one that earned him a following. He began holding anti-disco rallies.

As this was happening, Mike Veeck arranged a disco night at Comiskey Park, the home of the White Sox. The event drew a relatively good crowd, and select disco fans were allowed onto a dance floor on the field before the game. After the game Veeck went to a pub with his friend Jeff Schwartz, who also worked in the sales and promotions department at WLUP. The two laughed about the people in disco outfits who participated in the event, and Schwartz suggested that the White Sox have a night for rock and roll.

Not long after, Schwartz called Veeck and told him to turn on WLUP, as Dahl was blowing up a disco record on the air. Veeck said that within five minutes after the show ended, he called Dahl and asked, "Do you want to do that at Comiskey Park?"

The event was scheduled for Thursday, July 12, 1979. Fans who turned in a disco record upon arrival would be admitted for 98 cents, and Dahl would blow up the records on the field between games of a doubleheader with the Detroit Tigers.

The White Sox expected a lot of people to show up for Disco Demolition Night, but they weren't ready for an overflow crowd. Many of the 10,000 to 20,000 who couldn't get in through the turnstiles tried to scale the park's outside walls during the first game. Security was diverted to handle the crashers, leaving an understaffed force in the stands. Some of the disco haters who brought in records found they were effective as flying discs. "They [the anti-disco promoters] apparently forgot that records make wonderful Frisbees and fly twice as fast and hit twice as hard," wrote the *Chicago Tribune* the next day.

When the first game ended, Dahl took the field and blew up the supply of records that had been turned in. People then stormed the field. "Ninety minutes, 39 arrests for disorderly conduct, and a half-dozen injuries later, the second game was called off," reported the *Tribune*. The canceled game was eventually declared a forfeit victory for the Tigers.

For reasons unrelated to the disco fiasco, Bill Veeck sold the White Sox in the early 1980s, leaving Mike Veeck in need of another job. He still yearned to be in baseball. "I got a lot of job offers in soccer and radio because both those persuasions like riots," he said. But he didn't receive any baseball offers.

Just married, Mike Veeck moved to Florida to work for a friend's company and later became involved in advertising, eventually starting his own agency.

The Veeck family had a long tradition of fun and creative baseball promotions when Marv Goldklang first hired Mike Veeck in the early 1990s. As part owner of the Saints, Mike Veeck did much to foster an entertaining baseball experience at Midway Stadium in St. Paul.

The Disco Demolition Night catastrophe continued to gnaw at him as his life spiraled out of control. He soon got divorced and developed problems with drinking and drugs.

When Mike Veeck began to get his life back on track, he tried to return to baseball, again without success. He believes he was blackballed, both because of the disco event in 1979 and because baseball owners didn't want a Veeck back in the game. His father had ruffled plenty of feathers during his nearly half a century in organized baseball.

Then the younger Veeck got his chance. Goldklang, who had just purchased the Miami Miracle, was looking for a stadium for his team and was considering an abandoned spring-training facility in Pompano Beach, Florida, the same city where Veeck had his agency.

At Major League Baseball's winter meetings in 1989, Goldklang talked to longtime executive Roland Hemond, who had been general manager of the White Sox when Bill Veeck owned the team in the 1970s. Goldklang recalls Hemond telling him something to the effect of, "If you're crazy enough to buy that team [the Miami Miracle], you're probably crazy enough to hire Bill Veeck's son."

Goldklang followed up and hired Mike Veeck to operate the Miracle. Veeck recalled the initial meeting: "I knew Marv was desperate, and he knew I was desperate. It was a match made in heaven."

After a year the team relocated to Fort Myers, Florida, where the Minnesota Twins had just moved their spring-training headquarters. In 1993, the Fort Myers Miracle became a Twins affiliate.

When the team was still representing Miami, Mike Veeck wanted to sign Minnie Miñoso, who had started his professional baseball career in 1946 with the New York Cubans of the Negro National League. Miñoso's first major-league experience was with the Cleveland Indians in 1949, when Bill Veeck owned the team. He later played for Bill Veeck's White Sox in 1960 and 1961. In 1976, with Bill Veeck again in charge of the Sox, the fifty-year-old Miñoso played three games for the team; he returned for two more games in 1980. As a result, Miñoso's pro career extended into five decades, from the 1940s to the 1980s.

Mike Veeck hoped to revive the longtime connection between Miñoso and the Veecks by having him play in a game in 1990. But the idea was shot down by

THE WINFIELDS

Steve and Dave Winfield grew up in the Rondo neighborhood in St. Paul. Separated in age by fifteen months (Steve was born in July 1950, Dave in October 1951), the two were raised on athletics and demonstrated great skill in a variety of sports. They spent time on the nearby Oxford playground under the guidance of its director, Bill Peterson, and were later members of a pair of state-champion American Legion teams coached by Peterson. Both Winfields were multisport stars at Central High School.

Dave Winfield went on to a career that is familiar to most baseball fans. He played baseball and basketball at the University of Minnesota. On the diamond he stood out as a pitcher and a hitter and helped the Gophers reach the College World Series in 1973. The San Diego Padres drafted Dave Winfield with the fourth overall pick in the draft, and he never spent a day in the minors. He went directly to the San Diego outfield and played in the major leagues until 1995. After playing for the Toronto Blue Jays, with whom he won a World Series ring in 1992, Dave Winfield returned to Minnesota to play for the Twins. In September 1993, he collected the 3,000th hit of his career. He also hit 465 career home runs. Winfield was inducted into the Hall of Fame in 2001.

Steve Winfield, not as well known nationally, established a notable reputation in the Twin Cities that continues to this day. He was an outstanding hitter and outfielder in St. Paul amateur leagues for thirty-five years and was inducted into the state's Class A Baseball Hall of Fame in 2011. Steve Winfield played center field for West St. Paul and didn't hang up his spikes until the age of fifty-five.

Helping to form the Summit University Basketball Association as a means of promoting the sport, Steve Winfield began officiating basketball in the early 1970s and was still a referee as of 2015. His entire adult life he has been involved in promoting sports among youths and mentoring those who became coaches and sports officials. Steve Winfield is also involved in the Minnesota Twins–St. Paul Reviving Baseball in Inner Cities (RBI) program.

baseball commissioner Fay Vincent, who would not allow the sixty-four-year-old Miñoso to take the field.

Veeck said the rejection sparked a desire to be part of a team that was independent of the commissioner's office. At the same time, Goldklang was seeking to expand his growing baseball empire (which included several minor-league teams in addition to his piece of the Yankees), and he got involved in Miles Wolff's efforts to form a new league in the Upper Midwest.

BUILDING A NEW NORTHERN LEAGUE

Wolff was confident about the timing of his proposed new minor-league venture. "In the 1970s and '80s," he said, "running a minor league team was hand to mouth." But baseball economics were changing in the early 1990s, and Wolff noted, "the timing was right."

In early 1992 Wolff convened a meeting in St. Paul with potential owners who had experience in independent baseball, including Harry Stavrenos, who (as Harry Steve) had operated the San Jose Bees, and Bill Pereira, who had owned a team in Boise, Idaho. The mayors and recreation directors from interested cities also attended.

Among the candidates for teams were Duluth, Rochester, and St. Paul in Minnesota; Sioux City, Iowa; Sioux Falls, South Dakota; Fargo, North Dakota; Thunder Bay, Ontario; and Winnipeg, Manitoba.

Besides having potential ownership lined up, hopeful cities needed to have stadiums to accommodate the new venture. The league secured its first lease in April after an agreement was reached to renovate a ballpark in Sioux Falls, where Stavrenos would run the team. Negotiations weren't as successful in Fargo, and in Winnipeg potential owner Sam Katz "wasn't ready at that time," according to Wolff. Katz, who later became Winnipeg's mayor, may have been holding out for the possibility of a team within organized baseball.

The remaining owners, ballparks, and cities came through. Sioux City's mayor pledged to get a stadium, and Pereira took control of the team in that city. Thunder Bay owner Ricky May, who had worked for Wolff as general manager of the Durham Bulls, got a boost in his city soon after the Toronto Blue Jays won the 1992 World Series. Blue Jays president Paul Beeston came to Thunder Bay, Ontario, to speak and promote baseball. Within days, May's team, the Whiskey Jacks, sold all advertising space on the outfield walls of its Port Arthur Stadium.

In Minnesota, Rochester's Mayo Field was available as a ballpark, but Wolff had concerns about the team's ownership. A bid for the Rochester franchise had been made by Dick Jacobson, who had some involvement in amateur baseball and even more in a strip joint he ran to the south of the Twin

Cities. With rumors about shady dealings in a shady business (the strip joint, not amateur baseball), Jacobson didn't endear himself to Wolff. Instead, Wolff lined up former Atlanta Braves vice president Charles Sanders to take control of the Rochester team. (Jacobson finally made the independent baseball scene in 1994, with comical results, outlined in a future chapter.)

Duluth—which would operate as Duluth-Superior, recognizing the neighboring city in Wisconsin—had Wade Stadium and found an owner in Bruce Engel from Portland, Oregon. The original plan had been for Goldklang to run the Duluth-Superior team. However, logistics were an issue for Goldklang, who was concerned about the ease of traveling between Duluth and his home in New Jersey.

Goldklang was already having difficulties visiting one of his teams, in Erie, Pennsylvania, which required an airline connection through Pittsburgh. He had to abort one trip to Erie after getting stuck in Pittsburgh due to a flight delay. Soured by the experience, he wanted a team that he could reach by direct flights from the New York area. Wolff told Goldklang St. Paul was the only city in the new league that qualified, but because of its close proximity to the Minnesota Twins, it might not be the most desirable franchise. "Miles, if it's a direct flight," Goldklang told him, "I'll take St. Paul."

After hashing out the ballparks and ownership groups, by the end of 1992 the organization was set with the Sioux Falls Canaries, Thunder Bay Whiskey

PAUL MOLITOR

Paul Molitor grew up in St. Paul and, like the Winfield brothers before him, developed many of his athletic skills at the Oxford playground. He played baseball under Bill Peterson for Attucks-Brooks American Legion Post 606 and at Cretin (now Cretin–Derham Hall) High School. In high school Molitor lettered in soccer, basketball, and baseball and was all-state in the latter two sports. Molitor was drafted by the St. Louis Cardinals after high school but instead accepted a scholarship to play for Dick Siebert at the University of Minnesota. In his junior season he led the Gophers to the 1977 College World Series. Molitor was drafted by the Milwaukee Brewers with the third-overall pick in that year's amateur draft. He made the majors in 1978 and spent twenty-one seasons with Milwaukee, Toronto, and Minnesota. He set a record with 5 hits in the opening game of the 1982 World Series. Eleven years later Molitor was named the World Series Most Valuable Player as his Blue Jays beat the Philadelphia Phillies. Molitor finished his playing career in his home state and got his 3,000th hit as a member of the Twins in September 1996. He was inducted into the Hall of Fame in 2004. Molitor's place in the annals of Twin Cities baseball was further solidified when he was named as the new manager of the Minnesota Twins in November 2014.

Jacks, Sioux City Explorers, Duluth-Superior Dukes, St. Paul Saints, and Rochester Aces.

The new owners developed a framework for their operation, which was to be completely independent of organized baseball. Rosters, limited to twenty-two players, were broken into seven classes, from rookie to veteran, based on the number of years a player had spent in professional ball. Each team had to have at least five rookies with less than a year of pro experience, and a maximum of four players with six or more years.

Among the investors in the St. Paul Saints were Goldklang, Veeck, and Schley. Concerned about the great amount of independent-baseball experience Goldklang and Schley had, other owners feared a brainpower monopoly in St. Paul. Instead, for the first year, Schley served as director of baseball operations for the Northern League, drawing on his experience of obtaining players for other independent teams and working with league scouting director Nick Belmonte.

Another name in the Saints' ownership group was familiar for a reason other than his baseball experience. Bill Murray, Schley's longtime colleague and part owner of Goldklang's team in Fort Myers, was on board.

The league had a franchise fee of $50,000 for each team, but Wolff said the fee "wasn't required upfront. Owners didn't have to pay for a couple years." Goldklang expressed a philosophy that may have been common among all the owners: "We thought we'd lose money but have a hell of a lot of fun doing it." Over time, the Saints and most of the other teams found themselves having fun *and* making money. Goldklang said that he and Veeck have since asked themselves, "What the hell did we do right?"

Goldklang credits Veeck with the success of St. Paul and other cities in the Northern League. "Mike is a promotional genius," said Goldklang, adding, "He could have five ideas. Four would be great and the other could get you arrested."

CHAPTER 10

Unexpected but Intoxicating

PUTTING THE PIECES IN PLACE

The St. Paul Saints were to begin playing games in June 1993, but Mike Veeck wasn't waiting. He came to St. Paul frequently in order to get to know the city and its people. In late 1992 he appeared on a cable television program hosted by Dave Wright, a longtime fixture in the local sports-media community. Wright said that when the interview was complete, "I hit him up for a job."

As media-relations director, Wright became the first employee of the St. Paul Saints. Others with a similar love for baseball followed.

Bill Fanning was hired as general manager. Fanning had been a stockbroker and banker who left the financial business to work for minor-league teams before he ended up in St. Paul.

Attorney Tom Whaley kept his law practice going as he worked on the Saints sales staff on the side. He is now the club's executive vice president.

Annie Huidekoper grew up in New Canaan, Connecticut, a fan of the Boston Red Sox, and after college she lived in the Boston area. One day on her lunch hour, Huidekoper held the door for a large group of people and realized none of them had said thank you. She went back to her job, turned in her resignation, and decided she was going to move somewhere where people would at least say thank you. She had two other criteria for a new residence: it had to be an American League city, so she could see her Red Sox play, and it needed to be a community with good health care, the field in which she worked.

Huidekoper settled on the Twin Cities and moved to St. Paul in the fall of 1984. Eight years later, she read about the coming of the St. Paul Saints. Huidekoper had always had an itch to work in minor-league baseball. She decided to scratch that itch after hearing local sports columnist and radio

personality Sid Hartman predict that the Saints would be out of business within a month of their first game. Huidekoper called the team and said she wanted to help prove Hartman wrong. She was hired, initially on a commission basis. By the time the 1993 season opened, she was the team's director of community relations.

On a day-to-day basis, at the ballpark and throughout the Twin Cities, Huidekoper became and remains the most visible member of the organization. Her smile and cheerful manner were such familiar features at St. Paul's Municipal Stadium that a local publication did a front-page story on her titled "Saint Annie." Years later Veeck referred to Huidekoper as "the heart and soul of this operation since day one."

The small but growing staff crammed the office at Municipal Stadium. Veeck sometimes brought his young daughter, Rebecca, who anchored a spot in a playpen near the front door. She served as the greeter, shouting out "hi" to every person who came through the door—an initial indication of the fun and friendliness that would become trademarks of the team.

"We had no idea if this was going to work," recalled Wright. Then, in December 1992, a seemingly unrelated development across town provided a pivotal turning point for the team. The Minnesota Twins re-signed their star, Kirby Puckett, ending fears that he would go to another team. "It kicked in the baseball interest," Wright said. "We got momentum. It was snowing when the re-signing was announced, but people started coming to the stadium to see about tickets."

"We were making it up as we went along," Wright said in reference to how he and the others kept up with the increasing demand.

Although interest was clearly growing, no one knew how much staying power it would have or what level it would reach. Municipal Stadium's capacity was a little more than 5,000. Marv Goldklang projected that the team would need to average 2,500 tickets sold per game with an average turnstile count of at least 2,100 (since no-shows would not be contributing to other revenues, such as concessions) for the Saints to break even.

Veeck noted that an independent team, which doesn't have its player salaries covered by a parent club, has to draw more fans to cover costs. "I need to draw 2,220 fans to make the sort of money I'd get from 1,400 fans with an affiliated league," he said.

Early response to the Saints indicated that the attendance goals were realistic. "We should be OK," Veeck told *Star Tribune* columnist Patrick Reusse in late May 1993. "We've sold 1,000 season tickets. We've sold 28 of our 35 outfield signs at $2,750 apiece. If we can get a walk-up of 1,000 [single-game] tickets a night, we'll do it." Goldklang said they benefitted from the St. Paul–Minneapolis rivalry, from being able to offer outdoor baseball, and from a down cycle for the Twins, which had dropped to near the bottom of their division only a year and a half after winning a world championship.

BUILDING A TEAM

While some employees in the St. Paul front office worked on selling the Saints to the fans, others focused on building the team. Tim Blackwell was hired as manager. A catcher in the majors from 1974 to 1983, Blackwell stayed in the game and managed in the minors for the San Francisco Giants and New York Mets organizations. After leading the Columbia (South Carolina) Mets to the South Atlantic League title in 1991 and to the best regular-season record in 1992, Blackwell was fired. "My dream is to be fired as a big-league manager," he commented. Instead he would serve in St. Paul.

Among the players the Saints acquired were infielders Greg D'Alexander and Tommy Raffo, both of whom Goldklang had drafted for the Miami Miracle in 1990. The Saints also signed former major leaguers Jim Eppard, Dave Pavlas, and Leon "Bull" Durham.

Eppard, described by Wright as a "wise old soul," had been an outfielder–first baseman for the California Angels in the late 1980s. With the Saints, he served as a player-coach.

Pavlas had pitched briefly for the Chicago Cubs in 1990 and 1991 and then signed with the Pittsburgh Pirates organization before even having a chance to play for the Saints. He eventually made it back to the big leagues, playing for the New York Yankees in 1995 and 1996.

Durham was the big name of the bunch. During his ten-year career in the majors, he put together some big seasons for the Cubs in the 1980s. A two-time All-Star, Durham saw his career hampered and cut short by drug problems and back surgery. He tried to make a comeback with the Chicago White Sox in 1993 but fell short. Blackwell then contacted Durham, who was a former teammate of his from the Cubs, and convinced him to give St. Paul a shot.

"Leon gave us credibility," Wright said. Although Durham had only a few days to train with the Saints, he was ready for the season opener.

While the former major leaguers were the most familiar to fans in 1993, third baseman Kevin Millar was a player with the brightest future ahead of him. Mike Berardino, who later covered the Minnesota Twins for the *St. Paul Pioneer Press,* was with *Baseball America* in 1993 and toured some of the Northern League cities that year. He remembered being on the field during batting practice before a Saints game, and Veeck pointing toward Millar and saying, "That third baseman is going to make it to the majors." Veeck was correct.

Millar epitomized the Northern League's characterization as a "second-chance league" (or, as many have said, "a last-chance league"). A star at Lamar

University in Beaumont, Texas, under coach Jim Gilligan, Millar was twice passed on by teams in organized baseball in the annual amateur draft. Gilligan, who had been the pitching coach for the Miami Miracle when Goldklang and Veeck were involved with the team, called the pair and recommended Millar for St. Paul.

Millar wondered if he would be able to work his way into the Saints' crowded infield mix, and he sat on the bench for the team's first three games. Given a chance to start in the fourth game, he came through with the game-winning hit against the Thunder Bay Whiskey Jacks.

Kevin Millar and Mike Mimbs were two members of the 1993 Saints who eventually went on to bigger things in the major leagues. Millar spent more than a decade in the majors and won a World Series title with the Boston Red Sox in 2004.

KEVIN MILLAR
THIRD BASEMAN

MICHAEL MIMBS
PITCHER

Millar was signed by the Florida Marlins organization after the season and finally made his major-league debut in 1998. He went on to play twelve years in the big leagues and had several solid seasons, including with the Boston Red Sox when they won the World Series in 2004. Millar played his last major-league game in 2009, for the Toronto Blue Jays, but he returned to the Saints the following year, at the age of thirty-eight, in the hopes of jump-starting his career.

Millar was not the only player from the Saints' inaugural roster to make it all the way to "the Show," nor was he the first. The first to reach the majors was pitcher Mike Mimbs. After leading St. Paul with an 8–2 record in 1993, Mimbs was signed by the Philadelphia Phillies. He went 11–4 for the Class AA Harrisburg club in 1994 and then joined Philadelphia in May 1995.

KICKING OFF THE SEASON

The Saints traveled to Duluth, Minnesota, for the season opener on June 15. Duluth had a proud history in the previous Northern League, and the city and its fans responded enthusiastically to the return of the Dukes. Wade Stadium had been deteriorating in recent years, but the city invested in its renovation. The brick exterior was draped with red, white, and blue banners the night of the opener.

The first game sold out, and a block-long line of fans outside the stadium was hoping for standing-room tickets. The pregame barbecuing extended

The debut issue of the Saints scorebook and game program from 1993.

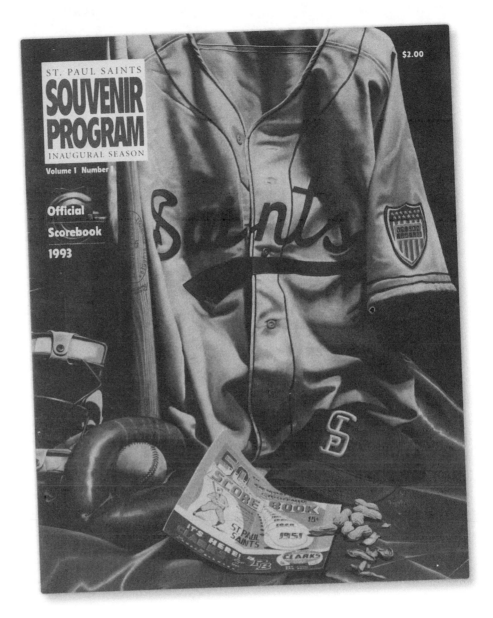

beyond tailgaters in the stadium parking lot. Residents along Grand Avenue, outside the ballpark, joined in the fun, whether they were going to the game or not.

The game was a good one, going into extra innings. In the top of the tenth the Saints got runners to second and third with one out. The Dukes intentionally walked Eppard to load the bases, and Duluth manager Mal Fichman brought in Wayne Rosenthal, who had pitched for the Texas Rangers during the previous two seasons, to face one of the other former major leaguers, Durham.

After falling behind with two strikes, Durham was looking for a breaking pitch that he could send deep enough to the opposite field to bring home the runner from third. Instead, Rosenthal delivered a fastball. Durham turned on it and sent it over the right-field fence for a grand slam.

St. Paul beat Duluth-Superior again the next night before the series finale was rained out.

The Saints came home to St. Paul, and the atmosphere for their Friday-night opener was just as festive as it had been in Duluth. Large crowds were assured for the weekend, and before the first game started, fans got an early introduction to what they could expect from Saints baseball. Fans could get a haircut while watching the game (an amenity that had been available at Comiskey Park when Bill Veeck owned the White Sox in the 1970s) or a massage from Sister Rosalind Gefre—leading to the slogan, "Sister Rosalind and the Saints—A Heavenly Combination."

The public-address announcer, Al Frechtman, brought an unconventional style to the ballpark. He drew on his background as a comedian, a member of local radio personality Garrison Keillor's troupe, and a department-store window dresser as he worked in one-liners amid player introductions.

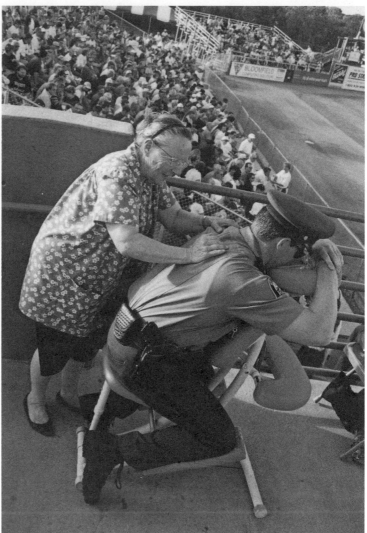

Sister Ros helps one of St. Paul's finest relax with a massage during a Saints game.

The Saints' mascot, a real pig, was introduced as the ball boy. Still in the piglet stage and named Saint, the pig was owned by Dennis Hauth of River Falls, Wisconsin. The plan was to have Saint perform his duty only at weekend and holiday games, but he grew in size and popularity to the point that the Saints arranged to have him present at every game. The team's $2,500 payment to the Hauths for the season made Saint one of the organization's highest-paid employees.

A number of former Saints from the American Association days—Angelo Giuliani, Leo Wells, Howie "Stretch" Schultz, Dwain Sloat, Mickey Rocco, and Lou Cardinal, as well as former public-address announcer Don Dix—were introduced before the game. Co-owner Bill Murray was on hand for the opening weekend and, in an expectedly unexpected manner, delivered one of the ceremonial first pitches by sailing it over the backstop screen.

The game itself, against the Thunder Bay Whiskey Jacks, was a tight one. The fans got loud early as, in the last of the first, Thunder Bay starter Brian Souza walked Rick Hirtensteiner, Greg D'Alexander, and Eppard to load the bases with no outs for Durham. However, the Bull popped out, and Souza struck out Tommy Raffo and Scott Meadows to get out of the jam.

The teams exchanged single runs in the early innings, and the game remained tied into the bottom of the ninth. D'Alexander and Eppard opened with singles and advanced on a wild pitch. After Durham lined out and Raffo was intentionally walked to load the bases, Meadows hit a grounder toward the hole. Shortstop Tom Arnold had no play on D'Alexander at home, and his only chance to prolong the game was to start a double play. He threw to second to Ty Griffin, who dropped the ball. D'Alexander crossed the plate with the winning run. Official scorer Tom Greenhoe credited Meadows with a game-ending hit.

The second home game, on Saturday night, was played in a steady rain but with enough interest and antics to keep the fans entertained. Murray got more involved in that game, donning a Saints jersey and coaching first base. He jockeyed for attention, once walking to the coaching box with a trail of toilet paper hanging out of his back pocket. He also inserted himself in an argument Whiskey Jacks manager Don Shwam was having with the umpires.

A PIG *for* PIG'S EYE, MINNESOTA

The idea of having a pig as the Saints' mascot fits with the history of the city of St. Paul. Back in the 1830s, Pierre "Pig's Eye" Parrant, the first European settler in what would become St. Paul, sold whiskey from a hovel near the entrance of a cave on the Mississippi River, upstream of what is now the city's downtown area. Local lore has it that, in 1839, a bar patron sent a letter with the return address of "Pig's Eye Landing," and with that, the unnamed city became Pig's Eye. Father Lucien Galtier later built a church, St. Paul chapel, above the landing and got the city name changed to that of his church.

St. Paul's connection to the city's origins as Pig's Eye, Minnesota, is evident in a local brew as well as the Saints' pig mascot.

PHOTO COURTESY OF THE ST. PAUL SAINTS

The subject of the dispute was the league's pitch timer. Wanting the umpires to enforce a rule requiring pitchers to deliver the ball within twenty seconds when the bases were empty, the Northern League had each team install a clock above the fence that was to be reset after every pitch. The pitch timer was an idea that went back to Bill Veeck's first time as owner of the White Sox. When he introduced an exploding scoreboard (with fireworks that went off after a home run), he included a "Pitch-o-Meter," designed to tick off the seconds between pitches. Even though the American League prohibited him from using it, Bill Veeck kept the feature on the scoreboard (a form of "silent protest," according to Mike Veeck), and it remained even after Bill Veeck sold the White Sox.

The pitch timer may have caused more delays in arguments than it saved. In this game, the operator had neglected to reset the timer after a pitch, and a ball was charged to Thunder Bay pitcher Yoshi Seo, leading to the argument.

"Miles Wolff and I loved it," Mike Veeck said of the pitch timer, "and we were a huge minority." Unpopular with the managers and umpires, the pitch timer was soon eliminated.

MAKING THE MOST OF PROMOTIONS

The Saints upped their season record to 6–0 with a 4–0 win over Duluth-Superior with Mimbs on the mound. More than extending the winning streak, that game is best remembered for the promotion "Silent Night," for which mimes were brought on the field for Mime-o-Vision. The promotion was to celebrate the fifty-first anniversary of the first lipreading competition. (Huidekoper said many of their promotions were matched to anniversaries, which they found in *Chase's Calendar of Events,* "our bible from the start.") Since the Municipal Stadium scoreboard didn't have video capability at the time, the mimes were to reenact plays for the crowd. Although the mimes were not a hit with the fans, their appearance has lived on as a memorable event.

The end of June was capped by an appearance by Minnie Miñoso, something Mike Veeck had been prevented from making happen three years earlier in Miami. Now free of oversight from the commissioner of Major League Baseball, Veeck and the Saints signed Miñoso. Wearing number 18, just as he did when he debuted with Cleveland in 1949 (and the same number actor Murray had worn when he coached first base two weeks before), the sixty-seven-year-old Miñoso came up in the first inning of a game against Thunder Bay. After taking two balls from right-hander Seo, Miñoso made contact and grounded out to Seo. Keith Gogos hit for Miñoso, who was the designated hitter, the next time through the order, but Miñoso had made his appearance in the 1990s. (He extended his number of decades when the Saints signed him again for a game in 2003.)

Media coverage was sporadic for the Saints during their inaugural season. The most reliable reporter was Mike Augustin of the *Pioneer Press*. The beat writer for the *Star Tribune*, Eric Pate, was sometimes present, but many of the game reports that appeared in the Minneapolis paper came from Dave Wright, packaged as "Special to the Star Tribune."

Beyond the hit-and-miss nature of game coverage, some of the reviews weren't complimentary. *Pioneer Press* columnist Bob Sansevere characterized the talent level in the Northern League as "dental-floss thin." Patrick Reusse of the *Star Tribune* was harsher. In the June 26, 1993, edition, Reusse wrote, "The romantic view is that this is a long-awaited return of outdoor professional baseball to the Twin Cities. How romantic can you get about a level of competition where the ball-delivering pig is getting a higher salary than many of the players?"

While this assessment wasn't out of line with Reusse's typical style, Wright acknowledged years later that Reusse's criticisms were "dead-on" and "harsh, but fair." Drawing more attention were comments from the Minnesota Twins.

LEGEND OF THE MIMES

The story of Mime-o-Vision at the Saints' Municipal Stadium became a grand and exaggerated legend of promotional disaster.

According to the stories that emerged after the event, the mimes were pelted with hot dogs from the crowd. Later Saints employees, who weren't even present at the event but heard the tales, passed on the story that the mimes stormed off the field, finally using their verbal skills to hurl f-bombs at the fans as they departed. Legend also claims that Mime-o-Vision received front-page coverage in the *Star Tribune*, and Mike Veeck himself wrote in his 2005 book, *Fun Is Good*, that "the paper devoted more than 40 column inches to how dumb the promotion was."

The truth, however, is rather more mundane. The Minneapolis paper, which devoted its front page to massive flooding in the area at the time,

had a single picture of a mime entertaining (or, perhaps, not entertaining) tailgaters prior to the game. The *St. Paul Pioneer Press* didn't even mention the event until two mornings later, when Veeck said he got calls from fans the next day saying the promotion was stupid.

Veeck acknowledges the story has been embellished in subsequent retellings but insisted the promotion was effective. He even had a follow-up in mind and invited the mimes to return the next year, but they declined. "They viewed themselves as artists and were not treated as such," said Veeck. He summed up the mime experience by saying, "It made you laugh. That's what made St. Paul."

Veeck got another laugh not long after, when Saints employees arranged to have mimes show up at his wedding.

The major-league team took a dismissive attitude to the newcomers. Twins executive vice president Andy MacPhail said fans who were interested in experiencing outdoor baseball should attend Minnesota Gophers college games, suggesting that the talent level was higher than what they would see with the Saints. MacPhail was also known to make references to "Mike's Beer League," referring to Mike Veeck, who took it in the spirit that it had not been intended. "I owe Andy a great debt," he later said. "Nobody cheers for Goliath."

About the time the Saints were getting started, the Twins were promoting a series against the Milwaukee Brewers to be played over Fourth of July weekend. An ad for the series, which would take place in the Metrodome, had a not-too-subtle shot at the Saints buried in the middle: "Why risk rain and mosquitoes?"

The Saints sought to take full advantage of the jabs. The attempts by the Twins to denigrate the Saints seemed to have the opposite effect on fans, who drew closer to the new team. Whaley said they were cheering on the Twins with each disrespectful comment aimed at them: "'Keep going,' we said."

Most attention the Saints received, though, was positive. One story tells of a woman who called directory assistance to get the phone number for the St. Paul Saints, adding that it was a baseball team. "Yes," the operator replied knowingly, "and a good one."

Among the amenities available to fans at Midway Stadium were in-game haircuts.

CELEBRITY APPEARANCES

Saints promotions regularly include special days for players and personalities from baseball's past. The first such promotion, held on the opening Sunday of the home season in 1993, was Joe Hauser Day, honoring a star from across the river. Hauser played five seasons for the Minneapolis Millers and set a record by hitting 69 home runs in 1933. Longtime WCCO-TV anchorman Dave Moore interviewed Hauser at the event. Moore didn't even try to hide his giddiness about getting to interview one of his boyhood idols. The fans were delighted by the ninety-four-year-old Hauser, especially after Moore asked him about being a teammate of Ty Cobb's in the 1920s and Hauser responded, "dirty, rotten son of a bitch."

Max Patkin, another celebrity, appeared at a Saints game in August 1993. The so-called Clown Prince of Baseball, Patkin continued his long tradition of entertaining fans at minor-league games. His antics date back to World War II, when he was pitching for a navy team in Honolulu. After giving up a home run to Joe DiMaggio, Patkin trailed the Yankee Clipper around the bases, aping his movements. After the war, Bill Veeck brought Patkin to Cleveland to coach first base, from where he would mimic batters and gyrate his body and neck into contortions of a rubber man. Patkin stayed with the Indians until Veeck sold the team in 1949. He then embarked on a barnstorming career in the minors. Patkin appeared in the 1988 movie *Bull Durham* and, at the age of seventy-three, came to St. Paul to perform for Mike Veeck's team.

Bob Cain was another player with a Veeck link who made an appearance at a Saints game. His connection dates back to 1951, when, while pitching for the Detroit Tigers, Cain drew the assignment of facing Eddie Gaedel on August 19 of that year. The three-foot-seven-inch Gaedel had been signed by Bill Veeck to a one-day contract with the St. Louis Browns. Wearing jersey number 1/8, Gaedel pinch-hit for Frank Saucier in the bottom of the first inning and, in his crouch, left a strike zone for Cain later described as "about the size of a baby's bib." Not surprisingly, Cain walked Gaedel on four pitches.

Gaedel died in 1961. But Cain was still alive in 1994, and Mike Veeck brought him in to re-create the event at Municipal Stadium. On July 31, Matt Blackwell, the ten-year-old son of Saints manager Tim Blackwell, donned a replica uniform and assumed the batting stance shown in a classic photo of Gaedel at the plate in 1951. Cain was a good sport with the re-creation, once again missing with four pitches, and the Gaedel stand-in trotted to first base with the crowd cheering both him and Cain.

Larry Doby, Sam Jethroe, and Buck O'Neil were among the stars of the Negro Leagues to whom the Saints paid tribute with days at the ballpark. In July 1947, just three months after Jackie Robinson debuted with the Brooklyn Dodgers, Doby became the first black player in the American League when Bill Veeck signed him with the Cleveland Indians. The Saints have retired number 14, the number Doby wore with the Indians.

The special service the Saints provided to their fans was illustrated in early July when a young man called and asked if he could have a wedding proposal flashed on the scoreboard. Mike Veeck felt that was too mundane and wanted something more memorable. So Huidekoper got to work concocting a plan. The young man, his fiancée to be, and a few friends were given tickets to the game. The young woman was informed that she had been chosen to throw out a ceremonial first pitch. The wannabe groom had already excused himself, presumably to use the restroom, but he was actually under the stands donning full catching gear, including a mask. He came out and took his position behind home plate to receive the pitch from his girlfriend, who was unaware of the true identity of her catcher. He then ran the ball out to her on the mound, took off his mask, and pulled from his pocket another ball, on which he had inscribed a proposal, along with a ring. Perhaps the best news of the entire affair was that she said yes. (Of course, the Saints often take pride in

MIKE AUGUSTIN

Mike Augustin was a versatile reporter, gifted wordsmith, colorful storyteller, and all-around good guy. He covered amateur sports, the small-college scene, and the pros for more than thirty years for the *St. Cloud Times* and *St. Paul Pioneer Press*.

Gregg Wong, a colleague of Augustin's at the *Pioneer Press* and now an official scorer for Minnesota Twins games, recalled Augustin's versatility: "Augie loved all sports and covered each one with the same zeal. But baseball, without question, was his real passion and love. He loved baseball because of the pace of the game, because you could analyze and comment between every pitch (and after the games over a cocktail or two), because you could see every play happen and develop. The game is a lot like the way Augie lived his life—laid back and unhurried with no time clock."

Augustin attended St. John's University in Collegeville, Minnesota, and later became a fixture around the Minnesota Intercollegiate Athletic Conference (MIAC). He had covered the old Northern League when St. Cloud was in the league, and years later he became the primary beat writer for the St. Paul Saints in the new Northern League.

Former Saints public relations director Dave Wright said that Augustin was a great writer who "understood the need for showmanship. Augie zeroed in on the stories of the players."

Augustin was diagnosed with cancer in December 1997 and was dead within a week and a half. In his memory, the MIAC created the Mike Augustin Award, which is presented annually to "recognize outstanding contributions to MIAC athletic programs and their student athletes." The St. Paul Saints named their press box at Midway Stadium after him.

"Augie was a sweet man," Mike Veeck told Jim Caple for the story in the December 20, 1997, issue of the *Pioneer Press*. "That doesn't mean he couldn't take a chunk out of your leg, but he loved what he did. He felt privileged to have his job."

promotions that don't work, and a refusal to the proposal may have resonated even more in Saints annals.)

Beyond the product on the field, the financial reports were also rosy. At midseason reporter Augustin revealed that the Saints had an average attendance of 4,800 fans per game, more than double their projected break-even point. David Brauer, in *Corporate Report America,* noted that the Saints would make more money than the Minnesota Twins in 1993, estimating a profit of $350,000 for the Saints and a 100 percent return on the original investment by the owners.

Brauer added that the Saints had enough discretionary revenue to spend $25,000 on extra fireworks shows (one of the most popular features with fans) and other promotions. "The Saints have established a business base that every big-league sales v. p. yearns for: revenues based on things under the team's control—entertainment, service—rather than winning and losing," wrote Brauer. "Meanwhile, the Twins were paying big salaries to formerly successful players during a miserable losing season."

Most of the teams in the Northern League were having similar success. Four other teams were averaging more than 2,200 fans per game. Rochester was the exception. Despite winning the first-half league title, the Aces' average attendance was just 1,547.

BUILDING RIVALRIES AND PROFITS

The Northern League teams fed off each other, generating interest with rivalries and mostly good-spirited jousting, and most clubs had their own colorful characters. Sioux City's Ed Nottle and Sioux Falls' Frank Verdi were among the more colorful managers, and were also known for their colorful language. Singin' Ed, as Nottle was called, enjoyed crooning and often sought out nightspots in St. Paul where he could perform after games. He also recorded an album, *To Baseball with Love,* and his music was often played at minor-league parks.

Verdi had a long career in the minors and a Moonlight Graham–like experience in the majors. His one appearance came in 1953 for the Yankees, when he went into a game to replace Phil Rizzuto at shortstop. Verdi had no chances in the field but was due to bat the next inning. However, after a pitching change, New York manager Casey Stengel sent up a pinch hitter for Verdi, who never played in the majors again.

While with the Rochester (New York) Red Wings of the International League in 1959, Verdi was coaching third base in place of ejected manager Cot Deal during a game in Havana, Cuba. The extra-inning game crept past midnight, into the morning of July 26, which was the anniversary of the 1953

The inaugural St. Paul Saints team proved successful at the ticket office and on the field.

attack on the Moncada army garrison in Santiago de Cuba by a band of rebels led by Fidel Castro. A raucous observance outside the ballpark included a burst of gunfire. A couple of stray bullets made it into Gran Stadium, one striking Havana shortstop Leo Cardenas and the other grazing Verdi's head. However, neither was seriously hurt, Cardenas because he hadn't been hit in a vital organ and Verdi because he wore a protective liner in his cap (something players used at the time instead of batting helmets).

Another notable Northern League manager in the early years was Doug Simunic of the Rochester (Minnesota) Aces. He was regarded as a good manager, though not a pleasant man. Former Saints announcers Kris Atteberry and Anthony LaPanta said Simunic had a "mean streak" and was a "whiner, who thought the whole world was out to get him."

The hardest feelings were aimed at Duluth-Superior, specifically Mal Fichman, the Dukes manager. Fichman became the frequent butt of jokes, especially out of St. Paul, and is mocked in Steve Perlstein's book about the first year of the Northern League, *Rebel Baseball: The Summer the Game Was Returned to the Fans*. Perlstein notes that Fichman—who had been the manager of a Rocky Mount (North Carolina) Pines team that had posted a record of 24–114 in the Carolina League in 1980—had earned the nickname "Mal Function." Perlstein might have had even more fun picking on the Dukes manager had he known about an item in the 1970 *Sporting News Official Baseball Guide,* which reported that in 1969 Fichman had been fired as general manager of Bakersfield in the California League and replaced by Paul Sheldon, the head usher. Mike Veeck also got into the act of mocking of Fichman, stating that the Dukes manager was known for his frequent complaints to commissioner Miles Wolff, including a grievance about the Saints' pig defecating on the field. "He needed something more monumental than that to complain about," said Veeck. "He took whining to a new level."

Managerial beefs and jests aside, as the season progressed, Northern League teams looked to selling players to organized baseball as a way of boosting both profits and prestige. "I said all along that the best example of our credibility would be when the major leagues showed enough interest to buy some of our players," Veeck told reporter Augustin.

Saints general manager Bill Fanning saw another benefit in having their players signed by organized baseball: credibility with players in the future. "The fringe players will know if they sign with our league they have the opportunity to keep their dream alive," Fanning explained. "It's a big selling point."

In mid-August the Saints signed two high-profile players who had attracted attention the previous month by escaping from a Cuban national team that was playing in the World University Games in Niagara Falls, New York.

Reports on the escapes vary, but one of the more colorful accounts has left-handed pitcher Eddie Oropesa, in full uniform, kicking off his spikes, scaling a twelve-foot-high chain-link fence at Sal Maglie Stadium, and jumping into a waiting car, yelling "Asylum! Asylum! Asylum!" Shortstop Rey Ordóñez also managed to get away from the Cubans during the tournament.

Oropesa and Ordóñez were talented players, and Marv Goldklang learned they were available from agent Gus Dominguez, who also represented the Saints' Eddie Ortega, another Cuban national. Several Northern League teams were interested in Oropesa and Ordóñez, but St. Paul had the edge, in part because of Ortega. The Saints signed both players a month after they defected. Both performed well for the Saints, and a number of major-league teams sent scouts to St. Paul to watch them play. (The Twins were not among the teams showing interest.) At the end of the season, the New York Mets signed Ordóñez, who made it to the majors in 1996 and was fifth in the balloting for National League Rookie of the Year. Oropesa ended up in the Los Angeles Dodgers organization and bounced around a bit before finally getting to the majors with the Philadelphia Phillies in 2001.

In addition to the Cuban duo, other Saints players also had their contracts sold to major-league organizations. Center fielder Rick Hirtensteiner was a popular player in St. Paul who batted .310 during the season. He had previously been in the Montreal Expos organization, and his contract was sold to the Marlins in 1993, but Hirtensteiner never got a chance to play in the majors.

Players moving up to the big leagues was not unique to St. Paul. Other Northern League teams bolstered their revenues by selling players into organized baseball, including youngsters trying to make a name for themselves as well as older players looking for a second chance. Rochester outfielder Kash Beauchamp was the son of Jim Beauchamp, who had played ten years in the National League in the 1960s and 1970s. Kash Beauchamp never made it to the majors, despite being the first player taken in the January 1982 amateur draft, and he had been out of pro ball since 1990. He made a comeback with the Northern League's Aces and was voted the league's Most Valuable Player. Rochester sold his contract to the Cincinnati Reds, and Kash Beauchamp finished the 1993 season with the Class AA Chattanooga Lookouts. Although the younger Beauchamp again fell short of the highest level, he played a few more years in affiliated and independent leagues and demonstrated the opportunity the Northern League gave to players such as him.

Jeff Bittiger had pitched for several major-league teams, including the Twins, in the late 1980s and had bounced around in the minors before joining up with the Aces. Rochester sold Bittiger to the Kansas City Royals organization during the 1993 season with the stipulation that he be returned to the Aces for the playoffs.

POSTSEASON PLAY

Bittiger and Beauchamp helped lead the Rochester Aces to the first-half league title in 1993. The Saints won the second half of the season, setting up a best-of-five series for the Northern League championship.

The teams split the first two games, in Rochester, and moved to St. Paul for the remainder of the series. The Saints brought in a couple of special guests to participate in throwing out the ceremonial first pitch before Game Three. One was former Twins owner Calvin Griffith, who seemed pleased by the response of the fans. Griffith's popularity in Minnesota had varied over his two-plus decades with the team. He had lamented how fans once waved at him when they saw him in his car with the TWINS license plates but later gave him the finger. No middle fingers were extended to him at Municipal Stadium. He received a nice ovation on the field and then sat in the stands signing autographs.

The other guest was Roger Awsumb, who had played Casey Jones the engineer on a long-running Twin Cities television show for kids. The Saints

After an unanticipated railroad delay, Casey Jones delivers the ceremonial first pitch before the third game of the 1993 Northern League championship series at Municipal Stadium.

PHOTO BY TOM OLMSCHEID; COURTESY OF THE ST. PAUL SAINTS

arranged a special entrance for Awsumb, having him arrive on a train outside the ballpark and then walk in through the outfield to the mound for the first pitch. Huidekoper said the performance required a lot of planning with the Burlington Northern railroad to have its train stop and drop Awsumb off.

As it happened, the train didn't arrive on time, and the ceremonies and the start of the game had to be pushed back. Rochester manager Simunic blasted the carnival atmosphere and blamed the distractions for the rough start by his pitcher, Bittiger. Simunic said he wasn't notified that the start of the game would be delayed until after Bittiger had begun his pregame warm-ups. "These are games of great magnitude," Simunic said. "One team knows when the game starts, one doesn't. It's a good product up here, but it takes a back seat to the carnival."

Bittiger walked two batters and hit another as the Saints scored 3 runs off him in the first inning. Wolff and Veeck acknowledged that Simunic had a valid point, but they couldn't change what had happened. Rochester never caught up after the bad opening inning, and St. Paul won the game 5–1.

The next night the Aces never had a chance. Mimbs pitched into the seventh inning without allowing a run. The Saints built a lead early and added to it. Durham homered in the fifth and singled the next inning. With the game's outcome all but assured, Durham was removed for a pinch runner, trotting off the field to a long ovation. St. Paul won 13–0 to clinch the series and the championship. Fans joined the team for a celebration on the field. When the players headed to the clubhouse, Veeck and Goldklang stayed on the field with the fans.

In addition to winning the title, St. Paul had sold out more than three-quarters of its games and had produced the biggest baseball buzz in the state. It wasn't achieved without criticism, however. "We were the New York Yankees of the league," said Goldklang, who as part owner of the Yankees understood the feeling. Occupying the largest city in the Northern League, the Saints were seen by others as the Goliath of the organization. Critics cited the close relationship between Goldklang and Van Schley, who worked with league scouting director Nick Belmonte, although Goldklang thought Belmonte, "if anything, showed favoritism toward other teams to the detriment of the Saints."

Whatever the reasons, the Saints emerged as the flagship team of the Northern League, although Veeck pointed out that the success was a group effort. "Everybody recognized starting out in this uncharted water that [the league] had to have total participation and cooperation among the early clubs," he said. "Every decision made by every member club in the early days was for the best return for the league."

The 1993 season exceeded even the most optimistic expectations of St. Paul and most other teams. Rochester was the exception, and with relatively little fan interest in its city, the team was dropped in favor of Winnipeg for the following season.

The Saints worked with the city of St. Paul to expand the grandstand at Municipal Stadium. They sought to keep up with the response that Stefan Fatsis, in *Wild and Outside,* called, "as unexpected as it had been intoxicating."

Veeck knew it would be tough to top the opening season, but he pledged that the Saints would not let up. "I can promise that we won't get spoiled or complacent," he told Tom Powers of the *Pioneer Press.* "We'll try twice as hard."

In his foreword to Perlstein's *Rebel Baseball,* Veeck reflected on what that first year with the Saints meant to him: "When I am old, toothless, and rocking on the porch, I will turn to whomever will listen and say, 'You should have seen St. Paul in '93. It was the greatest summer of my life.'"

CHAPTER 11

Spawns of Success

THE NORTHERN LEAGUE wasn't the only organization to give independent ball a try in 1993. But it was the only one that had any success.

The Frontier League operated in West Virginia, Kentucky, and Ohio, starting with eight teams in cities smaller than those in the Northern League. Two of the teams dropped out only a few weeks into the season, and the other six managed to hang on despite financial problems and sparse attendance.

The Frontier League experienced better times starting in 1994. The league had Kendra Hanes, the first woman to play professional baseball on a men's team since Toni Stone, Mamie "Peanut" Johnson, and Connie Morgan played in the Negro American League in 1953–54. Hanes had played softball at Oklahoma State and tried out for an all-women's baseball team, the Colorado Silver Bullets. She was signed as an outfielder by the Frontier League's Kentucky Rifles in 1994 but didn't last long. She came to the plate 11 times and had 1 walk but no hits.

The Frontier League also provided a chance for success for Mal Fichman, the much-maligned Duluth-Superior Dukes manager in 1993. No longer living up to his nickname of "Mal Function," Fichman managed three different teams to a total of four Frontier League titles over the next five seasons.

The strong showing of the Northern League in 1993 prompted the formation of several more independent leagues. Two of them featured at least one Minnesota team.

NORTH CENTRAL LEAGUE

George Vedder, who had been involved for a time in the formation of the Northern League, went in a different direction and started the North Central League in 1994. The league's West Division contained the Huron (South

Dakota) Heaters and two teams in Saskatchewan, the Regina Cyclones and Saskatoon Riot. The East Division comprised three Minnesota teams: the Brainerd Bears, Marshall Mallards, and Minneapolis Loons.

Owned by playwright Roger Nieboer, the Loons played at Siebert Field at the University of Minnesota. The home of the Minnesota Gophers since 1971, Siebert Field needed some work. The university was happy to accept Nieboer's money to make upgrades to the press box and seating areas, improvements it had been wanting to make but hadn't been able to afford.

The university, however, would not deviate from its policy of not allowing beer at the stadium. Nieboer tried to focus on the positive aspects of an alcohol-free atmosphere. At a neighborhood meeting attended by citizens with concerns about the team, Nieboer said, "We're trying to promote a family atmosphere at our games. People can bring their kids without having to worry about someone next to them who's had too much to drink." If the allusion to St. Paul wasn't obvious at that point, Nieboer also made a reference to the "anything goes, neighbor vomits in your lap" style at Saints games. (To be fair, there were never any documented cases of fans vomiting in one another's laps in St. Paul.)

The Loons didn't have beer, but they did have a couple of high-profile members on the team. The manager was Greg Olson, an Edina, Minnesota, native who had played for the Gophers and in the major leagues. Olson spent his last four seasons with the Atlanta Braves, one as an All-Star, before retiring as a player in the spring of 1993. (With the Loons, Olson was a player-manager and occasionally—very occasionally—grabbed a bat and pinch-hit.)

The Loons also signed local favorite Juan Berenguer, who had pitched for the Twins for several seasons, including the world champions of 1987. "Señor Smoke," as Berenguer was known, did well for the 1994 Loons, collecting a league-high 21 saves. He earned the save in a 1–0 win in the team's first home game.

The 1,500 fans on hand for the first game saw the types of antics the Loons were using to mirror the fun taking place at Saints games. They included a "Dash for Cash" that gave two fans the chance to pick up money scattered around the pitcher's mound after the first inning. More creative was a dunk tank, sponsored by the Culligan water-conditioning company. The tank was wheeled onto the field in the middle of the second inning, and Olson, wearing a Culligan uniform, got dunked. He then climbed out of the tank and resumed his duties—still dripping wet in the Culligan get-up—in the third-base coaching box. At the end of the second inning, Olson changed back into his baseball uniform. A few innings later he was driving around the warning track on a John Deere lawn tractor, which had been a gift from the Loons as an enticement to get him to manage.

The Minneapolis Loons line up for the national anthem at Siebert Field before the 1994 home opener.

The Loons had a top-notch play-by-play announcer, Ryan Lefebvre. The son of former major leaguer Jim Lefebvre, Ryan Lefebvre had come from Southern California to play for the Gophers, where he was an All–Big Ten outfielder. After a short playing career in the minors, Ryan Lefebvre came back to Minneapolis to pursue baseball announcing.

Lefebvre had teamed with Doug McLeod on Saints radio broadcasts in 1993, although Mike Veeck wanted him to play for the team. But Lefebvre stuck with broadcasting and would announce for the Loons from many different spots at Siebert Field. He once called an entire game from behind a screen on the field, not too far behind home plate. Another time, he announced from a perch partway up one of the light towers.

Lefebvre once convinced the team mascot, Looey the Loon (who, unlike the Saints' mascot, was a human being in a costume), to let him take his place for a routine on the field with team promotions director Paul Pruitt. The plan was for Looey the Loon to dance with Pruitt, but Looey Lefebvre eschewed the gyrations and squirted a bewildered Pruitt with a super soaker. Back in the press box, Pruitt fumed. "Looey was supposed to dance," he said, "and all he did was piss on me."

Lefebvre used his Loons broadcasting experience to launch an impressive announcing career with the Twins and then Kansas City, where he has been the voice of the Royals since 1999.

Even with some big names and their wild antics, the Loons had trouble drawing fans. While a major-league players' strike brought the Twins' season to a premature end, Nieboer mounted a marketing blitz for the Loons. It included hanging a large banner stretching across the main street in nearby Dinkytown, adjacent to the University of Minnesota campus in Minneapolis, to promote a pair of home stands to wrap up the season. The additional advertising and lack of major-league baseball didn't seem to make a difference, however. The Loons averaged just 769 fans per game, well below what they had hoped for.

The teams with the most success at the gate, Regina and Saskatoon, decided to break away from the North Central League after one year and join a new organization, the Prairie League. Another Saskatchewan team and one in Manitoba joined them in the Canadian Division. Minneapolis also joined the new league and played with three Dakota teams in the American Division.

As part of the Prairie League in 1995, the Loons secured a license to sell beer and drew slightly larger crowds—but they still averaged only about 1,000 fans a game. Unable to make their lease payments to the University of Minnesota, the team showed up for their final regular-season series and found themselves locked out of Siebert Field.

Finished in Minneapolis, the Loons moved to Austin, in the southern part of the state, and played the following two years as the Southern Minny Stars. Olson bought into the team and brought in three of his former Atlanta Braves teammates—Steve Avery, Tom Glavine, and John Smoltz—as investors. With the added funding, the Minny Stars were able to continue for a couple more seasons in the summer collegiate Northwoods League after the Prairie League disbanded following the 1997 season.

GREAT CENTRAL LEAGUE

Nieboer had hoped to name his team in the North Central League the Minneapolis Millers, the historic counterpart to the St. Paul Saints. However, someone else beat him to it. That man was Dick Jacobson, the strip-club owner who had previously tried to get the Rochester franchise in the Northern League.

Jacobson put up his money to back the Minneapolis Millers, as well as three other teams in the Great Central League, but his operation was far from ready for prime time. The four teams he backed spanned four different states. In addition to the Millers, the Great Central League had the Mason City (Iowa) Bats, Champagne-Urbana (Illinois) Bandits, and Lafayette (Indiana) Leopards.

For the Millers, Jacobson was able to produce one big name. It wasn't a player, however, but the manager, George "Boomer" Scott. Boomer had knocked 271 big-league home runs in thirteen seasons playing mostly for the

Boston Red Sox and Milwaukee Brewers. Scott may have been the origina-tor of the term "tater" to describe a home run, and he is also remembered for the string of puka shells he wore around his neck. When once asked what the necklace was made of, Scott replied, "second basemen's teeth."

Had he still been a player, Scott might have been a drawing card, but his appearance as a manager did little. The players didn't incite much interest from fans, either. However, a lack of organization was likely the biggest reason the team was doomed.

The Millers played at Parade Stadium on the western edge of downtown Minneapolis, a scenic spot with the Basilica of St. Mary as a backdrop. Once the center of sports entertainment in the city, the Parade Grounds had shrunk, much of its land usurped by the Walker Art Center's Minneapolis Sculpture Garden. The baseball diamond remained, but it had limited seating—not that much seating was needed for the poorly attended games.

The original general manager, Bill Williams, resigned before the season started and was succeeded by John King, who was making his initial foray into professional baseball. King was hired two days before the Millers' opener. His time with the team lasted only slightly over two weeks. King had reportedly tried to fire Scott as manager for reasons unknown, only to be told by Scott that he wasn't leaving. Instead, King departed, citing "differences with manage-ment and a lack of marketing and promotion."

King was certainly correct about the latter point. Few fans, it seemed, were even aware of the Millers, and the announced attendance of 491 for the opener was definitely an inflated figure. After his resignation, King told Rachel Blount of the *Star Tribune* that he had ordered a batting cage for the Millers but had to return it because the team couldn't pay for it. He also cited a shortage of pitchers as the reason for a loss in Mason City, when the Millers had to leave three hurlers at home because the team bus didn't have enough room for them.

The Millers opened at home on June 14, 1994, and it was only that morning that King found someone to throw out the ceremonial first pitch—the author of a book on the history of the original Minneapolis Millers. (Disclaimer: that author is also the author of the book you are now reading.) The author—aware that this "honor" probably came only after King had been turned down by the mayor and possibly every member of the Minneapolis City Council—was on the field before the game when he spotted Antonio Martinez, the Millers' starting pitcher, walking away toward the ivy-covered fence in foul territory in the outfield. "He's going to take a whiz," said the author to a colleague, an intended facetious remark that he quickly found to be not facetious at all. The baseball facility had no restrooms. The fans could go outside the park to a restroom, but the players usually followed Martinez's path to the ivy.

The Millers of the short-lived Grand Central League played at Parade Stadium on the edge of downtown Minneapolis.

The Millers also had Julian Martinez and Nino Martinez on the team. The trio at least gave radio announcer Kevin Murphy, who had a lot of trouble in his first foray into play-by-play work, one good line when he urged whatever listeners there were to "Come out to Parade Stadium for a three-Martinez lunch."

The station that carried the Millers' broadcasts, KYCR, was a Christian music station with other priorities. The station had certain shows it wasn't willing to preempt for the baseball game. As a result, listeners would hear a couple of innings of baseball, then an hour of "The Kingdom Has Drawn Near," and then the rest of the baseball game.

Teams in the Great Central League made little money, and several had difficulty making payroll. Most of the Mason City roster quit the team in mid-August after not getting paid; the Bats had to recruit new players (though not necessarily better ones) to make it through the rest of the season. The Millers had similar issues but made it to the end of the season.

Even after the season ended for the Millers, the issue of their final paychecks remained. Players showed up at the team's Minneapolis office only to find it locked. Erik Lovdahl, now director of training camps for the Minnesota Twins, was among the Millers who were stiffed. He filed a lawsuit against Jacobson on behalf of himself and several other team members. The players were successful and obtained a judgment, each of approximately $400, and had to go to Jacobson's strip joint in Coates, Minnesota, south of the Twin Cities, to collect. Lovdahl and Mark Wilson, a former Millers pitcher and now a Twins scout, both reported that they were paid in cash, in small denominations, mostly one-dollar bills.

The sorry chapter of the Great Central League came to a close, but Jacobson tried to stick it out. He carried on in 1995 with the Mid-America League, which included Great Central League holdover Lafayette and three other Indiana teams. But lack of planning, organization, and experience among the owners left the league as doomed as its predecessor.

The 1995 season was the peak for independents, with eleven leagues in operation that had no connection to organized baseball. The weaker ones were winnowed out quickly, and the number was reduced to six by 2014.

"Ideas are swimming upstream," said Veeck, adding that Major League Baseball imitates what the minor leagues do and imitates it "as soon as they can monetize it." Veeck also said that he has seen major-league teams importing more front-office talent from the minor leagues, rather than from corporate organizations, as they had done in the past.

"We grow fans," said Veeck of the independent leagues. "That's what the major leagues need from us—to develop fans."

CHAPTER 12

Down and Back Up Again

STRUGGLING TO RECAPTURE THE MAGIC

The excitement from the previous year's success remained in St. Paul as the 1994 season neared. When single-game tickets went on sale, the line of fans extended nearly a mile down Energy Park Drive. The Saints sold more than 20,000 tickets the first day.

Clearly Saints tickets were still a hot item and sellouts at Municipal Stadium would continue, even with increased capacity at the ballpark. The grandstand had been extended on each side, allowing the Saints to pack in more than 6,300 fans per game.

Despite the expansion of Municipal Stadium, there was talk of building a new ballpark for the Saints, one located along the Mississippi River adjacent to downtown St. Paul. The main cheerleader for a riverfront ballpark was the city's mayor, Norm Coleman, an inveterate civic booster. However, not all residents, fans, or team employees were big on the idea.

Crusty as it was, Municipal Stadium seemed to fit the Saints. No doubt the sight of barges and other watercraft cruising by would make a scenic backdrop to a baseball game, but regular attendees liked what they already had: a parking lot well suited for tailgating and a view of the state fairgrounds across the railroad tracks. The tracks themselves may have been the main attraction of the ballpark setting. Trains passing by were a reason to cheer, and trains passing simultaneously in opposite directions were a special occasion. Engineers quickly learned they could get a stronger ovation by blasting their horns (and a load of boos if they didn't). Trains were as much a part of Saints baseball as balls and strikes were. The riverfront stadium never happened, and most seemed satisfied with their snug but Spartan baseball home.

The team kicked off its 1994 season at its cozy home by honoring the 1993 champion Saints before the home opener on June 10, and the championship rings were distributed to the team. Leon Durham was back, now as a player-coach. A new star, Vince Castaldo, hit a bases-loaded triple to cap a five-run eighth inning as St. Paul beat Sioux City 6–3.

The Northern League had a new entry in 1994, as the Winnipeg Goldeyes took the place of the Rochester Aces. Baseball was a hit in Winnipeg, which drew 14,764 for its opener and more than 200,000 for the season, second only to the Saints.

Winnipeg not only brought in big crowds, but the Goldeyes won the 1994 league title under manager Doug Simunic. The Sioux City Explorers had won the season's first half with a 27–13 record, and Winnipeg matched that to finish first during the second half. The Goldeyes then beat the Explorers three games to one in the championship series.

The Saints were having a less successful season on the field. They finished third during the first half and dropped to fourth in the second half, missing the playoffs. However, the team did experience many memorable events once again. Early in the season, St. Paul was on the losing end of the Northern League's first no-hitter, pitched by Whiskey Jacks right-hander Rod Steph. The game, held in Thunder Bay, Ontario, just after the summer solstice, was played mostly under natural but diminishing daylight. Dave Wright, who added play-by-play announcing to his public relations duty, recalled that the stadium lights weren't turned on until the ninth inning, and the Saints batters had trouble seeing the pitches at this point. Steph fell behind in the count, 3–0, to Durham,

RETIRED and ROASTED

The opening weekend of the 1994 Saints schedule brought a transition of mascots, and Saint the pig, the 1993 mascot, was retired with a roast. The roast was of the celebrity-roast nature, with a series of tributes and good-natured ribbing. However, the announcement of Saint's roasting brought calls of protest by those fearing that the guest of honor was also going to be the main course. As Saint took his final bows, three-month-old Saint II was introduced. The new pig assumed official duties the next day as well as a new name, St. Paula.

SAINTS MASCOTS THROUGH THE YEARS
1993 – Saint
1994 – St. Paula
1995 – St. Patrick
1996 – Tobias
1997 – Hamlet
1998 – The Great Hambino
1999 – Hamilton
2000 – Hammy Davis Jr.
2001 – Kevin Bacon
2002 – Wilbur
2003 – The Notorious P.I.G. – Piggy Smalls

but the Saints hitter then watched three pitches go by for called strikes, ending the game. Darius Gash, with a seventh-inning walk, was the only St. Paul base runner, and Winnipeg won 1–0 behind Steph's gem.

Back in St. Paul two days later, on Saturday, June 25, the Saints played Winnipeg in a game that definitely needed artificial lights. The first pitch was at 7:08 PM. Seventeen innings and more than four and a half hours later, the game was suspended with the score tied 3–3. The teams returned early the next afternoon to resume the suspended game prior to the regularly scheduled one. In the top of the eighteenth Dann Bilardello squeezed home the winning run for Winnipeg.

Although Bilardello, a catcher in the National League from 1983 to 1992, won the game for the opposing team, he earned the admiration of Saints fans in another way. He had been designated as the K-Man, a popular staple at Saints games, although one of dubious sportsmanship. An opposing player is picked, and picked on, as the K-Man, meaning that the fans receive a prize if he strikes out in the game. Originally the award was a coupon for a two-liter bottle of soda pop at local Tom Thumb convenience stores, although the K-Man so often came through with a strikeout that the prize had to be changed to something of less value.

Some K-Men embraced the challenge, but many have been known to take umbrage as the fans hoot and the public-address announcer implores the hitter to whiff. Following a productive career in the major leagues, Pedro Guerrero signed with the Sioux Falls Canaries of the Northern League in 1993 and made his debut when the team was in St. Paul. Guerrero was pegged as the K-Man in

2004 – Squeal Diamond
2005 – Ham Solo
2006 – Bud Squealig
2007 – Garrison Squeallor
2008 – Boarack Ohama
2009 – Slumhog Millionaire
2010 – Brat Favre
2011 – Justin Bieboar
2012 – Kim Lardashian & Kris Hamphries
2013 – Mackleboar
2014 – Stephen Colboar

In 1995, St. Patrick was named the third in what would be a long and distinguished line of Saints "ball pigs."

PHOTO COURTESY OF THE ST. PAUL SAINTS

LITTLE BIG LEAGUE

In June 1994 the movie *Little Big League* premiered in the Twin Cities. Its first-unit production had been filmed over the previous year in the Twin Cities, with the Metrodome as the site for the baseball scenes. The movie featured career actors—including Timothy Busfield, Jason Robards, and Dennis Farina—as well as former major leaguers, such as Kevin Elster and Brad "The Animal" Lesley, portraying some of the players. The Northern League was represented in the film as well. Leon Durham had lines in the movie, and Saints teammates Ed Stryker and Scott Meadows also appeared in it. Longtime Twins radio announcer John Gordon played the part of play-by-play man Wally Holland.

his first full game and wasn't happy about being the subject of derision, especially when he struck out.

Bilardello, on the other hand, made it through the entire eighteen-inning game on June 25 without fanning (appropriately, the K-Man promotion was reportedly the idea of Saints general manager Bill Fanning). With his impressive feat of going the equivalent of two complete games without striking out, Bilardello was saluted by the Saints prior to the next game and presented with a two-liter bottle of soda.

The Saints had a few other memorable late-night games. One in July, against the Canaries, was delayed by rain and didn't start until 9:37 PM. The teams weren't able to complete it before the game was suspended by a curfew. Four days later, when the teams met in Sioux Falls, South Dakota, the Saints finally completed a 4–3 win.

Just over a week later, the Saints were in Thunder Bay for a game but were unable to play when, just before the game, the ballpark's electrical system was knocked out when lightning hit a transformer.

Although wins didn't pile up as frequently as the team and its fans would have liked, the Saints had some notable individual achievements in their second season. Matt Stark joined the club on July 29 and singled his first time up, the start of a 22-game hitting streak that set a league record. Castaldo was named the Northern League Most Valuable Player, thanks to a .316 batting average to go with his 16 home runs and 66 runs batted in.

St. Paul wrapped up its home season by giving the stadium a new name, one chosen by the fans, who suggested names and voted their preferences. Starting in 1995, the home of the Saints would once again be called Midway Stadium.

BOUNCING BACK FOR ANOTHER TITLE

For 1995, the Saints looked at all opportunities to improve following a disappointing season. Along with other independent teams, the Saints explored the possibility of signing Dwight Gooden, who had been a sensation with the New York Mets ten years earlier. Gooden had been the National League Rookie of the Year in 1984 and followed that with a Cy Young Award in 1985. Drug problems derailed his brilliance and eventually brought him a pair of suspensions that put him out of organized baseball for the 1995 season. Gooden sat out the year and decided not to play with any independent teams.

The Saints also made a play for one of the best catchers in the college game, Jason Varitek. Varitek was taken by the Minnesota Twins in the first round of the 1993 amateur draft but decided to return to Georgia Tech for his senior season. He was then drafted by the Seattle Mariners, who initially didn't have any more luck in getting him to sign than the Twins had.

Baseball America dubbed Varitek the "Holdout from Hell" when he refused the Mariners' offer. In January 1995 the Saints made their move, signing Varitek to play for them with the agreement that he could still sign with Seattle if he so chose.

Varitek's agent, Scott Boras, was looking for more than leverage with the Mariners. He claimed that his client's signing with an independent team meant he was no longer an amateur and was free to sign with any major-league team. Those in organized baseball disagreed, contending that any player who had not signed with a major league or affiliated minor league would continue to be subject to the amateur draft. Boras countered by citing the language in organized baseball's own operating procedures, which described the "Rule 4 Amateur–Free Agent Draft." He was quoted in the *New York Times* asking why, if baseball intended for the draft to include professional players, which Varitek now was, did they use the word *amateur* in describing the draft? "Why not just Rule 4 Draft?" Boras asked. "Nobody but an amateur has ever been drafted in that draft."

If the issue went to the courts or an arbitrator, the decision could have had far-reaching ramifications. In 1975 an arbitrator's ruling had opened the door to free agency for existing major leaguers. A similar outcome in Varitek's case could have had a similar impact for players coming out of high school and college.

But the question wasn't answered, at least not at that time. Varitek and the Mariners finally reached agreement on a contract in April. The catcher was off to a pro career within organized baseball. Boras, meanwhile, stuck around as a hard-line negotiator for his clients, ready to fight such a battle again.

The Saints hadn't been looking to upend organized baseball's draft structure; they just wanted a good catcher. They didn't get Varitek, but they had a few other newcomers in 1995. One was a public-address announcer. Al Frechtman decided to leave because he felt that the Saints were no longer allowing him to use his freewheeling style behind the mic. Bob Yates, a local radio personality, replaced Frechtman. Wright characterized Yates as "more traditional" than Frechtman but "too subtle for this crowd." Tim Blackwell was also gone, having landed a managing job in the Baltimore Orioles organization, and Marty Scott took over as skipper of the Saints. Scott had played and then managed in the Texas system before becoming the Rangers' director of player development for ten years. Let go as part of a front-office shuffle, Scott came to St. Paul with hopes of someday making it back to the majors.

The Saints also added prominent outfielder Darryl Motley, who had spent time with the Kansas City Royals and Atlanta Braves from 1981 to 1987. Motley kept playing in the minors and had several seasons in the Mexican League, as well as one in Japan, before he signed with St. Paul. An on-base

Dan Peltier batted .366 for the Saints in 1995 and drove in 56 runs in 83 games. He played in the San Francisco Giants organization in 1996 and then returned to St. Paul briefly in 1997.

machine for the Saints in 1995, he also belted 13 homers, second to only Doug O'Neill's 17 for St. Paul.

First baseman Dan Peltier was a fearsome slugger and the team's top hitter, with a .366 average. The Saints also brought back a couple of their stars from 1994: Castaldo and Stark, who both produced again. With these big bats, St. Paul finished second in the league in runs scored and won both halves of the Northern League season in 1995.

A championship series was still played, as the Saints faced defending-champion Winnipeg. The teams split the first two games in St. Paul and then headed north for the remainder of the series. The Saints took the next two, winning the deciding game 4–0 behind pitcher Steve Morales's eight innings of one-hit ball, to earn their second title in three years.

TWIG

When Marty Scott was hired to be the new
manager of the St. Paul Saints in 1995, he had
received an endorsement from a popular new
addition to the team's coaching staff, Wayne
Terwilliger. The two had been together in Texas
before "Twig," as Terwilliger was known, went to
the Minnesota Twins as a coach in 1986.

Terwilliger had worked in the Twin Cities
before, having played for both the St. Paul Saints
and the Minneapolis Millers during a professional career that started in 1948. He had served
in the marines during World War II, landed on
the southern end of Iwo Jima, Japan, in 1945,
and saw the American flag flying on Mount
Suribachi. After the war, Terwilliger played
baseball at Western Michigan in Kalamazoo and
then for a semipro team before signing with the
Chicago Cubs.

Terwilliger was popular when he coached for
the Twins. The team held a retirement ceremony
for him just before the end of the strike-shortened
1994 season, even though retirement hadn't been
Terwilliger's choice.

"The first few years that I worked with [Twins
manager] Tom Kelly we were fairly close, but we
drifted away from that relationship," Terwilliger
says in his autobiography, *Terwilliger Bunts One*,
written with Nancy Peterson and Peter Boehm. "I
respected his managing and the way he treated the
players, but as the years went by he talked to me
less and less, and when he did say something, it
often sounded like a put-down."

Peterson and Boehm were regulars at Saints
games, and, after Terwilliger's forced retirement
from the Twins, Boehm lobbied for St. Paul to
hire him. The Saints were already on it and hired
Twig as first-base coach. "Mike [Veeck] said
he thought my presence would help the team

Wayne Terwilliger was a longtime presence in Minnesota
baseball before becoming a coach with the Saints in 1995.

PHOTO COURTESY OF THE ST. PAUL SAINTS

build credibility," writes Terwilliger. After eight
seasons in St. Paul, Terwilliger eventually left
the Saints but stayed in baseball, managing and
coaching in Texas and putting more than sixty
years of his life into pro ball. His number, 5, was
retired by the Saints.

St. Paul won another Northern League championship in 1996. But the season is best remembered for two players who weren't even around at the end.

In April the Saints signed Jack Morris. A St. Paul native, Morris pitched in fourteen seasons for the Detroit Tigers and then came home and helped the Twins win the World Series in 1991. He went to Toronto and was on two more champion teams before finishing with Cleveland in 1994. Morris tried to catch on with the Cincinnati Reds in 1995, but when that didn't work out, he took some time off. A year later he opted to join the Saints, figuring a strong showing with the team could get him another offer to pitch in the majors.

Although some Minnesota fans had been bitter back when Morris left the Twins and signed as a free agent with the Blue Jays for 1992, Morris said his hope was to stay in Minnesota following his comeback with the Saints. "The Twins needed pitching bad, and I wanted to come back and maybe finish my career right here again," he said. "But they didn't come across the street to even look at me. I guess they were still mad that I left. I don't know what happened there."

Twins general manager Terry Ryan said they had no interest in Morris but that it had nothing to do with events of the past. "I could see where a veteran contending team would be interested [in Morris]," Ryan explained. "We weren't that."

A contending team did consider Morris, as well as another newcomer on the Saints, Darryl Strawberry. A sensation even before he starred at Crenshaw High School in Los Angeles, Strawberry was the first player taken in the 1980 amateur draft, by the New York Mets. The National League Rookie of the Year in 1983, he was one of the top players in baseball through the rest of the 1980s.

With a leg kick and sweet swing at the plate, Strawberry hit 280 home runs before he was thirty years old and appeared to be on a sure track to the Hall of Fame. But injuries slowed him down, and his cocaine use drew him a suspension for the first part of the 1995 season. Later in the year, the New York Yankees signed Strawberry, but they bought out his contract after the season. Strawberry was a free agent who had trouble finding takers.

Looking for another shot, Strawberry came to St. Paul. Although Mike Veeck was big on giving second chances, he wavered when it came to Strawberry. He didn't know if he wanted to take on Strawberry's baggage, which included issues with alcohol, domestic disputes, and tax evasion. However, Marv Goldklang used the magic word: blackball. When Goldklang said he thought Strawberry was being blackballed from the majors, Veeck, ever the champion for the outsider and underdog, converted.

Strawberry signed with the Saints on May 3, 1996, and two weeks later he was in training camp with Morris, as well as a player who had little shot at making the team. Dave Stevens was born without legs, but he didn't let that stop him from playing sports. He was on the football and wrestling teams at Augsburg College in Minneapolis and also had the chance to practice a few days with the Dallas Cowboys of the National Football League. St. Paul Saints manager Scott, a Texas native and Cowboys fan, liked Stevens's story.

JACK MORRIS

Jack Morris lived in several Twin Cities suburbs before his family settled into the Highland Park neighborhood of St. Paul. In addition to playing baseball, Morris was a ski jumper for the St. Paul ski club when he was in junior high and was on the varsity basketball team for Highland Park High School. On the diamond, Morris was a third baseman and shortstop. His younger brother, Tom, was the school's top pitcher. However, Jack's strong arm got him a scholarship and the chance to pitch at Brigham Young University, where one of his teammates was Harmon Killebrew's son, Cam. After lettering for two years, Morris was drafted by Detroit and signed with the Tigers after his junior season. With the Tigers in the 1980s, Morris won 162 games, more than any other pitcher in the majors. He had 20 wins for Detroit in 1983 and 19 more the next season, when the Tigers won the World Series. Morris came to the Twins in 1991 and won 18 games during the regular season and 2 more in both the American League playoffs and World Series. He capped his year with the Twins with a ten-inning shutout over the Atlanta Braves in the seventh and deciding game of the World Series. Morris went to Toronto and won 21 games in 1992 as the Blue Jays went on to win the World Series. He finished his major-league career with 254 career wins.

Forty-one-year-old Jack Morris prepares to fire one in during a Saints game in 1996.

PHOTO COURTESY OF THE ST. PAUL SAINTS

He brought Stevens to camp and promised him an opportunity to play in an exhibition game.

That season Strawberry and Morris put on a show from the start. The Saints dropped the opening game of the season in Duluth on Friday night, May 31, despite two hits from Strawberry. A large media contingent had come up for the first series, and a busload of fans headed north from the Twin Cities for the Saturday night game, only to be disappointed when it was fogged out.

The game was made up as part of a doubleheader on Sunday, and Morris made his Saints debut in the first game. However, he was only a footnote in the game account, as Strawberry blasted a memorable two-run home run in the fifth inning. The drive cleared the fence to the left of a light tower in right-center field and sailed over the backstop of an adjacent Little League field. David Haglin, president of the West Duluth Little League, was grooming the diamond and saw the ball land near second base. Along with a New York writer who had come out to check on the distance, Haglin measured the divot on his field to the wall of Wade Stadium and came up with a distance of 147 feet. Adding that to the 380 feet from home plate to center field at Wade Stadium, Strawberry's clout was listed as 527 feet.

After Strawberry's monumental blast, St. Paul's Marty Neff and Kevin Garner homered on the next two pitches from Duluth-Superior right-hander Pat Ahearne. The three homers on three pitches gave the Saints a seemingly comfortable lead, but the Dukes tied the score in the bottom of the inning with 4 runs off Saints relievers Joe Miller and Jim Manfred. Strawberry wasn't done, though; his two-run single in the sixth gave St. Paul its winning margin and the start of a doubleheader sweep.

Strawberry stayed hot through June, and the Yankees became interested in him again. Goldklang, also a part owner of the Yankees, provided reports and recommendations on Strawberry to New York boss George Steinbrenner. Yankee general manager Bob Watson, in town for a Yankees series with the Twins later that month, said he was nearly 100 percent sure he would not sign Strawberry. Within a week, though, he changed his mind, influenced at least in part by the team's scouting director, Gene "Stick" Michael.

On July 2, in his twenty-ninth game with the team, Strawberry hit his final home run for the Saints, bringing his total to 18. The ball shot over the center field batter's eye at Midway Stadium. Strawberry came out of the game in the fifth inning and got an offer of a minor-league contract, reportedly with no guarantee of a call-up by the Yankees. Assigned to New York's top farm team, in Columbus, Ohio, Strawberry homered in his first two at-bats the next night. He had another homer in his next game and got the call to join the Yankees in New York.

Goldklang recalls Steinbrenner's words to him when the Yankees signed Strawberry: "If he f**ks up, it's your ass." Strawberry didn't "f**k" up anything, though, and instead brought the team success. He hit 11 home runs for New York and helped the Yankees win the World Series for the first time since 1978.

Strawberry was gone, but Morris was still in St. Paul, along with a continuing Yankee presence in scouting director Michael. Michael approached Morris, who later said he didn't "have a ton of interest in playing in New York."

The Saints ended the first half of the season in a first-place tie with the Madison Black Wolf in the East Division. (The Northern League had expanded to eight teams with the addition of a team in Madison, Wisconsin, and the Fargo-Moorhead RedHawks.) A one-game playoff was held at Midway Stadium on Thursday, July 18. Morris was on the mound and a still-hopeful Michael was in the stands.

As he had done in the seventh game of the 1991 World Series, Morris pitched 10 innings. But this time he didn't get the win, and the game continued on as a tie. The Saints finally beat the Black Wolf in twelve innings to capture the first-half title. Morris celebrated with his teammates, but the next day he went into Scott's office and said he had pitched his last game for the Saints. Where he would go—back to the majors or home to his ranch in Montana— was still up in the air.

Morris became more receptive to joining the Yankees but balked at Michael's insistence that he make a number of tune-up starts at Columbus. "'Bullheaded Jack' told Stick I was already pitching in the minors and didn't want to do it," Morris recalled in 2014. "I wasn't even thinking of who was on the Yankees roster and how good the team had become."

Morris packed up and went west rather than east. He later called the decision his "only regret" in baseball. "If I had one thing to go back and do again, I would have signed with the Yankees and probably put two or three more [championship] rings on my finger."

The Minnesota Twins' lack of interest in signing Morris may have been, in part, a lingering sign of the team's dismissive attitude toward the Saints. However, by this time there was some thawing of the icy relationship. Andy MacPhail and his "beer league" references were gone, and Twins marketing consultant Pat Forceia pushed for a cross promotion between the teams in 1996.

On Sunday, June 9, the Saints played in the afternoon and had longtime Twins announcer Herb Carneal throw out a ceremonial first pitch. Fans with Saints ticket stubs were able to use them to gain admittance to the Minnesota-Oakland major-league game that night, as a two-for-one cross-team package. The Twins honored Wayne Terwilliger, then with the Saints, before their game, and the Saints' mascot Tobias the pig attended as well, making the rounds of the plaza outside the Metrodome and stopping in to visit one of the suites

A brief turn with the Saints in 1996 helped to revive the major-league career of Darryl Strawberry (center, holding bat).

during the game. Over time, Veeck said he developed a warm relationship with MacPhail's successor, Terry Ryan, Twins president Dave St. Peter, and others in the organization. A measure of détente between the teams had been established, although it was still years before the Twins signed anyone who had been on the Saints' roster.

Morris's departure left a spot open for another veteran, and the team filled it by signing Glenn Davis, a former National League slugger who had been playing for the Hanshin Tigers in the Japan Central League. For St. Paul, Davis hit 9 home runs and drove in 50 runs in 39 games.

With their first-place finish in the first half and a playoff spot assured, the Saints continued playing hard while also entertaining their fans. Even Scott got into the act, along with longtime nemesis Simunic, who was now managing Fargo-Moorhead. Both managers were ejected in a game at Midway Stadium on August 20. Under the stands they met and had the idea to put on the sumo-wrestler suits, which were usually used by fans for between-innings frivolity.

At the end of the eighth inning, the two came onto the field in the suits and began bumping oversized bellies (a result of the padding in the suits, although each manager contributed his own girth to the contest). Fans loved the exhibition, but umpires Don Grimaluskus, Jerome Krueger, and Wes Kenny did not.

Commissioner Miles Wolff had no choice but to take action, fining both managers. Wolff said he also fined the Saints "more than a little" for the team's complicity in the stunt. Veeck, when approached by Scott and Simunic, had okayed the gag and even helped set up the wrestling mat on the field. However, Wright recalled that when Wolff notified the Saints of the fine, he also asked for a videotape of the event, not because he needed it for evidence or further study but because he was amused by it.

Amusing antics aside, the Saints and Black Wolf again tied for first place in the second half of the season. This time, no tiebreaker game was held, and both teams were headed to the playoffs.

As the regular season wound down, Scott set up his rotation for the playoffs. To keep other arms rested, Scott gave a start to Joe Miller, a converted out-fielder who had worked out of the Saints bullpen all year.

Miller took his 7.01 earned-run average to the mound on Sunday, August 25, and got plenty of run support from his teammates. He didn't need it, as he had no trouble putting down the Thunder Bay batters and racking up goose eggs on the scoreboard. Miller retired the first 21 Whiskey Jacks before walking the leadoff batter in the eighth.

The perfect game gone, Miller still had a no-hitter going, and he retired the next three batters in the inning. In the ninth Miller struck out the first hitter and walked the next one. The next batter, Jarvis Brown, who had played on the Twins world-championship team in 1991, hit a ground ball toward the left side. Shortstop Lance Robbins moved to his right and booted the grounder. The fate of the no-hitter now rested with official scorer Tom Greenhoe, a colorful character who worked in the sports information department of the University of Minnesota. Wright said Greenhoe took his time making a decision. Wright finally prompted him on what his call would be. "Greenhoe said, 'I got this one.' He just wanted the crowd to look up at him, and then he announced an error."

The no-hitter still intact, Miller retired the final two batters to complete it. Some called it the unlikeliest no-hitter ever.

The Saints celebrated with Miller and then headed for a nearby watering hole to watch the premiere telecast of *Baseball Minnesota,* a twenty-two-part reality-style series on the Saints produced by the FX cable network. The Saints had let the network into their dugout and locker room for an inside look at life in the low minor leagues. Scott gave the film crew incredible access, sometimes to the point of discomfort for the players. He wanted the behind-the-scenes material to be authentic. Director Rob Klug described the players as "tragic heroes on the first leg of a nearly impossible journey. . . . They are the underdogs in each one of us."

With two divisions, the Northern League had two rounds of playoffs in 1996, and St. Paul was unbeatable in them. The Saints swept Madison in two games and then faced Fargo-Moorhead for the championship in a best-of-five series. After winning the first two games at home, St. Paul headed to Fargo

SAINTS ON THE SMALL SCREEN

Baseball Minnesota wasn't the first documentary exposure the Saints had received. Morley Safer had come to St. Paul for a *60 Minutes* segment on the Saints in August 1995. Even though little was needed to make the Saints look good, Safer made a point of juxtaposing the local major-league team, showing the lifeless atmosphere at the Metrodome during another bad season for the Minnesota Twins. Safer contrasted the festive nature in St. Paul with what he called the "big-time summer of discontent" in Minneapolis.

It is often noted that the Saints outdrew the Twins on Wednesday, September 6, 1995. However, an apples-to-apples comparison is not really possible. The Twins, playing in the afternoon, had a paid attendance of 7,845 and an in-house crowd of only 2,742, smaller than the paid attendance, which was 4,637, for the Saints game that evening. Dave Wright noted that the Saints' turnstile counts were "notoriously inaccurate" in the early years, so the team counted only the number of tickets sold, regardless of how many no-shows there were. He still believes the Saints had more butts in the seats than the Twins that day, but added, "Our view at the time was that it was a statistical fluke. We didn't make a very big deal out of it."

and finished it off quickly. The game was tied after eight innings. Jeff Bittiger pitched a strong game for the RedHawks, striking out 10, but his fielders let him down. With two out in the top of the ninth, Joe Biernat reached on an error. Carlton Fleming followed with a triple to bring Biernat home with the decisive run, and St. Paul had another title.

Klug had used the term *underdogs* to describe the Saints players, and individually they may have been that—men at the lowest rung of baseball playing for the joy of the game as well as for nearly impossible hope. However, as a team, St. Paul was hardly viewed as an underdog by the other teams in the Northern League. Three-time champions, the Saints were at the top of the heap.

Final Years of the Northern League

BIG NAMES IN ST. PAUL AGAIN

Not content to sit still after winning three of the Northern League's first four titles, the Saints looked at bringing in more attention-grabbing players in 1997.

One of the big names considered by St. Paul was Steve Howe, a twelve-year major-league veteran and former National League Rookie of the Year. The left-handed pitcher had been suspended from organized baseball seven times for drug and alcohol problems. On top of that, when Howe looked to the independent leagues for another chance, he was on probation for having tried to go through airport security with a handgun in his carry-on bag the previous June. Howe might have been pushing his luck even with a last-chance league, but he did sign with the Sioux Falls Canaries, only to have his season cut short by an injury.

Another player the Saints considered was thirty-year-old right-hander Hideki Irabu, who had pitched the last eight seasons in the Japan Pacific League. Irabu's ambition was to pitch for the New York Yankees. However, the San Diego Padres had acquired his rights from the Chiba Lotte Marines, his team in Japan. In case a trade between the Yankees and Padres couldn't be worked out, Irabu explored other options. Reportedly St. Paul was an interested suitor, although the Saints carefully avoided comment. Marv Goldklang said only, "We're always looking for quality starting pitching." Irabu did get his trade to New York and pitched for the Yankees and two other teams through 2002 before returning to Japan.

While the Saints may have demurred on Howe and been usurped by the Yankees on Irabu, the team ended up with two players who were as prominent as Darryl Strawberry and Jack Morris the year before. The first was a left-hander, Ila Borders, who had pitched at Southern California College and

Whittier College in California. She was one of the first women to play in a college baseball game. Borders went to Saints training camp in mid-May and, along with thirteen other pitchers, competed for one of the ten spots on the staff. A few days before the opener, Borders made the team, becoming one of the few women to play on an otherwise all-men's team in professional baseball.

Borders had a rough start on May 31, failing to retire a batter in her first appearance, although the next day she was brought into a game in relief and struck out the side. Less than a month into the 1997 season the Saints traded Borders to Duluth-Superior. The following season the Dukes started Borders in eight games, figuring advance notice of a mound appearance would draw fans. It did, although she was hit hard during the year. Her struggles continued in 1999, and the Dukes traded Borders to the Madison Black Wolf. There, manager Al Gallagher (full name Alan Mitchell Edward George Patrick Henry Gallagher but known merely as "Dirty Al") found a way to get maximum value from Borders. He started her and often let her get through the opposing lineup one time. After nine batters, Borders was relieved by a harder-throwing pitcher. In 15 games with Madison (including 12 starts), Borders had a 1.67 earned-run average.

Borders pitched one more season, in 2000 in the independent Western League, before retiring from pro baseball, having left a significant mark on the game. She returned to Southern California and became a firefighter in Long Beach.

A week after trading Borders to the Dukes in 1997, the Saints made headlines again by signing J. D. Drew, a star out of Florida State University. Drew had been the second player taken in the amateur draft, but it was apparent that the Philadelphia Phillies would have trouble signing him.

Two years earlier the Saints had signed Jason Varitek when he was resisting contract offers from the team that had drafted him, the Seattle Mariners. Drew followed the same route to St. Paul and with the same agent, Scott Boras.

Players taken in the draft, especially those who had completed their college eligibility, didn't have much leverage with the teams that drafted them. They were offered salaries and signing bonuses significantly lower than what they could get if they were able to negotiate with all organizations.

In between Varitek and Drew, the true value of top draft picks on the open market became clearer. In 1996 three top players were declared free agents after the teams that had drafted them failed to tender an offer within the required time period. One was first baseman Travis Lee, who had been taken second in the draft by the Minnesota Twins. Once allowed on the open market, Lee signed a deal worth around $10 million with the Arizona Diamondbacks. His package was about $8 million more than what the number-one pick, pitcher Kris Benson of Clemson University, had received from the Pittsburgh Pirates.

In 1997, Ila Borders made history as the first woman to play in the Northern League. Her stay with the Saints was brief but memorable.

(In 1996, freed from the clutches of one team, two other players, Matt White and Bobby Seay, reportedly ended up with around the same money that Lee had received.)

The open-market value of a coveted player entering the pro ranks became known as "Travis Lee money," and Drew made it clear before the 1997 draft that this was the compensation he would be seeking. The Phillies' initial offer of $2.05 million, reportedly the highest ever presented to a drafted player who had completed his college eligibility, was still well short of Travis Lee money. The Phillies increased their offer, but a wide gap remained, and Boras and Lee decided to sign with a team in a league independent of organized baseball.

As Drew worked out with the Saints and then debuted with a home run, Boras worked a couple angles to make him a free agent. One involved a claim that the Phillies had failed to deliver a contract offer to Drew's permanent address. By the end of July, baseball's executive committee rejected the claim. It was hardly surprising that baseball would side with one of its own, so Boras tried another route—one he would have pursued in 1995 had Varitek not eventually come to terms with Seattle. Boras had been prepared to claim that since Varitek had signed a professional contract (with St. Paul), he was no longer eligible for the draft and would become a free agent. Although Seattle and organized baseball dodged this showdown, the major leagues changed the draft rules (or, in their language, clarified them) to prevent such a situation from happening again. The "clarification" meant that players who signed with an independent-league team were still subject to the draft and could not become free agents.

On behalf of Drew, the Major League Baseball Players Association (MLBPA) filed a grievance, contending that Major League Baseball could not change the draft rules without the consent of the union.

Meanwhile, Drew dominated the Northern League, just as Strawberry had in 1996. Drew hit 18 home runs in 44 games with the Saints, and, as his grievance dragged on, he prepared to start the 1998 season with them.

On May 19, 1998, arbitrator Dana Eischen upheld the MLBPA grievance, ruling that baseball violated the collective-bargaining agreement by unilaterally changing the draft rules. However, Drew and all other future draftees lost the overall battle, since Eischen also determined that Drew's rights weren't subject to arbitration because he wasn't a member of the union, leaving his status to be determined by Major League Baseball's executive committee. With Eischen's two-way ruling, baseball averted a disaster, one that would have opened the door to more options and bigger paydays for all incoming players.

Drew had won the grievance on its merits but lost on a technicality. A court case might have produced a different outcome, but a lengthy legal battle wasn't feasible for a young player. Drew's options for entering organized baseball remained only with the Phillies and then, after the 1998 draft a few weeks later,

J. D. Drew attracted a lot of media attention in St. Paul in 1997. Most of the attention focused on his contract holdout, but Drew also excelled on the diamond, batting .341 with 18 home runs in just 44 games with the Saints.

PHOTO COURTESY OF THE ST. PAUL SAINTS

with the St. Louis Cardinals, who took him with the fifth overall pick. Drew stayed with the Saints, making about $750 a month, and drew the wrath of many within baseball, including fans at Northern League games as well as his future colleagues in the majors.

Drew stuck to his convictions, pointing out that he was only asking for the same rights that nearly everyone else in the country enjoyed when entering the workforce. Not only that, baseball players outside the United States and Canada had those rights, not being stuck with only one potential employer, and had the benefit of choosing which team to join and receiving a contract based on open-market value.

Unfair or not, the system was still in place, and Drew lacked leverage. After St. Louis drafted him, Drew went through the same negotiations with the Cardinals that he had had with the Phillies over the past year. This time, the offer was more to his liking, although not quite Travis Lee money. After hitting 9 home runs (including one off Borders) in 30 games for the Saints, Drew signed with St. Louis on July 3 for a four-year deal worth a reported $7 million in guaranteed money and up to $9 million with incentives.

Drew left St. Paul during the 1998 season to join the St. Louis system, playing first in the Class AA Texas League. Despite missing more than two weeks with a knee injury, Drew was called up by the Cardinals after two months in the minors. He made his major-league debut on September 8, 1998, entering the game as a pinch hitter two innings after Cardinals teammate Mark McGwire hit his record-breaking 62nd home run of the season.

Drew hadn't been around long enough to be picked for the first Northern League All-Star Game in 1997, which was played at Midway Stadium on August 4 before another St. Paul sellout of more than 6,300 fans. The event featured a home-run hitting contest, and the East Division (the Saints' division) won the game 2–1 on a two-run, seventh-inning home run by Nate Vopata of Madison.

The Saints also had a new radio broadcast team in 1997, Jim Lucas and Don Wardlow. Both were thirty-four years old, and Wardlow was blind. They got their chance to announce professional baseball when Mike Veeck hired them to announce games for the Miami Miracle in 1990. Veeck fired them in 1992 on the premise that they needed to "prove they could do it without me." The pair broadcast games for the Minnesota Twins' Class AA affiliate in New Britain, Connecticut. In 1997, Veeck hired them again, this time for St. Paul, and they called Saints games for the next three seasons.

The Saints won the 1997 East Division first-half title easily with a record of 24–18, six games ahead of Thunder Bay. In third place were the Duluth-Superior Dukes, who had gotten off to a bad start, losing 17 of their first 21 games. The Dukes came back strong in the second half and finished first in the

Andy Nelson's murals at Midway Stadium celebrate the heroes and great moments from Minnesota baseball history.

ANDY NELSON

An artist and ardent baseball fan, Andy Nelson combined his loves and left his legacy in drawings and murals for the Society for American Baseball Research (SABR), *Minneapolis Review of Baseball,* and the St. Paul Saints.

Raised in McIntosh, Minnesota, Nelson was born in Milwaukee and was fascinated by the scrapbooks his dad compiled during the Braves' pennant-winning seasons in 1957 and 1958. An art major at Bemidji State in Minnesota, Nelson took a children's literature class and had the idea for an ABC primer for young readers. In the 1980s, he provided the artwork for the SABR annual directory and combined his illustrations with a baseball drawing based on each letter of the alphabet. Soon after, Nelson teamed with Ken LaZebnik and Steve Lehman on a book,

A Is for At Bat: A Baseball Primer. LaZebnik and Lehman had founded the *Minneapolis Review of Baseball,* and Nelson became the illustrator for the publication.

In 1993, Nelson captured the magic of the Saints' first season with a mural on the walls of the team's stadium. The mural included other local baseball history, but the most popular feature, just inside the ticket gates, was a panorama of the opening year at Municipal (later Midway) Stadium. Nelson deviated from his normal practice of drawing generic people. He had renditions of actual fans, who for years after delighted in seeing their images in the mural. Nelson continued providing artwork for the Saints for their programs and other publications. He died in 2008 at the age of fifty-two, and his funeral was held at Midway Stadium.

division by one game over the Saints. These teams met in the first round of the playoffs, and Duluth-Superior eliminated St. Paul in five games. The Dukes went on to beat Winnipeg in the finals for their first Northern League championship.

ST. PAUL SLUMP

After falling short in the 1997 playoffs, St. Paul went into a championship drought that extended several years into the twenty-first century. The Saints weren't bad, just not good enough to take another title. But they continued to entertain their fans.

Catcher Matt Nokes joined the Saints in 1998. As a rookie with the Detroit Tigers in 1987, Nokes hit 32 home runs, made the All-Star team, and finished third in Rookie of the Year voting. He never had another season like that one, and he retired in 1995. After being out of baseball for more than two years, Nokes made a comeback in St. Paul and put up good numbers in 1998, including a .351 batting average. He also hit a home run that sent the Saints to the title round of the playoffs.

However, Nokes may be best remembered for an incident in Winnipeg in July 1998. The Goldeyes' mascot, Goldie, was annoying the Saints by jumping on top of their dugout and pounding the roof with a broomstick. Nokes said he told Goldie to knock it off, but the mascot was at it again the next night. As is usually the case, accounts vary on what happened next, most of them reporting that Nokes jumped on top of the dugout, chased Goldie, pinned the mascot against a wall, and choked him (or her) with the broomstick.

Nokes's account was that he came outside the dugout and became concerned when Goldie jumped off the roof and onto an adjacent trampoline. Feeling threatened, Nokes said he grabbed the broom and "squeezed it up against him."

The Northern League fined Nokes $25 and suspended him for one game. Meanwhile, sports mascots in Manitoba planned to rally in support of Goldie at the end of August, when the Saints next came to town. The mascot mob, estimated at a half dozen, confronted Nokes, with Goldie holding a broomstick and calling the catcher out of the dugout. Nokes came out waving a white Saints flag, apparently a universal sign of peace to sports mascots, and embraced Goldie as the crowd applauded.

Soon after, back in St. Paul, Nokes hit his game-ending home run to give the Saints a three-games-to-two win over Thunder Bay in the first round of the playoffs. Nokes's blast also ended the Northern League history of the Whiskey Jacks, which had drawn little more than 54,000 fans that season to their home games. A team in Schaumberg, Illinois, had already been tabbed to take Thunder Bay's spot in the league in 1999.

In the league finals, Fargo-Moorhead swept St. Paul to win the championship. Managed by Doug Simunic, the RedHawks were dominant during the regular season, winning 64 of 85 games. They were led by the hitting of Darryl Motley, who had played for St. Paul in 1995 before being traded to Fargo-Moorhead before the 1996 season. After many years in the major leagues and the Mexican League, Motley settled into independent leagues and was a star. He retired in 2002 at the age of forty-two.

Another key member of the RedHawks was a local athlete, Chris Coste, who was born in Fargo and played at Concordia College in Moorhead. Undrafted out of college, Coste went the independent route starting in 1995. The next year he joined Fargo-Moorhead as a catcher (a position he hadn't played before) and was an all-star in the Northern League. Signed and then released by the Pittsburgh Pirates during the 1998–99 offseason, Coste returned to the RedHawks and had another solid season, earning him another chance in organized baseball, one that stuck this time.

Coste played in the minors and finally reached the majors at the age of thirty-three, with the Philadelphia Phillies in 2006. He was a member of the Phillies' world-championship team two years later and played through 2009. Coste came back to his alma mater as an assistant coach and took over as head coach of Concordia in Moorhead in 2014.

Veeck and Goldklang operated a number of teams in different leagues, and in 1998 they were involved in two teams in the Northern League. The Goldklang Group bought into the Sioux Falls Canaries with announced intentions to sell the Saints. Veeck explained that he went to Sioux Falls because he "felt tired and run-down . . . wanted something different." He said the league imposed certain waivers and conditions on them for owning two teams, such as limitations on baseball operations.

Despite the group's professed plan to sell the St. Paul team—and even though Veeck also worked for several major-league teams over the next few years—Veeck and Goldklang are still with the Saints.

The 1999 season brought a new look of sorts to the Northern League, although it was hardly noticeable. The Northeast League—with eight teams based in Connecticut, Massachusetts, New York, New Jersey, and Pennsylvania—was looking for an alliance as it tried to fend off another independent league from encroaching on its territory. With independent leagues operating according to their own rules, unlike affiliated leagues operating under an umbrella organization, territorial rights and other issues were hard to coordinate.

Commissioner Miles Wolff hoped to bring unity to the independent leagues—there had been seven of them in 1998—and establish guidelines that covered them all. In the meantime, the Northeast League was absorbed into the

Northern League. The existing Northern League teams played in the Central Division and the incoming teams in the Eastern Division.

The merger was mostly invisible since there was no interdivisional play during the regular season, only a postseason title series between the division champions. Some had concerns over a talent gap between the two divisions, the feeling being that the Central Division had much stronger teams. Not that a five-game championship series once a year was enough to prove otherwise, but a team from the Eastern Division won the league championship every year of the alliance, which ended after the 2002 season.

The manager of the champion New Jersey Jackals in 2001 and 2002 was George Tsamis, who had pitched for the Minnesota Twins in 1993. After his playing career, he started managing in the Northern League East Division, moving to New Jersey in 2001. With two championships on his resume, Tsamis moved up again, becoming manager of the St. Paul Saints in 2003.

The Saints had been through a revolving-door period of managers. Marty Scott moved from managing into the front office after 2000. Doug Sisson managed in 2001 before heading back to organized baseball and was succeeded by Jim Johnson, a longtime baseball man who, like Sisson, had little experience in independent ball.

Tsamis stuck around longer than his predecessors and became another in a line of talented and colorful personalities associated with the Saints. He was once described as a "vulgar David Puddy," after the laconic character on

Seinfeld with a monotone speaking delivery. Concerned that his conversation might be too strong for a new female employee, Tsamis warned her that he swears a lot. Her reply of "Who the f**k doesn't?" put the manager at ease.

The Saints didn't have their best years during this period, and although the team continued to draw well at the box office, St. Paul was no longer the attendance king of the Northern League. In 2001, Winnipeg drew the most fans in the league, marking the first time that the Saints did not lead in attendance. Schaumberg, a relatively new entry to the league, also did well at the gate.

One team that struggled was Duluth-Superior, whose on- and off-field ups and downs were often related to changing ownership. After the 2002 season, the Dukes were lured to Kansas City by a new ballpark. They vacated the aging but charming Wade Stadium, a true Duluth landmark that, as of 2015, was home to a team in the collegiate Northwoods League.

Other new teams with new ballparks joined the Northern League. The Saltdogs of Lincoln, Nebraska, took the spot of the Madison Black Wolf in 2001. The Northern League expanded in 2002 with the addition of two cities with new ballparks: Joliet, Illinois, and Gary, Indiana. Gary, however, went through construction delays and political problems with its ballpark, forcing its team to spend its initial season entirely on the road.

The trend for shiny new stadiums was perhaps another indication of the success and significance of the Northern League. By 2003 the Saints were the only Northern League team playing in a ballpark that was more than ten years

JOE MAUER

Many regard Joe Mauer as the best athlete ever from Minnesota, although he had plenty of competition for the title within his own family. The Mauers have been one of the most prominent sports families in St. Paul and all of Minnesota. Mauer's mom, Teresa Tierney, was a great volleyball and basketball player at Central High School and the College of St. Catherine in St. Paul. At Cretin–Derham Hall High School, Joe Mauer played football, basketball, and baseball. As a senior he was named the *USA Today* High School Player of the Year in football and baseball. Mauer received a scholarship to play quarterback at Florida State University, but he instead signed a baseball contract with the Minnesota Twins after being the first player taken in the 2001 draft. Mauer was in the starting lineup for the Twins on Opening Day in 2004. Two years later, he led the American League in batting average for the first of three times and received the league's Silver Slugger award at catcher (his first of five). In 2009 Mauer had a batting average of .365 and on-base percentage of .444 while hitting 28 home runs. In leading the Twins to the Central Division title, Mauer was named the American League Most Valuable Player. Through his first eleven seasons in the majors, he had a career batting average of .319.

old. (Sioux Falls Stadium, home of the Canaries, was built in 1964, but it had been extensively renovated in the early years of the Northern League.) The Saints soon were looking to change that distinction, with hopes for a new ballpark constructed in the downtown area of St. Paul. The quest was eventually successful.

BUILDING UP TO THE "MIRACLE AT MIDWAY"

As the Saints struggled to keep up in the standings and attendance, the team continued to push the "Fun Is Good" mantra to create an entertaining ballpark experience.

On Wednesday, July 16, 2003, St. Paul brought Minnie Miñoso back again, ten years after he first suited up for the Saints, extending his pro baseball playing career into a seventh decade. At the time, the seventy-seven-year-old Miñoso was working in community relations for the Chicago White Sox, who had hosted the major-league All-Star Game the night before. Miñoso flew to the Twin Cities the next day to take part in the Saints' annual tribute to the Negro Leagues. St. Paul offered Miñoso a standard league contract—for a prorated salary of $32.26 for one day—and made him the designated hitter for that night's game against Gary.

As part of the tribute, both teams wore replica jerseys of Negro League teams. Miñoso, wearing a New York Cubans uniform, led off the bottom of the first. Gary left-hander Tim Byrdak, who had pitched for the Kansas City Royals a few years earlier, got in the spirit by employing an exaggerated windup, similar to those used during Miñoso's era. Byrdak was low with his first three pitches, then got one in for a strike. Miñoso fouled off a pitch and then walked on the next one. He went to first and then trotted off the field to an ovation as Jeff Brooks came in to run for him. Afterward, Miñoso said that was enough for him as a player and that he was done making token appearances in games.

The Saints hadn't won the Northern League championship since the mid-1990s, but 2004 produced a championship run with its share of wackiness along the way. In June, Tsamis was vulgar but hardly laconic after a reversed decision by the umpires. St. Paul's Tonayne Brown had been called safe on a slow roller when umpire Brad Beedle ruled that Sioux City pitcher David Glick, covering first, had missed the bag. However, plate umpire Brad Hungerford overruled Beedle and called Brown out (a decision that also snapped Brown's 16-game hitting streak). Tsamis and coach Ben Fleetham argued vehemently against the call, and both were ejected. Before leaving, Tsamis removed his shoes and placed them near, but not on, the base as a way of indicating that the original call had been the correct one, a demonstration that was picked up by

Wearing a New York Cubans uniform in honor of the Negro League team, seventy-seven-year-old Minnie Miñoso jogs to first after drawing a walk for the Saints on July 16, 2003. It marked the seventh decade in which Miñoso appeared in a professional baseball game.

PHOTO COURTESY OF THE ST. PAUL SAINTS

national media. Tsamis's shoes made highlight shows and eventually even got their own baseball card.

The Saints twice set attendance records in 2004, first with a crowd of 7,401 on June 30. Jason Verdugo pitched a four-hitter in an 11–0 win over Gary. Then the head baseball coach at nearby Hamline University, Verdugo had pitched in the San Francisco Giants organization beginning in 1997 but retired after the 2000 season. He came back as an active player with the Saints in 2004 and won five games during the regular season.

St. Paul decided to shoot for an even greater crowd in late July and announced that they wouldn't turn anyone away for a game against Sioux Falls. With many fans sitting and standing in a roped-off area along the outfield warning tracks, a record crowd of 8,514 watched the Saints beat the Canaries 15–10.

St. Paul continued to build up its roster as well as its crowds. Late in the 2004 season the Saints, nervous about shortstop Chas Terni's sore hamstring, acquired Marc Mirizzi in a trade with Sioux Falls. The versatile Mirizzi could play all four infield positions, and he got a steady spot in the lineup during the playoffs because of a thumb injury to third baseman Billy Munoz.

St. Paul defeated Fargo-Moorhead in the opening playoff round to advance to the title series against the Schaumberg Flyers. The Saints won one of two in Schaumberg, the second on a tenth-inning run-scoring double by Mirizzi. The series moved to St. Paul, and the Flyers took the next game to put the Saints one game from elimination in the best-of-five series.

Verdugo pitched another gem in the fourth game, shutting out Schaumberg in a 7–0 triumph. It would be Verdugo's last professional game as a pitcher. He continued coaching, though, for Hamline in the spring and as pitching coach for the Saints in the summer. Verdugo set a Hamline record for wins by a coach before stepping aside to become the school's athletic director in 2011.

The Schaumberg–St. Paul series came down to a winner-take-all final game. The Flyers built an early 6–2 lead at Midway Stadium, and the Saints scored one more in the seventh. Leading 6–3 entering the last of the ninth, the Flyers brought in relief ace Brett Weber to finish it off. He almost did.

Tim Marks doubled to lead off the inning, but Weber retired Terni and Josh Renick. Justin Hall doubled home Marks and then scored on a single by Adam Olow to make it 6–5. A small turnout—1,100—had gotten smaller over the first eight innings as some fans abandoned hope and, ultimately, the ballpark. However, with the tying run now on base, those who remained stirred and then buzzed when Nick Gretz followed with a hit.

Chants of "T! T! T!" greeted Tonayne Brown as he stepped to the plate with two on and two out. After fouling off three pitches, Brown singled to bring home pinch runner Kris Cox with the tying run. Lou Lucca walked to load the bases, and Schaumberg manager Andy McCauley made a pitching change,

bringing in left-hander Lyle Pampas to have the switch-hitting Mirizzi swing from the right side.

Mirizzi pulled a 1–1 pitch to left field. The drive cleared the fence for a game-ending, and season-ending, grand slam. The Saints celebrated their fourth Northern League championship. It was also the third league title in four years for Tsamis, who had won the first two with the New Jersey Jackals. The phrase "Miracle at Midway" was coined to describe the comeback. The moment lives on as one of the team's greatest memories out of a collection of many.

Acquired as infield insurance, Mirizzi gave St. Paul much more than that, and the Saints rewarded him by agreeing to trade him to San Angelo, Texas, of the independent Central League, where he had the opportunity to be a player-coach and be closer to his wife's family.

Mirizzi later returned to St. Paul as a visiting player. His first time back, he was honored before the game and then designated as the K-Man in the game. The K-Man has sometimes been used as a shot at an unpopular player, and

Saints teammates mob Marc Mirizzi after he delivered the game- and championship-winning home run against the Schaumberg Flyers in the 2004 Northern League championship.

PHOTO COURTESY OF THE ST. PAUL SAINTS

some even get the tag for an entire series. In Mirizzi's case, however, the K-Man status was given as a salute to the man with the big blow.

Always on the lookout for novel and new, the defending-champion Saints brought other innovations to Midway Stadium in 2005. St. Paul scheduled an exhibition game on Mother's Day that started at 5:35 AM. General manager Derek Sharrer had wanted to schedule a predawn game three years before when he was with a Veeck-Goldklang team in Charleston, South Carolina, but the parent club vetoed the idea. With the independent Saints, Sharrer was free to do what he wanted.

The crowd of 2,253 at the so-called sunrise game included approximately 500 people who had come for the game the previous night and stayed overnight at the stadium. Some pitched tents in the outfield and others found spots in the parking lot and under the grandstand. A bugler blasting reveille and a rooster cock-a-doodle-dooing signaled fans to clear the field. The sun could be seen rising beyond the right-field fence as the game got underway.

In 2005 the Northern League added two teams in Alberta: Edmonton and Calgary, cities that previously had Class AAA teams in the Pacific Coast League. However, the Northern League would change drastically within a year with the departure of some of its core clubs.

Northern League mainstays Sioux City, Sioux Falls, and St. Paul all abandoned the league following the 2005 campaign. They joined up with several clubs from the Texas-based Central League, along with an expansion team in St. Joseph, Missouri, to form a new league starting in 2006.

Veeck cited "philosophical differences" with other Northern League owners and a "different vision of where independent baseball should be going" as reasons for the break. Wolff, the first commissioner of the Northern League in 1993, had been the commissioner of the Central League since 2002 and stayed on when it merged with his former group.

The lights were on at Midway Stadium not for a night game but for a very-early-morning game on May 8, 2005. First pitch was at 5:35 AM.

PHOTO COURTESY OF
THE ST. PAUL SAINTS

The new organization became the American Association, adopting the same name of the league in which the earlier St. Paul Saints had played from 1902 to 1960 and which continued operations until 1997. Though a drastically different organization than the earlier teams that represented the capital city, the 2006 St. Paul Saints were returning to their roots, in a sense.

Midway Stadium illuminated for a night game in 2006.

CHAPTER 14

From Midway to CHS Field

BATTLING FOR THE AMERICAN ASSOCIATION CROWN

The American Association featured two five-team divisions in 2006. The Saints were in the North along with Northern League transplants the Sioux Falls Canaries, the Sioux City Explorers, and the Lincoln Saltdogs, plus the newly formed St. Joe Blacksnakes. In the South were the teams from the Central League—the El Paso Diablos, Coastal Bend Aviators (in Robstown, Texas), Fort Worth Cats, Pensacola Pelicans, and Shreveport Sports.

The Cats had won the Central League championship in 2005 under manager Wayne Terwilliger. Terwilliger stepped down as Fort Worth manager but remained with the club as a coach as he approached his sixtieth season in professional baseball. In the first two seasons of the new league, the Saints faced the Fort Worth Cats in the title series, which went the limit both years.

In addition to Terwilliger, the Cats had other former Saints, including Marc Mirizzi. In the first game of the 2006 championship series, Mirizzi had 3 hits, scored 2 runs, and drove in 2 as Fort Worth won 6–3. St. Paul took the next two games but couldn't finish it off at Midway Stadium, where the Cats won the fourth game to stay alive.

The final game was tied 1–1 in the sixth inning when Mirizzi doubled home the go-ahead run in a 2–1 Fort Worth victory. It was the second time in three years that Mirizzi had the game-winning hit in a championship finale.

The excitement continued after the game, when some of the Saints players went to Half Time Rec, a bar located about a mile and a half east of the stadium, to celebrate the birthday of coach Jackie Hernandez. Some Fort Worth players who had been on the Saints before showed up as well. The event was peaceful until the arrival of another Cat, pitcher Steve Wilkerson, who was belligerent, according to Half Time Rec owner Louie Walsh. A shoving match

Outfielder Brian Buchanan, who had spent parts of several seasons in the majors, joined the Saints in 2006 and was the team's top home-run hitter that year with 11.

escalated to a fistfight and the arrival of St. Paul police. During the melee, Kris Zacuto of the Cats began choking a fifty-four-year-old cop who was two days away from retirement. Other officers had to subdue Zacuto with pepper spray and batons.

Afterward, Walsh stuck by the Saints, saying they "never, ever caused anything but happiness" when they were at Half Time Rec. St. Paul general manager Derek Sharrer, though relieved his players hadn't instigated the brawl, noted that the Cats were in town to play the Saints, "and from that standpoint, we do take responsibility to the community."

The Cats and Saints met again—on the field, not in a bar—in the championship series in 2007. This time the series started in St. Paul and finished in Fort Worth, but the pattern was the same. The Saints dropped the first game, won the next two—with the help of home runs by first baseman–outfielder Fernando Valenzuela Jr. in each game—and then were unable to win another. In the decisive fifth game, Fort Worth's Jordan Foster broke a 1–1 tie with a solo homer in the seventh. The Cats scored 2 more in the inning and won 4–1 for their third straight league title.

The Saints next returned to the title series in 2011, facing the Grand Prairie AirHogs. This time the Saints took the first 2 games and needed only one more win to clinch as the series shifted to Grand Prairie, Texas. As had happened a few years earlier against Fort Worth, St. Paul could not get the final win. Jason Jennings, the National League Rookie of the Year in 2002, was the winning pitcher for the AirHogs in the finale.

During its first few seasons, the American Association produced a number of future major leaguers. The 2006 champion Fort Worth Cats briefly had Luke Hochevar, who made it to the majors the next year and remained on the Kansas City Royals pitching staff through 2013. Max Scherzer, a future Cy Young Award recipient with the Detroit Tigers, pitched a few games with the Cats in 2007.

Several Saints pitchers also found success at the major-league level. Reliever Tanner Scheppers pitched four games for St. Paul after being drafted by Texas and before being signed by the Rangers three months later. Spotted by a Milwaukee scout during the 2009 American Association All-Star Game, Brandon Kintzler was purchased from the Saints and became part of the Brewers bullpen crew the next year.

Left-hander Caleb Thielbar pitched for the Saints in 2011 after being released by the Brewers organization. In August of that year Thielbar signed with the Minnesota Twins and made it to the majors with them two years later. Thielbar was outstanding out of the Twins bullpen, not allowing a run in his first 17 appearances, and he was named the team's top rookie in 2013.

Thielbar's signing was the first time the Twins pursued a player off the Saints roster. Although the relationship between the teams had warmed over time, the signing marked a major departure from the disdain the Twins had shown during the early history of the Saints. The Twins took on another Saints player near the end of the 2013 season, signing Mark Hamburger, a hard-throwing right-hander who had attended local Mounds View High School. The Twins had signed Hamburger out of a tryout camp in 2007 and traded him to the Texas Rangers organization the next year. Hamburger briefly made it up to the majors in 2011, but he had problems with marijuana that knocked him out of organized baseball. After going through drug treatment at Hazelden in Center City, Minnesota, Hamburger pitched for the Saints in 2013 and got another offer from the Twins. He had to serve a fifty-game suspension at the start of the 2014 season and then pitched for Twins farm teams at the AA and AAA level.

"The independent leagues used to be where careers went to die," wrote Tom Powers in the *St. Paul Pioneer Press* in September 2013. "More and more it's

becoming a place where careers are resurrected or even launched. Big-league organizations now routinely look to independent baseball for help."

Like the 1993 squad, the Twins were a poor team in need of help in 2013. By then, however, they no longer let pride get in the way of acquiring players who could assist them and had several players who had played in independent leagues.

Infielder-outfielder Chris Colabello had played seven seasons in the independent Can-Am League before signing with the Twins organization in early 2012. He went on to be runner-up for the Most Valuable Player award in the Class AA Eastern League in 2012, and he was named the MVP of the Class AAA International League in 2013, the same year he debuted in the majors with the Twins.

Left-hander Andrew Albers had signed with the Twins in March 2011 after pitching one season in the Can-Am League in 2010. He came up to the Twins in 2013 and kicked off his major-league career with back-to-back wins, including a shutout.

From Mike Mimbs and Kevin Millar in the early years to later players such as Scheppers, Kintzler, and Thielbar, the Saints have been a stop for a number of players who needed another boost to make it to the major leagues. Other members of the organization also honed their skills in St. Paul and were rewarded with jobs at the top levels.

Caleb Thielbar starred out of the bullpen for the Saints in 2011 before getting signed by the Minnesota Twins organization. He made his big-league debut in 2013.

PHOTO COURTESY OF THE ST. PAUL SAINTS

Kris Atteberry broadcast games for the Sioux Falls Canaries and Saints from 1999 to 2006. In 2007 he went to the Twins as a studio host and play-by-play announcer. Atteberry is a veteran who clings to the stories of life in the minors. He remembers that for years the Saints stayed at a Best Western hotel when they were in Sioux City, Iowa. One year, however, the team switched its lodging to the Cardinal Inn across the border in South Sioux City, Nebraska. The Sioux City Bandits arena football league team lived at the Cardinal Inn during the season. Atteberry recalled that the football players were "friendly" with the housekeeping staff, who allowed the players access to other rooms. One night after a game the Saints returned to find their rooms bereft of personal items, such as computers. Manager George Tsamis decided that was enough of the Cardinal Inn and made sure the team was back in better quarters in Sioux City.

Rusty Kath is one of many Saints public-address announcers who were hired for their ability to entertain. Kath had done public-address announcing in college at the University of Minnesota–Morris for terrible teams, and he tried to lighten the mood with backhanded compliments and subtle humor. "As dumb luck would have it," he said, "it was just on-the-job training for working with the Saints."

Kath had never been to a Saints game, but he accompanied a friend to auditions being held for a new announcer, which took place at Acme Comedy Club. Kath's combination of stand-up comedy and improvisation earned him a second interview and then the job. Initially he alternated games with Maggie Faris, a local comic, but soon had the booth to himself. "She was a phenomenal stand-up," Kath said of Faris, "but her baseball knowledge was lacking. That was the beauty of the Saints—they don't mind taking a chance on something that might not go well."

Kath's popularity at Saints games was evidenced by the "Rusty Kath Bobblejaw" giveaway the team held at the ballpark in 2007. "We have this vision of minor-league baseball being this beautiful piece of Americana," Kath recalled of his time with the Saints. "And it is. However, the stories that are less-often written are more interesting and not quite as Norman Rockwellian."

After three years of announcing with the Saints, Kath got a job with the Tampa Bay Devil Rays in 2007 hosting pregame ceremonies and between-innings events.

HAVING FUN AND GROWING FANS

Mike Veeck is proud of those members of the Saints organization who made it to the majors or other levels of organized baseball, but he knows the team can't make it solely on these achievements. The atmosphere at Midway Stadium and Veeck's "Fun Is Good" philosophy have long made Saints games an attractive destination to a wide range of fans. Veeck said making people laugh is "the great unifier. Fun is a great healer."

Antics and "ushertainers" are staples of Saints games to help fans have a few hours of fun and escape from whatever troubles and pressures exist in their everyday lives. The ushertainers roam the stands and the field, working the crowd from the moment the gates open. The Saints consider them "hosts of a party" and tell them to be on the prowl to bring a smile to anyone who doesn't have one. One of the ushertainers, Seigo Masubuchi, performs nightly to the organ music of Andy Crowley in an act called "Karaoke with a Real Japanese Guy."

A 2014 Saints press release referred to the team and its ballpark environment as a "circus on steroids." It is an apt description that could also apply to other teams owned by Veeck and Marv Goldklang. Still, there are limits.

The "Fun Is Good" philosophy has stuck with Mike Veeck and the Saints since the beginning.

A Vasectomy Night with the Charleston (South Carolina) RiverDogs, part of the Goldklang Group, scheduled for Father's Day in 1997 was snipped because of opposition from Catholics, including a bishop who was a RiverDogs season-ticket holder.

In St. Paul, however, the limits can apparently be pushed a bit further. In 2001, the Saints hosted Inflatable Bat Night, sponsored by Viagra. There was no explanation, and none was needed.

In 2008, the team's marketing campaign slogan was, "We'll Stoop to Anything to Get Attention!" One of the promotions that year was a "bobble-foot" night, ostensibly in conjunction with National Tap Dance Day. However, the giveaway item, which featured a restroom stall with a bobbling foot visible at the bottom, was an obvious allusion to a recent scandal. Idaho senator Larry Craig had been arrested the year before for soliciting sex in the men's room at the Minneapolis–St. Paul airport, giving a foot tap intended for a man in the next stall, who was actually an undercover cop. The Saints kept it tongue-in-cheek, characterizing the giveaway as a tribute to "toe-tapping friends and fans from around the nation who may ever have set foot in Minneapolis–St. Paul . . .

Ushertainer Seigo
Masubuchi is one of
the unique features at
Saints games, providing
entertainment and fun
for fans.

even for just a change of planes." Like the scandal itself, the Saints' promotion generated huge publicity, and the bobblefoots immediately became a hot item on eBay.

Not as hot, but perhaps even tackier, was the 2011 giveaway of men's "tweeting wiener" underwear, with a drawing of a hot dog holding a Saints pennant and having its picture taken by a bird. This came after US representative Anthony Weiner tweeted a photo of his bulging tighty-whities to a woman and the incident became national news.

Politicians aren't the only targets of the playful yet mocking Saints promotions. Sports figures and teams provide ample fodder, and the Saints were fortunate to have the Minnesota Vikings around for that.

In September 2002 Randy Moss, the Vikings' star receiver, was trying to make an illegal turn while driving in downtown Minneapolis. Traffic officer Amy Zaccardi tried to prevent it by standing in front of his car. That didn't stop Moss, who edged forward, bumping Zaccardi and knocking her to the ground. From that came "Randy Moss Hood Ornament Night" at Midway Stadium.

Under the guise of the anniversary of the *Love Boat* television show, the Saints held a "Love Boat Night" in 2006 at which they gave away small rubber boats to fans. With the boats colored purple and gold and featuring the name "Minnetonka Queen" on the bow, the true meaning behind the promotion was pretty clear. It was another not-so-subtle jab at the Vikings, whose team outing on Lake Minnetonka the previous October had turned into a sex party involving prostitutes and came to be known as the "Love Boat Scandal." "They were good at blatantly saying it without saying it," said Kath of the Saints' ability to mock offenders in an indirect manner.

A less subtle attack was directed at Atlanta Falcons quarterback Michael Vick, who became a pariah, and a felon, for engaging in a dog-fighting ring at his Virginia home. After the story broke in 2007, the Saints were ready with a Michael Vick Chew Toy for dogs. Shaped like a pig, the rubber toy featured Vick's name and his number, 7, on the back.

The Saints and other Goldklang-Veeck teams have been holding bobblehead nights during presidential-election years since 2004, each time letting fans vote by picking the bobblehead of a particular candidate. The idea for the first "Bobblelection" on August 2, 2004, was credited to front-office employee Steph Harris. With the presidential election between John Kerry and George Bush three months away, all the teams owned by Veeck and Goldklang made bobbleheads of the candidates. At Midway Stadium and elsewhere, random fans were selected to choose one of the bobbleheads. The first bobblehead to run out was declared the winner. "The publicity we got for that—brilliant," said Dave Wright. The Saints also invited both parties to send a representative to throw out a ceremonial first pitch at a Saints game. Democratic Senator Tom Harkin of Iowa led a pregame rally for Kerry in the stadium parking lot and then served as his party's representative for the first pitch. "Harkin got it," said Wright. "With open collar and beer in hand, he walked out to the mound to throw out the first pitch." Kerry beat Bush at the St. Paul game, although Bush took the overall vote among all Goldklang-Veeck teams. The Saints claim that the event was recognized as one of the first polls for the Bush-Kerry election.

In May 2009 the Saints gave away a Count von ReCount bobblehead in the midst of the protracted recount to determine the winner of the previous fall's election for senator from Minnesota between Norm Coleman and Al Franken. The recount included court battles and wrangling over a voter's intent on disputed ballots. The Saints' bobblehead was dressed like Count von Count of *Sesame Street* and allowed fans to turn the head to show the face of Franken or Coleman. Lawyers were on hand to help determine the fans' intent.

Ideas for Saints promotions occasionally emerge from late-night get-togethers at bars and are sketched out on cocktail napkins. Even those that come out of structured think tanks can result from freewheeling brainstorms.

Amanda Rodriguez, who has served as an intern for the Baseball Hall of Fame, St. Paul Saints, and Minnesota Twins in successive years starting in 2012, tells of a postseason meeting to determine promotions for the coming season. Tinder, a matchmaking mobile app, was gaining popularity in 2013. One employee was known for his frequent dates with women through Tinder. One of the Saints outfielders that year left these names on the team's pass list: "Tinder girls Megan, Susan, and Cindy. IDK [I don't know] last names." (Rodriguez said they made sure Megan, Susan, and Cindy got tickets apart from one another.)

From this came the idea for "Tinder Loving Care Night," held at Midway Stadium on May 22, 2014. The night included a between-innings event featuring a woman and five male potential date candidates. As the young men lined up, the woman swiped right or left to accept or reject each one, mimicking the swiping feature on the Tinder app.

Despite the occasional adult-oriented promotion, Saints games are family-friendly affairs with lots of kids in attendance. The players show their appreciation for the younger fans by generously signing autographs before and after games.

Everything about the evening was aboveboard, but in the brainstorming meeting that led to Tinder night, employees joked about including a three-way as part of the promotion. No such ménage à trois came to fruition, but the joke did lead to an idea for an exhibition game between three teams. For "Three-Way at Midway Night" in early May, the Saints got their preseason opponent, the Fargo-Moorhead RedHawks, to agree to bring in a third team, the amateur Minneapolis Cobras, for a so-called XXXhibition Game, sponsored by KINKY Cocktails. The Saints faced the RedHawks for six innings and then sat out while the Cobras took on Fargo-Moorhead in innings seven through nine. The twelve-inning game concluded with three innings between the St. Paul and Minneapolis teams. The Saints were the winners, scoring 20 runs as compared to the RedHawks' 10 and the Cobras' 4.

Trains and fireworks are special attractions that have always been a part of Midway Stadium. Fans yell at each passing train, sometimes getting a salute from the engineer blowing his horn. Fireworks are popular, too, and a frequent postgame event.

Mudonna has been delighting crowds at Midway Stadium, and now CHS Field, since 2003.

PHOTO COURTESY OF THE ST. PAUL SAINTS

During the seventh-inning stretch, Saints staff members toss bags of peanuts from the press box to eager fans below. (A new official scorer had a bag placed in front of him by an employee in the top of the seventh during one game. Not knowing the routine, instead of waiting to throw the bag to a fan during the next inning break, he tore open the bag, cracked the peanut shells, and munched the innards. "Rookie mistake," said the veterans in the press box as they clued him in on the purpose of the peanuts.)

In the early years of the Saints, the Sammy Davis Jr. version of the theme from *Shaft* was used as a rally song. Original public-address announcer Al Frechtman, who also handled the music at the time, played the tune between pitches when the Saints needed runs.

A real pig has always been the Saints' mascot. But in 2003, the team introduced a human in a pig costume, named Mudonna, as a secondary mascot. Mudonna isn't allowed to speak but has been known to play charades as a means of communicating.

More than once the Saints have had a game sponsored by the Minnesota Atheists, and on those nights they drop the "S" from their team name, so the front of the jerseys reads "Aints."

The Saints are quick to honor people by allowing them to throw a ceremonial first pitch, sometimes having a line of them at the mound before a game. A greater honor may be the occasional ceremonial last pitch. At game's end, as

BOB KLEPPERICH

The closing of Midway Stadium after the 2014 season brought an end to nearly sixty years of Bob Klepperich working in ballparks used by the St. Paul Saints. While a student at Cretin High School in St. Paul, Klepperich became the equipment manager for the visiting teams at Lexington Park. "No salary, just tips," he said of the time he spent wire-brushing shoes, hanging uniforms (sometimes after his mom washed them), and cleaning the locker room. When the Saints moved to Midway Stadium the next year, Klepperich followed and started drawing a weekly salary in addition to the tips. He also ran his own concessions for the players, buying everything from beer to chewing tobacco to pop and milk and selling it for a slight profit.

When major-league baseball came to Minnesota, displacing the local minor-league teams, Klepperich interviewed with the Twins, but the job of visiting clubhouse manager went to Jim Wiesner, who had been in charge of the Saints' clubhouse at Midway Stadium.

Klepperich stayed busy at Midway Stadium, however, as the Minnesota Vikings used it for their practice field. He was the assistant to the equipment manager, Stubby Eason, for five years. During this period, Klepperich received his degree at the College of St. Thomas and started a thirty-six-year high school teaching career in St. Paul. He still spent his out-of-school hours at Midway Stadium, working on the grounds and taking on greater duties, which he continued performing at the new Municipal/Midway Stadium—scheduling, rental agreements, recruiting events, and payroll. Klepperich passed his test to be a facilities supervisor in 1980 and became a permanent employee for the city of St. Paul, also working in food and beverage operations for the municipal swimming pools and golf courses.

He has probably been the most regular attendee of Saints games since the team began in 1997, estimating that he has been at about 97 percent of their games. Even after retiring from teaching, Klepperich continued working long days and nights in a setting that may have become more familiar to him than his own home.

The Saints, rather than the city, run the new Lowertown ballpark, and Klepperich's job was eliminated with the move. He's thought about what he can do with his coming free time but lamented the end of a big part of his life: "I've had a ballpark to go to for fifty-nine years."

the fans are filing out, one person takes the mound to throw out the final pitch of the night.

The fans of Section F, the "Section F-ers," have been among the most prominent at Midway Stadium. The group solicits a dollar from the crowd each time one of the Saints homers. The money is donated to research for retinitis pigmentosa, the disease that has robbed Veeck's daughter, Rebecca, of her sight. The Section F-ers have raised well over $60,000 through this collection.

While more traditional baseball minds have shown disdain for the high jinks at Midway Stadium over the years, some of the team's critics eventually copied them. "Ideas are swimming upstream," Veeck has said, referring to the major leagues picking up on the promotions. Activities once considered over the top are becoming mainstream at ballparks at all levels of baseball through-out the country.

During the early years of the Northern League, the Saints and other teams in the league brought in a number of big-name players—Leon Durham, Pedro Guerrero, Darryl Strawberry, Jack Morris—to mix in with the youngsters on their rosters. The twenty-first century hasn't seen the same level of star power being signed, although big names do pop up in discussions, sometimes generated by media speculation. A sports column in 2013 suggested that former slugger Jose Canseco, who had been playing in independent leagues for a number of years, would be a great match for the Saints. Although it wasn't a serious suggestion, it did get a response from Canseco, who teamed with Mark McGwire as one of the Oakland Athletics' "Bash Brothers" of the late 1980s and early 1990s. Canseco tweeted a reply on Twitter that read, "hey @stpaul-saints i would give my left nut to play for you guys." (Canseco presumably still has all his lower body parts because the Saints didn't take him up on his offer.)

Saints executive vice president Tom Whaley says it has become harder to land players, in part because of the proliferation of independent teams. The look of the independent leagues has changed, too. After the Saints and three other teams moved to the American Association in 2006, the Northern League hung on for a few more years but folded after 2010. Four of its teams—Fargo-Moorhead, Winnipeg, Gary, and Kansas City—were absorbed by the American Association.

After the Shreveport-Bossier Captains dropped out of the South Division before the 2012 season, the American Association was left with an uneven number of teams. The league solved the scheduling problem by playing a handful of interleague contests with the Can-Am League.

Through it all the Saints have stuck with their formula of what Annie Huidekoper calls the three Cs: conversation, connection, community. She asserts that in 1993 the Saints joined bars and churches as a source of community in the Twin Cities. "Midway Stadium became a gathering place," she said, adding that many fans made friends and even developed second families while attending games.

A NEW DOWNTOWN BALLPARK

As for the future of Saints baseball, it was destined for change when the team left their home of twenty-two years after the 2014 season. A new ballpark in the Lowertown section of St. Paul was nearing completion as the team wrapped up its run at Midway Stadium on August 28. A crowd of nearly 9,500 turned out for the last game at the ballpark. Kevin Luckow, a fan who for years has documented his experiences and insights in a blog called *The 10th Inning Stretch*, captured his thoughts on the end of the stadium: "As I have evolved into a 44-year-old that kind of has a better grasp of life priorities than he did as a Zubaz-wearing 23-year-old, Midway Stadium was always there for me as a getaway from life. Not sure what discussions in the parking lot consisted of in 1993 but nowadays it consists of topics such as home improvement, career, and several conversations consisting of the words, 'Remember when?' . . . I'm going to cherish the memories of my days at Midway Stadium where I grew up and look forward to creating new ones in Lowertown."

For the Midway Stadium finale, St. Paul mayor Chris Coleman delivered a ceremonial first pitch, which was caught by Bill Murray at home plate.

PHOTO COURTESY OF THE ST. PAUL SAINTS

The quest for a new Saints ballpark had been brewing since the early 2000s, but it picked up steam in 2012. In April of that year, ballpark supporters organized a Wiffle-ball game on the grounds of the state capitol while the legislature was in session. The following month, the St. Paul Port Authority struck a deal to buy the land for the ballpark, at the site of the abandoned Diamond Products/Gillette building on the eastern edge of downtown in the Lowertown Historic District. Soon after, in mid-July, the St. Paul City Council approved initial funding for the ballpark. By September the city received a grant from the state of Minnesota for $25 million—more than half of the total state economic development grants awarded—to build the park.

Finally, the Lowertown ballpark was becoming a reality. Demolition of the Diamond Products/Gillette building began in the summer of 2013, and initial design drawings for the 7,000-seat ballpark were released in December. The

On August 28, 2014, Midway Stadium was packed for the final game of the Saints season. It would be the last Saints game held at the beloved ballpark.

Backers of a new ballpark for the Saints held a Wiffle-ball game in front of the state capitol in April 2012 to help drum up support from legislators.

first concrete for the new structure was poured in April, and by October, the sod for the field was being rolled out.

In September, Veeck had announced that the stadium would bear the name CHS Field following a naming-rights agreement with CHS Inc., a farm and agricultural cooperative based in Inver Grove Heights, Minnesota. Goldklang noted that CHS had built a reputation around the concepts of "fun, family, farms," a good match with the Saints' "Fun Is Good" philosophy and the team's emphasis on creating a family-friendly ballpark experience (Viagra Inflatable Bat Nights notwithstanding).

The total cost for the ballpark project was $63 million, about 17 percent of which was needed to remove contaminated soil at the site. In addition to the $25 million state grant, the Saints put in $11 million. The city of St. Paul, the Metropolitan Council, and Ramsey County provided the rest of the money.

Public funding for sports facilities is always a divisive issue among citizens, sports fans and nonfans alike. The team has been quick to emphasize the regional nature of the ballpark and that, in addition to Saints games, it will be used for amateur sports and other regional events, including Hamline University baseball games. Supporters also touted the more than 400,000 visitors the ballpark would bring to downtown St. Paul each year, generating an estimated $10 million in revenue annually for the city.

The stadium features a premium-seating area behind home plate, which brought complaints from fans who had season tickets behind the plate at Midway Stadium and saw the cost of these seats more than double in the new ballpark. Some fans lamented the loss of a parking lot and feared the end of the tailgating experiences that had been a staple at Midway Stadium. Other features of the downtown location offer new opportunities for Saints fans, however. A number of bars and restaurants are located within easy walking distance. The Metro Transit light rail drops fans off about a block away from the ballpark. Huidekoper noted that the other end of the Central Corridor Green Line is at the Minnesota Twins' Target Field, conjuring the days when streetcars ran between the Millers' Nicollet Park in Minneapolis and the Saints' Lexington Park in St. Paul.

Home plate of the new ballpark is in the northwest corner of the site, and the orientation offers fans sitting in the outfield a view of the downtown skyline. Broadway Street runs parallel to the first-base line, and the Metro Transit light-rail maintenance facility is beyond right field. The other two sides of the ballpark are hemmed in by highway and freeway approaches.

Public art is an integral component of the new ballpark. A row of twenty-eight decorative pillars meanders on the plaza in a manner reflecting the course of the Mississippi River. The pillars contain silica and lime harvested from the river valley and are capped by lights that illustrate the changing water conditions of the river.

When the design was unveiled in late 2013, St. Paul mayor Chris Coleman praised the ballpark for how it "complements Lowertown's natural beauty and brings in a new, important perspective."

The new space also received its share of criticism, but no matter where the Saints play, the team continues to create a unique and lasting legacy of independent baseball for the city of St. Paul.

St. Paul's downtown skyline provides a backdrop to the Saints' new CHS Field, shown here under construction in October 2014.

PHOTO COURTESY OF THE ST. PAUL SAINTS

Sources

TWIN CITIES NEWSPAPERS as well as *The Sporting News* were the source of much of the information on the Saints. Interviews with people noted in the acknowledgments were another rich source. In addition, the following websites and publications were significant:

All-Time Records and Highlights of the American Association, annual guide of the American Association.

Anderson, Kristin M., and Christopher W. Kimball. "Designing the National Pastime: Twin Cities Baseball Parks." *Minnesota History* (Fall 2003): 338–51.

Baseball-reference.com. Sports Reference, 2014. Web.

Bouton, Jim. *Ball Four: The Final Pitch.* Champaign, IL: Sports Publishing, 1970, 1981, 1990, 2000.

Brink, Carol. *The Twin Cities.* New York: Macmillan Company, 1961.

Carneal, Herb, with Stew Thornley. *Hi Everybody!* Minneapolis: Nodin Press, 1996.

Christensen, Ray, with Stew Thornley. *Golden Memories.* Minneapolis: Nodin Press, 1993.

Evans, Bob. "Larry Rosenthal." *Minnesotans in Baseball,* 196–201. Ed. Stew Thornley. Minneapolis: Nodin Press, 2009.

Fatsis, Stefan. *Wild and Outside: How a Renegade Minor League Revived the Spirit of Baseball in America's Heartland.* New York: Walker and Company, 1995.

Haag, Ken. "The Saga of Eric the Red." *Sports Collectors Digest,* 24 Aug. 1990, 120–22.

Hinman, Jim. "Brief History of the St. Paul Saints" (unpublished manuscript). 1998.

Johnson, Lloyd, and Miles Wolff, eds. *The Encyclopedia of Minor League Baseball.* Durham, NC: Baseball America, 1997.

Jones, Mel. "The St. Paul Municipal Stadium." *ACE: Athletic Club Events* (a publication of the St. Paul Athletic Club), Mar. 1957, 20–21.

Kahn, Roger. *Good Enough to Dream.* Lincoln: University of Nebraska Press, 1985, 2000.

Kane, Lucile M., and Alan Ominsky. *Twin Cities: A Pictorial History of Saint Paul and Minneapolis.* St. Paul: Minnesota Historical Society Press, 1983.

Kemp, David, and Miles Wolff, eds. *The History of Independent Baseball Leagues 1993–2002.* Sioux Falls, SD: Moriah Press, 1993.

Koblas, John J. *A Guide to F. Scott Fitzgerald's St. Paul: A Traveler's Companion to His Homes & Haunts.* St. Paul: Minnesota Historical Society Press, 1978, 2004.

Larson, Don W. *Land of the Giants: A History of Minnesota Business.* Minneapolis: Dorn Books, 1979.

Luckow, Kevin. *10th Inning Stretch.* n.p., n.d. Web. [http://10thinningstretch.blogspot.com]

Maccabee, Paul. *John Dillinger Slept Here: A Crooks' Tour of Crime and Corruption in St. Paul, 1920–1936.* St. Paul: Minnesota Historical Society Press, 1995.

Mugalian, Art. "Walt 'Moose' Moryn." *Minnesotans in Baseball,* 163–75. Ed. Stew Thornley. Minneapolis: Nodin Press, 2009.

O'Neal, Bill. *The American Association: A Baseball History 1902–1991.* Austin, TX: Eakin Press, 1991.

Perlstein, Steve. *Rebel Baseball: The Summer the Game was Returned to the Fans.* Minneapolis: Onion Press, 1994.

Peterson, Armand, and Tom Tomashek. *Town Ball: The Glory Days of Minnesota Amateur Baseball.* Minneapolis: University of Minnesota Press, 2006.

Peterson, Todd. *Early Black Baseball in Minnesota.* Jefferson, NC: McFarland & Company, 2010.

Pluto, Terry. *The Greatest Summer: The Remarkable Story of Jim Bouton's Comeback to Major League Baseball.* Englewood Cliffs, NJ: Prentice-Hall, 1978.

Reichard, Kevin. "Living the Dream." *Corporate Report: The Magazine of Minnesota Business,* Sept. 1998.

Riehle, David. "Say It Ain't So, Charlie! The 1897 Dispute between Charles Comiskey and the St. Paul Trades and Labor Assembly over the Opening of Lexington Park." *Ramsey County History* (Summer 2004): 14–18.

Salin, Tony. *Baseball's Forgotten Heroes.* Lincolnwood, IL: Masters Press, 1999.

Sullivan, Neil J. *The Minors: The Struggles and the Triumph of Baseball's Poor Relation from 1876 to the Present.* New York: St. Martin's Press, 1990.

Terwilliger, Wayne, with Nancy Peterson and Peter Boehm. *Terwilliger Bunts One.* Guilford, CT: Insiders Guide, 2006.

Veeck, Bill, with Ed Linn. *The Hustler's Handbook.* New York: G. P. Putnam's Sons, 1965.

Veeck, Mike, and Pete Williams. *Fun Is Good: How to Create Joy & Passion in Your Workplace and Career.* Emmaus, PA: Rodale, 2005.

Wright, Marshall D. *The American Association: Year-by-Year Statistics for the Baseball Minor League, 1902–1952.* Jefferson, NC: McFarland & Company, 1997.

Index